HOME OFFICE

REVIEW OF PRISON SERVICE SECURITY IN ENGLAND AND WALES AND THE ESCAPE FROM PARKHURST PRISON ON TUESDAY 3rd JANUARY 1995

By General Sir John Learmont, KCB, CBE.

Presented to Parliament by the Secretary of State
for the Home Department
by Command of Her Majesty
October 1995

LONDON: HMSO
Cm 3020 £24.50 net

The Rt Hon Michael Howard QC MP,
Secretary of State for The Home Deparment,
50 Queen Anne's Gate,
London,
SW1H 9AT.

27 September 1995

Dear Home Secretary,

This is the report of the Review of Prison Service Security in England and Wales and the escape from Parkhurst Prison on Tuesday, 3rd January 1995.

I have interpreted the terms of reference widely, which you encouraged me to do, in order to provide as comprehensive a picture as possible of the many areas which could affect security.

I have been at pains to ensure fairness to those who might feel personally criticised in this report. Whilst no individuals are named, those who I considered could feel identified have been provided with a copy of the relevant part of the report to enable them to challenge factual accuracy. This procedure has closely followed the guidelines emerging from the Royal Commission on Tribunals of Inquiry (1966) under the chairmanship of The Rt Hon Lord Justice Salmon. Such "Salmon letters" have been sent to individuals at many levels involved in and with the management and organisation of the Prison Service. I have applied a liberal interpretation of these rules to ensure, as far as possible, that absolute fairness has prevailed. Such procedures have touched as high as Prisons Board level illustrating that I have endeavoured to identify where reponsibilities have ultimately reached and where the criticism stops. The responses have resulted in a number of further interviews being carried out plus amendments and additions being made to the report.

Within the report I have identified and recommended that there is a need for a further study to be carried out to improve the liaison between the Prison Service and the Home Office. Time has not allowed this area to be explored in any depth but in view of the fact that the Prison Service has been an Agency for two and a half years, it now seems appropriate to re-examine ways of devolving greater operational independence to the Service.

I feel I should also say a few words about the cost of my recommendations, which is contained at Appendix Q. The information in this Appendix has been arrived at as a result of information received from the Prison Service, professional Prison Service advice from within my Inquiry Team, input from a private sector architect (in relation to the new High Security and Control Prisons), a Home Office management accountant and the judgement of the assessors. Of the 127 recommendations, in my view only 21 carry a cost tag, with some of the cost of these offset by other recommendations. We have taken great care to keep these to a minimum realising the difficulty of increased expenditure. However, I feel that where additional costs are incurred these are essential to bring the Prison Service up to the standard required to meet its obligations to society.

I have been asked on several occasions whether I have been put under any political pressure to slant the Inquiry or its recommendations in any particular direction. I feel it appropriate to record that from the outset you have given me a totally free hand to express my views without fear or favour and I end by expressing my gratitude to you for affording me this privilege.

I now submit this report to you.

Yours Sincerely,

John Learmont

General Sir John Learmont KCB CBE

Contents

Section	Content	Paragraphs

Appendices

Appendix	Content
A	BACKGROUND AND HISTORICAL INFORMATION
B	THE LEARMONT INQUIRY TEAM
C	REFERENCE DOCUMENTS
D	PRISON ESTABLISHMENTS VISITED
E	PERSONS INTERVIEWED AND SUBMISSIONS RECEIVED
F*	CORRESPONDENCE REGARDING GEOPHONES
G*	BACKGROUND INFORMATION ON ESCAPEES
H*	EXISTING PARKHURST MANAGEMENT STRUCTURE
I	PRISONS BOARD 'ACHIEVEMENTS LIST'
J	KEY PERFORMANCE INDICATORS
K	THE ORGANISTION OF THE PRISON SERVICE (AS AT START OF THE INQUIRY)
L	LIST OF PRISON SERVICE INITIATIVES
M	PAPERWORK CALCULATION
N	CATEGORISATION - A NEW APPROACH
O	WOODCOCK ENQUIRY RECOMMENDATIONS
P	LEARMONT INQUIRY RECOMMENDATIONS
Q	COSTING OF LEARMONT INQUIRY RECOMMENDATIONS

Note: * - those marked with an asterisk refer to the Parkhurst Inquiry

Illustrations

Figure

Note: * - those marked with an asterisk refer to the Parkhurst Inquiry

SECTION 1: OVERVIEW

INTRODUCTION

1.1 The escape from Whitemoor Prison, on 9th September 1994, of six of the very highest security prisoners, shocked and stunned the staff and severely dented public confidence in that establishment, despite their almost immediate recapture. When the findings of the Inquiry, carried out by Sir John Woodcock, were published three months later, they caused severe reverberations throughout the Prison Service, in Parliament and across the country.

1.2 In addition to criticising specific procedures and practice at Whitemoor, the Woodcock Report pointed to widespread problems in the Prison Service generally, in particular with regard to security. On 19th December 1994, the Home Secretary made the following statement to the House of Commons in response to the Report:

> *"Sir John Woodcock's Report reveals a dreadful state of affairs at Whitemoor. I shall tell the House this afternoon what happened, the extent of the problems that exist, and the radical action which I believe needs to be taken to remedy them."*

1.3 In outlining the radical action required in respect of the wider problems, he said:

> *"I am therefore appointing General Sir John Learmont, formerly Quartermaster General for the Army, to conduct a comprehensive, independent and authoritative review of security throughout the Prison Service. His terms of reference will be:*
>
> *In the light of the Report of the Inquiry into the attempted escape from HM Prison Whitemoor on 9 September 1994, to review physical security and security procedures in the Prison Service in England and Wales, and to make recommendations."*

1.4 In the same statement, he also asked that the need for 'closed visits' within Special Security Units should be considered as part of the Inquiry. A 'closed visit' is one in which the prisoner and visitor are totally separated by screens which preclude any possibility of physical contact, and hence any passage of unauthorised items.

1.5 The Inquiry Team started work on 9th January 1995. Meanwhile, the Prison Service had rarely been out of the headlines, with the suicide of Frederick West, at Winson Green Prison on 1st January, the disturbances at Everthorpe Prison, on 2nd January, and the escape of three prisoners from Parkhurst Prison, on 3rd January.

1.6 In the light of the obvious security implications of the escape from Parkhurst, the terms of reference were extended by the Home Secretary, in a further statement to the House:

> *"As the House knows, Sir John Learmont is already reviewing physical security and security procedures throughout the Prison Service in England and Wales, and Sir John, accompanied by Sir John Woodcock, who reported on events at Whitemoor and who is acting as his assessor, will be visiting HMP Parkhurst this week. I have asked them to carry out an independent assessment of events at Parkhurst. They will have available to them the report made by Mr Tilt* [the Prison Service Director of Security] *which they will be able to take into account. In view of the detailed information about security at Parkhurst in Mr Tilt's report, it would not be appropriate for me to publish it, but the examination of it by Sir John Learmont will ensure that it is independently reviewed. Sir John Learmont and Sir John Woodcock will not be bound by it and the scope of their Inquiry will not be limited in any way. It will be open to them to bring forward proposals for early action without waiting for their formal report to me. The findings of their report will be published."*

(Hansard 10 January 1995)

SCOPE OF THE INQUIRY

1.7 The full Report of the Learmont Inquiry is presented in one document. The Report covers both the examination of security in the Service as a whole and the more specific investigation into the escape from Parkhurst. The Report consists of seven sections. Section 1, the Overview, provides the background to the Report and describes the methodology adopted. To assist the lay reader, historical background information and definitions of relevant terminology have been included at Appendix A.

1.8 Section 2 is dedicated to the findings of the Parkhurst Inquiry and sets out a number of specific security recommendations as well as raising some wider issues requiring further examination.

1.9 Many of the broader issues raised by the Parkhurst escape emerged again during the wider examination of prison security. These issues are dealt with in Section 3 of this Report, providing a backdrop for the examination of specific subjects.

1.10 Sections 4 and 5 address problems of prison security, encompassing the prison population, its accommodation and management. Section 4 examines the basics. Section 5 presents proposals for the way forward. Section 6 draws some conclusions.

1.11 Recommendations are made throughout the Report and are set out in a consolidated format in Section 7, grouped under subject headings. A full list of the 127 individual recommendations, in the order in which they appear in the Report, is at Appendix P. For ease of reference the full list of recommendations from the Woodcock Report is at Appendix O.

METHODOLOGY

The Inquiry team

1.12 The Inquiry was conducted by three assessors (General Sir John Learmont; Sir John Woodcock; and Mr G J Dadds, a former Governor/Area Manager/Regional Director, HM Prison Service) supported by three advisers (Mr M S Heath, Director General, the Engineering Council; Mr P J Leonard, a Governor 1, HM Prison Service; and Sir Peter Wallis, formerly of HM Diplomatic Service). The secretariat was drawn from Bedfordshire Police and the Home Office.

1.13 The Parkhurst escape was investigated by a team of Police Officers, led by Deputy Assistant Commissioner A Fry, from the Metropolitan Police, and drawn from the Metropolitan, Sussex and Dorset police forces. Secretarial support was provided locally by Hampshire police. The full membership is listed in Appendix B.

The main Inquiry

1.14 A security review of the six Dispersal Prisons was conducted, which provided essential information about physical security and security procedures and formed the basis for many subsequent recommendations. Current Prison Service practices in England and Wales were compared with those in operation in Holland, the USA, Spain, Scotland and Northern Ireland. Ideas were tested with a wide range of personalities both inside and outside the Prison Service, including inmates themselves.

1.15 Further information was obtained from a variety of sources. This included written submissions from individuals, groups and the Prison Service, together with a number of significant source documents, listed in Appendix C. The Inquiry visited over 50 prisons, predominantly in England and Wales but also in other countries. Many hundreds of prisoners and prison staff were interviewed in depth and these interviews contributed to a broad understanding of the Service, covering its good practice as well as its difficulties and problems. The comments and opinions in this Report are therefore put forward with confidence. In addition, the Inquiry has had the benefit of the considerable Prison Service experience of two members of the team, which has assisted the judgements on professional issues contained in the Report. Lists of prisons visited and individuals interviewed appear at Appendices D and E, respectively. The Inquiry extended over a period of nine months which included consideration of the financial implications of implementation. The Inquiry's costings appear at Appendix Q.

1.16 The procedures adopted by the Inquiry, when investigating both the escapes from Parkhurst Prison and the wider security issues, have followed the pattern established in the Woodcock Enquiry. The strategy has been to seek out the truth and, to achieve this, witnesses have been guaranteed confidentiality and anonymity. In order to remove any question of scapegoats being sought for any errors or omissions, emphasis has constantly been placed on the fact that the Inquiry has no disciplinary function. Comprehensive notes have been taken of interviews, for the exclusive use of the Inquiry and, in particular, to assist in compiling this Report. These notes will not be supplied to anyone, not even to individuals requesting notes of their own interviews. This stance has been taken to ensure the protection of witnesses and to avoid the embarrassment, suspicion and distrust which would otherwise inevitably arise if some witnesses circulated the record of their own interviews to colleagues, whilst others refused. These procedures have been explained to witnesses, who have not been precluded from being accompanied or legally assisted during interviews and who have been allowed to make their own written records. All assertions in the Report are supported by substantial written or oral evidence and judgements have been formulated from this material.

The Parkhurst Inquiry

1.17 Immediately after the escape from Parkhurst Prison, the Hampshire Constabulary opened a criminal investigation into the event and the Prison Service Director of Security undertook a non-disciplinary inquiry into the circumstance of the breakout.

1.18 At Parkhurst, 198 interviews were conducted by the Inquiry. It was surprising how many people asked to be seen and care was taken to strike a balance between volunteers and those identified for interview. The interviews were semi-structured, allowing the interviewers to focus on relevant topics while at the same time enabling the interviewees to freely express their views. Many interviews lasted several hours.

1.19 The interviews covered a cross-section of employees of all ranks, including ten Governor Grades and personnel at area and central Headquarters. Eight weeks were spent at Parkhurst conducting interviews and visiting all sections of the prison. Many hours were spent in the prison observing different working practices.

1.20 An open letter was circulated throughout the Prison Service, locally and nationally, explaining the terms of reference of the Inquiry. The letter emphasised that the Inquiry had no disciplinary function and assured the confidentiality of any written or oral statement made by prison personnel.

1.21 Section 2 of the Report seeks to provide as complete an account of the issues surrounding the escape as is possible, given the constraints of time and the need to avoid compromising the criminal investigation. It was essential to ensure that police primacy was maintained with no breach of sub judice rules. The criminal investigation continues.

The Salmon procedures

1.22 Every effort has been made to ensure fairness to those who have contributed and to anyone who might feel themselves to be the subject of criticism in the final Report. Throughout the information-gathering stage, every opportunity was taken to test provisional findings, criticisms and likely recommendations with individuals at all levels of the Prison Service.

1.23 It was agreed that, if a POA member wished, he or she could have a POA representative, a legal representative or 'Friend' present during interview. Agreement was also reached with the Prison Governors Association (PGA) concerning the conduct of interviews with Governor Grades. The PGA requested that prior notice of the topics to be covered in each interview be sent to the Governor Grades and this was done. No objections were raised if PGA members wanted a legal representative or 'Friend' to be present during an interview. The same practice was adopted for more senior Area and Headquarters Grades and for main-grade Civil Servants.

1.24 Whilst no individuals are named in the final Report, criticisms are frequently made of practices and procedures, which relate to specific posts and which could lead to the identification of the postholders, at least within the Service. In accordance with the best practice emanating from the Royal Commission on Tribunals of Inquiry (1966) under the chairmanship of Rt Hon Lord Justice Salmon, relevant extracts from the draft Report were circulated to 131 people who might believe they could be identified as the subject of criticism. The circulation offered an opportunity for individuals to comment before the Report was finalised.

1.25 During the Salmon procedures, requests have been received for details of evidence and identities of witnesses. These requests have not been met, for to do so would violate the confidentiality and absolute anonymity guaranteed to all. The Inquiry has collected a considerable amount of evidence from people at many levels within the Service who would feel extremely vulnerable if the pledge which has been given was not honoured.

ACKNOWLEDGEMENTS

1.26 To examine such a wide range of issues within the time available has required full co-operation from many people and thanks are due for the help and co-operation received from the Home Office, the Prison Service, HM Chief Inspector of Prisons, the Prison Ombudsman, senior industrialists, some previous authors of Prison Service Reports, the Commissioner of the Metropolitan Police Service, the Chief Constables of Bedfordshire, Dorset, Hampshire and Sussex, Prison Service staff associations and Governors and staff of the prison establishments that were visited, both within the UK and elsewhere.

SECTION 2: THE PARKHURST INQUIRY

THE STORY OF THE ESCAPE

2.1 At 6.00 pm on Tuesday 3rd January 1995, a Prison Officer entered the main corridor of D Wing at Parkhurst Prison where ten inmates were impatiently milling around by the exit, waiting to be escorted to the sports hall. The Officer had no idea how many or which prisoners to expect; and so began the train of events which led to three of those inmates escaping from what should have been one of the highest security establishments in the prison estate, holding some of the country's most notorious, organised and dangerous criminals.

2.2 The Officer was carrying out a routine task, collecting prisoners to take to the sports hall. The group, including some not noted for regular attendance, trailed from Wing to Wing, collecting more inmates en route, until they reached a total of 31. No prior notification of attendance had been given to staff. They did not know how many to expect in the group, had no idea of their security classifications and did not take any form of roll call to see who was present. Despite the high turn out and the membership of the group, suspicions were not aroused.

2.3 The unwieldy crocodile of inmates was escorted by three members of staff throughout the journey to the sports hall, with a dog handler in the vicinity. Because of on-going building work, they had to cover a distance of about one-quarter of a mile and pass through a series of security gates (see Figure 1). The staff unlocked one gate after another and shepherded the group through. They should have opened one gate at a time, held the group at each gate and counted the prisoners but they did not do so. The weather was reasonable but darkness had fallen and parts of the route were very dimly lit. The inmates wore their customary mixture of sports kit and personal outdoor clothes. There was no attempt to search any of the group, either on leaving the Wing or on arrival at the sports hall.

Fig.1 **Movement to Sports Hall**

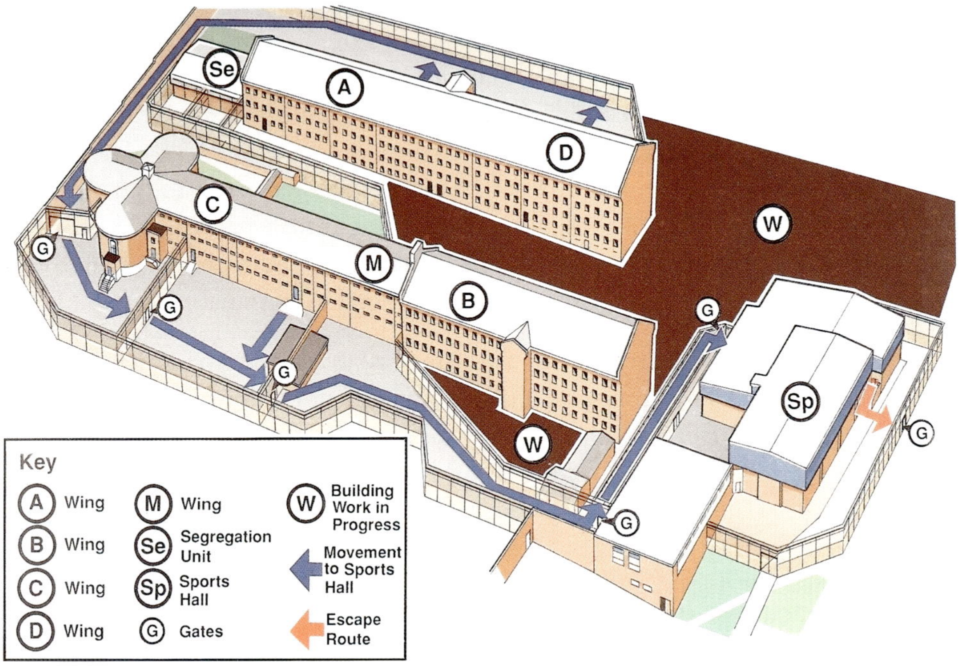

2.4 Once at the sports hall, a number of inmates peeled off into the weight-lifting area, with one instructor, whilst the rest spread around the main gymnasium engaging in 5-a-side football, supervised by a second instructor. For the first and only time that evening, a full roll call was taken by one of the instructors. Throughout the session, the accompanying Prison Officer remained in an observation box overlooking the two areas. Thirty-one active and demanding inmates would be a difficult group to control in the best of conditions. The poor design of the sports hall meant that conditions were far from ideal. There were a number of blind spots, some countered by strategically placed mirrors, but from the observation box it was still impossible to see the rear door of the sports hall and neither instructor could view his colleague's group (see Figures 2 and 3).

2.5 By the time the gym session was called to a close, at 7.00 pm, three of the prisoners were outside the prison perimeter, with prison staff totally unaware of their absence. The remaining inmates wandered around within the sports hall making control difficult. Some expressed their anxiety to return to Wings in time for their favourite TV programmes, others distracted

Fig. 2 Plan of the Sports Hall

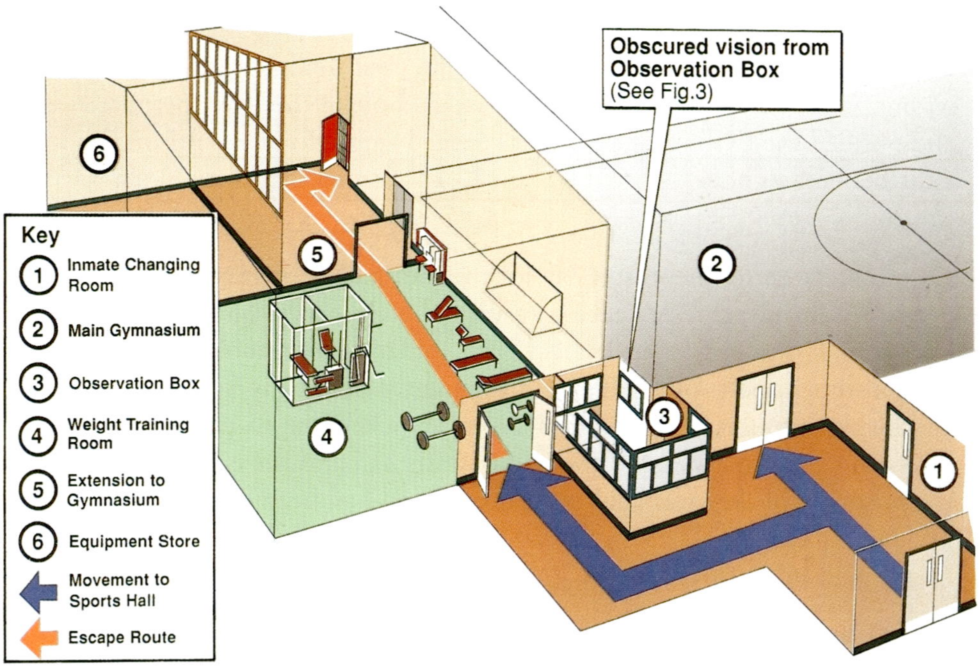

Fig. 3 Observation Blind Spot

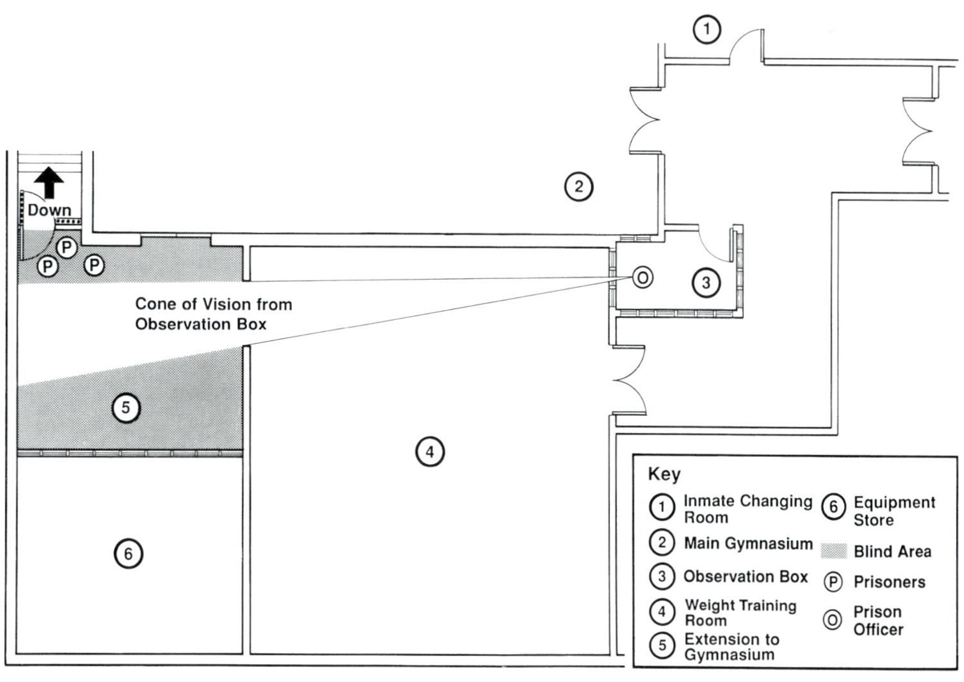

staff by gathering towards the exit door. No attempt was made to count them as they left the hall and Wing staff accepted the number that re-entered D Wing. As far as the Officers and the Emergency Control Room (ECR) staff were concerned, all was well and another routine task had been completed.

2.6 It was over an hour before staff had the first inkling that something was wrong. A patrolling dog handler discovered a hole in the inner perimeter fence and notified the ECR. Frantic activity ensued throughout the prison but it was a further half an hour before it was finally confirmed that three inmates were missing.

2.7 The hitherto uneventful day for the staff had been anything but uneventful for the three escapees. It was the culmination of activity over a long period, during which they had been able to fashion tools, manufacture the constituent parts of a ladder and apparently arm themselves with a gun and blank ammunition. They had also made a key that would open all the doors and gates that stood between the sports hall and the outer defences of the prison. This key was vital to their plan and had been tested several times prior to the escape. The key, the ladder rungs and perhaps a gun should have been found in routine searches.

2.8 The escapees' preparation and testing had not stopped there. They knew that they would need to cut through sections of the weld-mesh fencing and so had tested the wire cutters on a piece of fencing unwittingly provided for them in the metal workshop as a guard to a guillotine cutter.

2.9 The three inmates wasted little time in organised exercise once the roll call was over. They soon moved to the area of the unobserved rear door of the sports hall and made their exit. During a walk of about 200 yards, they used their key on a compound gate and two doors to enter the training workshop. Provided to give purposeful training, the workshop proved a God-send to the would-be escapers. The ladder uprights had been stacked beneath a bench, with other tubing and the connecting brackets and rungs hidden elsewhere in the workshop. It took little time to assemble the parts. The remaining elements of the escape equipment, consisting of a step ladder, wire snips, pliers and other small hand tools, were taken from the workshop store. Although locked, the door to this room was easily forced.

2.10 Once fully equipped, the three moved to a pre-determined area of the inner perimeter fence and put their earlier practice to good use by cutting a hole through an upper section of single-thickness weld-mesh. The approach to the fence and the area beyond were both open ground and they should have been seen by the prison's closed circuit television (CCTV) cameras, controlled from the ECR. The staff in the ECR were expected to form the central co-ordinators of CCTV coverage and ultimately of prison security. They consisted, on this night, of inexperienced and largely untrained Officers. Either the cameras did not adequately cover this particular section of fence or the staff did not notice the escapees on their monitors.

2.11 The final perimeter wall was scaled using the ladder and the three descended outside the establishment using lengths of hosepipe and electric cable (see Figure 4). This area was covered by cameras but again the escapees went unnoticed by ECR staff. Once outside the prison, the three were well-set; they wore their own clothes and had ample cash and a substantial head start on the authorities.

Fig. 4 **The Escape Method**

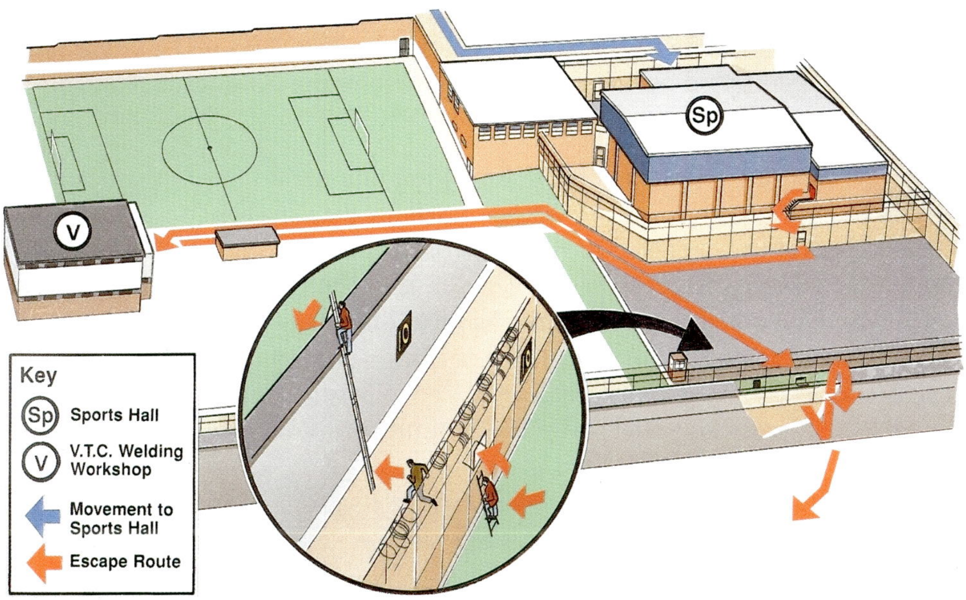

2.12 They walked into the centre of Newport and hired a taxi to Sandown, some nine miles away. Although they had in the meantime been spotted by an off-duty Prison Officer, they were not immediately recognised and it was to be the following morning before that Officer connected his sighting with the then highly publicised escape.

2.13 One of the escapees was a qualified pilot and the plan had been to use a tool, made in the workshop, to 'pull' the ignition of a light aircraft. The tool had been forgotten and the escapees had to find an alternative. They left the taxi at a filling station and purchased food, drink and three screwdrivers before walking a short distance to Bembridge airfield. Their clumsy efforts to enter and steal an aircraft were unsuccessful and they decided to try a seaborne escape. They walked along a railway line to Ryde but could not locate a suitable boat and went to ground in a summer house in the garden of a detached house occupied by a lone woman.

2.14 During four days and nights in hiding, one of the escapees shaved off his distinctive beard, which allowed him to venture out into the town to buy food. On the evening of 8th January, under cover of darkness, they made their way towards East Cowes to search again for a suitable boat. Shortly before 7.00 pm, they were spotted walking along the road to Cowes by off-duty Prison Officers who quickly alerted police. Two were detained almost immediately and the third was chased across open land towards a marina on the River Medina.

2.15 The chase was taken up by a Police Special Constable, an unpaid volunteer working in his own time, who caught up with the fleeing prisoner but lost him after a short struggle. About half an hour later, a police dog picked up a scent leading from the rear garden of a house and over a field towards the marina. The dog handler challenged a man who fled and jumped into the water, followed by the handler who, despite the deep water, was able to catch and handcuff him.

2.16 The three arrests marked the culmination of a period of great concern to the residents and authorities on the Isle of Wight, thankfully without injury to any of the personnel involved or members of the public. The significant danger posed by the escapees was reflected in the effort to recapture them, which was maintained throughout five days and nights, involving considerable manpower and resources both on the Isle of Wight and elsewhere. Public anxiety was further heightened because of previous threats made by one of the prisoners involved. The Trial Judge and a number of Police Officers and witnesses involved in his case were placed under 24-hour guard until the prisoners were back in custody.

THE ISSUES RAISED

2.17 This escape involved three dangerous inmates of one of the highest security prisons. They managed to carry out considerable preparations, obtain or manufacture tools and possibly a gun, and leave the establishment totally unobserved. The escape raised a number of critical questions, which formed the basis of the Parkhurst Inquiry:

- How did the inmates manufacture or obtain the escape equipment and carry or store it without being detected?
- How did they manage to breach the physical security measures and reach the outside of the perimeter wall?
- Why did it take almost two hours to detect the escape?
- Would improved intelligence handling have prevented the escape?
- Did the building works contribute in any way to the escape?
- Were there other factors in the management of the prison regime which affected the escape?
- Were there any previous warning signals?

How did the inmates manufacture or obtain the escape equipment and carry or store it without being detected?

2.18 The inmates had collected a number of articles for use in the escape. The following list shows the extent of the equipment obtained by the escapees:

- 6 x 12 foot lengths of 1 inch diameter metal } ladder parts
- a number of brackets } ladder parts
- slide hammer
- a key
- handgun and 9 rounds of blank .22 ammunition (see para. 2.27)
- in excess of £200 in cash
- 2 pairs of wire-cutting snips
- 2 pairs of pliers
- screwdriver
- 2 adjustable spanners
- copper hammer
- wooden step ladder (approximately 6 feet high)
- length of hosepipe
- length of electrical cable

2.19 Most of the tools and equipment were taken from the workshop store during the escape. Simple measures such as secure doors, locks and intruder alarms, would have prevented this. Of greater concern is the acquisition of the other items in the above list. They must either have been made in the prison or smuggled in by visitors, by staff or with inmates' personal property.

(a) Facilities for manufacture

2.20 Parkhurst provided opportunities for inmates to work in the laundry, tailors' shop, charity shop or welding workshop and to carry out cleaning duties. Inmates should be allocated to particular types of work by a Labour Board, chaired by a Governor Grade, taking into account the suitability of the work and a prisoner's history. These procedures were not always followed at Parkhurst. The main facility for manufacturing the escape items was the Vocational Training Course welding workshop (usually referred to as the VTC).

2.21 The VTC was staffed by a permanent Instructor, supported by a part-timer, and was fully equipped with metalwork tools, welding equipment and materials. There was no detailed audit of materials. In addition to the Instructor, a Prison Officer was detailed to book in the prisoners; report the roll to the ECR; ensure that Exceptional and High Risk Category A inmates were appropriately logged; monitor activities in the workshop; complete the occurrence sheet; and inform the ECR that the workshop was clear of prisoners at the end of each session. The Officer would be located in an observation box affording a view of the workshop.

2.22 An average attendance would be eight inmates and the Instructors were not able to supervise closely all the prisoners. They normally received little help from the Prison Officers, many of whom failed to carry out all their duties and preferred to sit in the security box reading or writing reports. There were very few supervisory visits.

2.23 Most Prison Officers had no knowledge of metalwork and were not able to monitor activities, especially of those inmates trained and experienced in sheet-metal work. Officers supervising such work must have sufficient knowledge and understanding of the work to ensure that they can identify security problems. Additionally, when prisoners were welding, they worked in cubicles hidden behind rubber safety screens, which gave them ample opportunities to make illicit items. It is clear that security in the workshop was compromised by an inability to observe all prisoners at all times.

2.24 One of the escapees was a qualified sheet-metal worker. In January 1994, he was assessed by the workshop instructor as being suitable to work in the welding workshop to gain National Vocational Qualification (NVQ) certificates in welding. He was judged to be capable of possessing the necessary welding skills to accomplish any task asked of him and was left to work without interference or supervision. He became a regular attender in the VTC and was consistently one of the highest paid inmates.

2.25 In the summer of 1994, he started work on the construction of metal goal posts for the sports hall. Among the materials he used were six twelve foot lengths of one inch diameter metal. This work had been commissioned and paid for by the Physical Education Department but was later abandoned. When approached by the other two prisoners in October or November, to help with the escape, he had little difficulty in converting the rods into a substantial ladder by making a number of brackets to connect the rods and form rungs. The tubing was stored under a workbench while the brackets were, according to an instructor, hidden in the tool store behind overalls and other items of clothing, in a metal cupboard.

2.26 During the relevant period, one of the other escapees gained admittance to the VTC as part of an art course with the Education Department. He had full access to the equipment and materials and was able to work unsupervised. He was not on the VTC roll and his admittance to the workshop was granted by a Governor Grade without full knowledge of the contents of his security file. He was responsible for making the key and the slide hammer. This tool was made from parts taken from an old exercise bicycle and was designed to facilitate the theft of a car and/or an aircraft. At one stage, it was found and removed to the office by an instructor who did not know what it was. He failed to report the matter or attach any significance to it and the prisoner soon reclaimed the tool. The instructor found the second inmate to be "demanding and pushy" and the inmate's behaviour led to him being banned from the workshop.

2.27 It is alleged that one of the inmates manufactured a hand gun but no gun has been recovered. For reasons of confidentiality, it is not possible to debate this allegation in this Report but, on the evidence available, the Inquiry believes that the escapees were able to fashion a gun and were in possession of blank ammunition.

2.28 There is no evidence that the inmates had access to a Prison Officer's key. However, from drawings found in the property of one of the prisoners, it appears that the key they used could have been made from memory after seeing keys handled by staff. The key was tested at various times and on one occasion taken back to the workshop for strengthening.

2.29 The escapees took full advantage of the workshop facilities to make the component parts of the ladder, slide hammer, gun and key. The ease with which these prisoners were able to work unsupervised, in a fully equipped workshop, highlights the security implications of providing such a facility without any check on materials or proper security procedures. Establishments with workshops require reliable procedures to guarantee daily audit of tools and materials. The Director of Security concluded in his Inquiry into the escape that it was inappropriate for a maximum security prison to have an engineering or welding workshop for training prisoners, a conclusion which this Inquiry supports. Further, the Service should review all work and training available to inmates in Dispersal Prisons, with emphasis on the central importance of security. In addition, workshops across the whole prison estate should be examined to ensure that prisoners can be observed at all times and that, subject to health and safety regulations, safety screens are made of transparent material.

(b) Items brought in by visitors

2.30 The majority of items listed in paragraph 2.18 could have been obtained within the prison but two items would have had to come from outside. These were the cash and the blank ammunition. The most likely route was through visits. Visitors to Category A prisoners are governed by the Approved Visitors Scheme under which only vetted visitors are permitted. In addition, all visitors, regardless of the category of the prisoner, are supposed to receive written visiting orders which they bring with them to present to gate staff. It was common for visitors to arrive at Parkhurst without an order and, on those occasions, an order would be filled out by the Wing staff and sent to the gate or the visit would be allowed to proceed without an order. There was no restriction on the number of visits allowed to an inmate.

2.31 The entrance containing the main reception area, X-ray machine and metal detector portal could not properly accommodate more than a few visitors at any one time and it was often overwhelmed, particularly at weekends. There should be sufficient accommodation and equipment at the main gate of an establishment holding Category A prisoners, to allow searching of all visitors and staff at all times. Observation of procedures, and thus security, would be enhanced by CCTV coverage of the reception area. The problems at Parkhurst were compounded by the fact that an insufficient number of staff was trained to operate the X-ray equipment properly and with full knowledge of procedures and relevant legislation. The communication between the main reception area and the visits reception area needed to be improved. If anything of interest was found, the fact could not be easily communicated to staff who searched the visitors and dealt with any personal property.

2.32 Visitors were admitted to the visits reception area, where they passed through another metal detector portal and were 'rub-down' searched, and their personal property was left in lockers before they moved through to the main visits room, passing toilets on the way. Prisoners at Parkhurst have in the past complained about the over-zealous searching of visitors. HM Chief Inspector of Prisons in June 1991 recommended that the arrangements for searching visitors should be reviewed. The Chief Inspector queried the need for a 'rub-down' search in all cases. His view was not accepted by the Governor or the Area Manager but there were a number of problems in practice. Visitors will always resent being searched but Governors must be supported in implementing existing instructions, in accordance with the recommendations of the Woodcock Report, in particular in maintaining 'rub-down' searches and X-ray examination of any items taken into the prison by visitors.

2.33 Searching of visitors took place in a small locker room which was inappropriate for the task. Once the visitor was in the visits room, an Officer was sent to collect the inmate, who should have been searched by Wing staff before leaving his Wing but this was rarely done. Prisoners were 'rub-down' searched by security staff before entering the visits room and a description of their clothing was noted. There was a serious weakness in the arrangements on which Officers have commented that:

> *"... because of the design, prisoners who have been searched pass those waiting to be searched, often unseen by Officers."*

2.34 Visits took place in the large visits room on the ground floor of the gate lodge. One corner of the room was partitioned off for the high risk prisoners. Tables and chairs were loosely spread around the room and there was a children's area and canteen. The two private visiting rooms were closed pending installation of large viewing windows, which meant that police and legal visits took place in the main visits room. There was no CCTV observation of this area. It should be covered by 360° fixed CCTV, with a recording facility.

2.35 The open nature of the visits room, which is not peculiar to Parkhurst, produced an unacceptable situation. Supervision of the room was often inadequate. It was not unknown for the staff to be busy fetching inmates or searching visitors and inmates and, in doing so, leaving the visits room undermanned. Prisoners and their visitors routinely pushed tables together to form groups. To prevent this practice, furniture should be fixed in a formal and easily observable layout. In addition, prisoners were not required to wear any item of distinguishable clothing, eg a tabard, with the result that Officers frequently found it difficult to identify inmates from visitors. An identification system is in place in some establishments and should be extended to all secure prisons. It was known by Officers that, in the confusion and noise, illicit items were regularly passed to the inmates. Officers witnessed objects being passed which were immediately hidden in a prisoner's anal passage or underwear.

2.36 The absence of any formal identity check of visitors entering and leaving the visits room increased the concerns of staff about not being able to distinguish inmates from visitors. This was highlighted by one Officer who recalled:

> *"Civilian clothes made visits very difficult; on one occasion a prisoner was visited by his identical twin. You could not tell them apart."*

2.37 The identity of visitors should have been verified before they left the prison and there is a need for a formal recognition system. The road to freedom from the visits room was barred by only two doors. Following the completion of its draft Report, the Inquiry received a copy of the HM Prison Service Security Audit Report on Parkhurst, giving the results of an audit carried out between 22nd February and 9th March 1995. The Audit Team reported:

> *"We were also concerned about the lack of identification of inmates and visitors. Photographs of inmates are available in visits but were not being used by staff. We observed that visitors are allowed to leave the prison before inmates are accounted for."*

2.38 Additionally, a Governor has expressed concern about a design brief which placed the visits room on the perimeter of the establishment without a sterile area between it and the gatehouse.

2.39 If an inmate was suspected of receiving items during a visit, he should have been strip searched. The Manual on Security reminds Governors that they have the discretion to authorise strip searches but that this must be exercised reasonably. It means in practice that '... searches should be conducted only where the interests of security or of good order and discipline so require.' Strip searches of prisoners suspected of receiving illicit articles during visits were, therefore, within the rules but they were regarded as pointless by some staff because prisoners frequently concealed items internally.

The intimate searches necessary to discover items hidden in this way could not, by law, be carried out by Officers, and doctors would only perform them with the consent of the prisoner or when health was seriously threatened. This left one Officer with the feeling that:

> *"All Officers could do was use what they had seen as intelligence and hopefully cell searches would follow."*

2.40 Inmates suspected of receiving goods from visitors can be restricted to 'closed' visits. These were very rarely imposed at Parkhurst and it was observed that the closed visits room was badly constructed, requiring prisoners and visitors to stand in order to see each other through the high window. The room was also used as a storeroom for sports mats and as a place for strip searching the high risk inmates. The facility should be reconstructed and closed visits should be re-introduced for prisoners suspected of receiving illicit items or identified as likely to attempt escape.

2.41 There can be little doubt that goods were regularly smuggled in by visitors despite the belief that policies were in place to address the problem. The disparity between theory and practice would have been alleviated had a clear written policy on searching been available to staff, inmates and visitors. This policy must be monitored and supervised to ensure implementation. It was illogical that Parkhurst visitors, after being searched, could go directly, or at any stage during a visit, to the toilets, where objects hidden in underclothing or body passages could be retrieved and pocketed without any fear of further searches. Any visitor going to the toilet should be subject to further searching on the way to and from the toilet area and this principle should also apply to inmates. In addition, all toilets should be searched before the end of a visits session and before the inmates and visitors are allowed to leave.

2.42 The suggestion that prisoners should not have access to toilets at all during visits was raised by a Principal Officer at Parkhurst in September 1994, as part of his investigation into a serious assault on a prisoner believed to be dealing in drugs. A senior Governor said he was "... not sure we can insist on this" and it was not pursued. The smuggling of drugs into the prison was the major issue in that case but the arguments would equally apply to the smuggling of ammunition or cash. No limit was imposed on the amount of cash visitors could carry and money being paid in or out of prisoners' accounts was passed in the visits room. This system was open to abuse and any such transactions should take place away from visits rooms, removing the need for visitors to carry more cash than they need to spend in canteens or vending machines in the visits room.

Family visits

2.43 The concept of 'family visits' was introduced at Parkhurst in October 1993, as a result of the Woolf Report, and was endorsed by Prison Service Headquarters. The idea was to allow Category A and B inmates with young children to meet their families in a 'different environment'. The visits were held monthly on a Wednesday, for eight prisoners, and were booked in advance by inmates, through Wing Governors. The visits started at 10.00 am and were held in the sports hall, where inmates could be involved in activities such as trampolining with their children. At 11.45 am, the families, inmates and staff moved to the visits room where lunch was brought in by other prisoners. The visits continued through the lunch period, during which time all the other prisoners were locked up, with only a skeleton staff left in the prison.

2.44 Certain high security prisoners soon dominated the family visits scheme and started to complain about the security imposed on normal visits because, on family visit days, they could mingle openly with other prisoners and their families without restriction. The prisoners delivering lunch to the families were not searched, either on entering the visits area or on leaving, despite having freely mingled with the inmates and their visitors. Families were allowed cameras but the films were developed and checked by the prison. One film was found to have pictures of an area of the prison that should not have been photographed. One Officer pointed out that the most dangerous inmates were wandering around the prison, together with numerous members of their families, making proper supervision extremely difficult.

2.45 The rationale for 'family visits' was laudable but the system was abused by those prisoners who were most capable of taking advantage of lax security. Although the concept was successful in other prisons with very different security problems, it is not an appropriate concept for a Dispersal Prison, like Parkhurst, where a few dominant inmates soon used it to their own advantage.

2.46 The potential advantages of 'family visits' were far outweighed by the abuse. They were seen as wrong in principle by the majority of staff. One Officer stated:

> *"Family visits are not suitable for Parkhurst. No inmate should be out during State A, ie lunch time ... High risk prisoners used to intimidate other inmates so that they could monopolise family visits."*

2.47 Visits to prisoners are important and play a role in maintaining family ties and reducing control problems. However, the situation at Parkhurst was lax and unprofessional, offering little or no effective obstacle to visitors determined or compelled to smuggle illegal goods to inmates. 'Family visits' in their existing format should be stopped altogether in Dispersal Prisons. As with other visits, effective measures are required to ensure that inmates and visitors meet in a secure, sterile and properly supervised environment.

Children

2.48 Parkhurst quite properly resisted attempts to relax the instructions to search children but there had been a problem with children taking toys into the visits rooms. There was documentary evidence of three separate occasions when children had been in the visits area with toy guns. This may seem innocuous and irrelevant to the realities of security but toy and imitation weapons can provide determined inmates with a means to facilitate escape.

2.49 It has been intimated that the gun in the possession of the escapees from Parkhurst consisted of parts of a toy gun adapted, with other materials, to make a weapon capable of discharging blank ammunition. There were other occasions, not detailed within this Report, when toy guns had provoked potential security breaches.

2.50 The way to solve the problem depends on the type of prison. In high security prisons, visiting children should be prohibited from bringing their own toys and restricted to those provided in the children's area. In lower category establishments, imitation weapons should be banned and the Prison Service should institute appropriate systems for checking other toys.

(c) Items brought in by staff

2.51 No evidence has been produced that any member of staff assisted with the escape yet the possibility that a member of staff could be coerced into bringing items into the prison for inmates cannot be ignored. As they arrived for work, staff were required to pass through the metal detector portal at the main gate and to have their bags X-rayed. Their metal key chains almost always triggered the metal detector but this never resulted in further checks. Dog handlers, prison and police escorts and other regular official visitors using the vehicle entrance did not pass through the X-ray or metal detector portal facilities.

2.52 About once a month, staff were subjected to complete searches on arrival at the prison and the visits room was utilised for this purpose. The procedures at Parkhurst were more effective than in some other establishments but were no substitute for the safeguards, against coercion or the passing of illicit items via staff, that would be provided by the implementation of the Woodcock recommendation for the searching of all staff at Dispersal Prisons each time they enter the prison; and there should be random searches of staff leaving these prisons. Facilities should be provided for all staff to leave personal clothing and possessions outside the establishment perimeter.

(d) Items brought in within inmates' property

2.53 It is possible that inmates brought illicit goods into the prison with their legitimate property. After the escape, two spanners and a battery charger were found hidden inside a radio cassette player belonging to one of the escapees. The photographs at Figures 5 and 6 show other items kept in his cell.

Fig. 5 & 6 **Property in Prisoner's Possession**

2.54 Reception Officers at Parkhurst had the use of an X-ray machine but not all had received training. The problem was compounded by the large volumes of property held by some prisoners, which often arrived separately to the inmates and with inventories which varied in accuracy and degree of detail. Security checks by untrained staff were unlikely to provide a comprehensive screening. Once property passed through reception, it was considered to be clear of illicit goods. Consequently the property was rarely, if ever, re-checked, using an X-ray machine, during a cell search. It was encouraging to learn that, when the Security Audit Team visited in February 1995, all items entering the prison through reception were being passed through the X-ray machine and that Parkhurst procedures were described as consistent with best practice.

'Rub-Down' Searches

2.55 'Rub-down' searches of prisoners should have taken place whenever prisoners moved from one building to another or between areas. This is not explicitly set out in the Manual on Security but was stipulated in the 1994/95 Parkhurst Establishment Contract. Officers and Governor Grades accepted that 'rub-down' searches were rarely done. Prisoners leaving the workshops, or leaving for and returning from the sports hall, were not normally searched. Hand-held metal detectors were available to assist with 'rub-down' searching but were not used. Both these factors had a bearing on the escape. HM Chief Inspector of Prisons commented in October 1994 on:

> *"... an almost complete absence of proper 'rub-down' searching whenever members of management are not present."*

2.56 The Governor contended that the requirement to undertake 'rub-down' searches was unrealistic because they were time-consuming, manpower-intensive and impractical in a prison undergoing major structural reorganisation. Despite the difficulties, 'rub-down' searches must be carried out consistently and to a standard specified in the annual security audit, agreed with the Area Manager.

Cell searching

2.57 The Manual on Security stipulates that Category A prisoners should have their cells searched fortnightly but there was no written instruction at Parkhurst to endorse this, other than in the job description for the Principal Officer in charge of the Security Department. The Manual further states that accurate records of cell searches, including the reason for the search, should be maintained. The Parkhurst Establishment Contract 1994/95 laid down a target of searching each cell, on average, once every 28 days.

2.58 Cell searching failed to meet targets throughout the prison. Wing staff showed a marked reluctance to search the cells of prisoners on their own Wings, while the Security Section found it impossible to maintain targets, due to constant abstractions for other duties.

2.59 This issue was raised in the 1991 Hadfield/Lakes Report of an Audit of the Custody of Category A Prisoners. It was considered that efficient searching was a most important security tool and the Report strongly recommended that prisons holding Category A prisoners should have dedicated and fully equipped searching teams, capable of maintaining a viable searching programme and supported by dogs trained to search for firearms, explosives and drugs. The importance of such teams was re-stated in the Woodcock Report and is fully supported by this Inquiry.

2.60 A senior Governor Grade at Parkhurst addressed the issue in February 1993 in a memorandum to Headquarters:

> *"Within HMP Parkhurst we have a dedicated Security Department which has search teams. We also have a responsibility within individual areas for searching of cells to take place by Wing staff. As indicated in the Hadfield/Lakes Report because it is a flexible task, in the past search teams have been regularly deployed to cover Wing duties. We have not been maintaining our searching targets, this is now improving but is not yet perfect."*

2.61 Further evidence that cell searching was not taking place was found in the minutes of the Parkhurst Security Committee meeting, held on 13th September 1994, where comments were made about searching having 'fallen away'. This was followed by a memorandum from a senior Governor Grade reminding staff of the need to search and record searches. The minutes of the following Security Committee meeting, on 27th September 1994, stated:

> *"Searching - this has not improved, the staff seem to think that the full search conducted on 19, 20, 21 September had obviated the need for cell searching this week, A and D Wings will be further pursued."*

2.62 The minutes of a meeting on 8th November 1994 recorded nil ordinary searches on A and D Wings, although other parts of the prison were on target. These findings and comments were mirrored by HM Chief Inspector's letter of October 1994 which stated that:

> *"The searching of Category B and C inmates and their cells hardly happened, that of Category A prisoners seriously behind target."*

2.63 To search a cell properly, including examination of the furniture and prisoner's property and a strip search of the prisoner as recommended in the Manual on Security, could take as much as three hours and sometimes more. The resentment this caused, quite apart from the time involved, brought pressures on Wing staff not to search cells. The Area Manager commented about searching cells in September 1994:

> *"This appeared to be a difficult procedure as some prisoners were in bed."*

2.64 In November and December 1994, 'lock down' searches were instituted because searching targets were not being achieved. These searches were described by a Principal Officer as follows:

> *"To meet our searching quota, once a month we locked down the prison and used all the staff to search all prisoners' cells. These are not full, quality searches but just a cosmetic exercise to keep quotas up..."*
>
> *"..There are definite signs and evidence of a reluctance by Wing staff to confront inmates."*

2.65 The Audit of February 1995 also found many instances of poor security and staff intimidation and, in regard to the searching of cells, reported:

> *"The standard of cell searching we observed, in particular by residential staff, was so poor that it amounted to little more than staff entering a cell, checking it briefly for about 3-5 minutes and leaving. The inmates were not strip searched and rarely rubbed down."*

Property held in cells

2.66 One factor in the inability to search cells effectively was the amount of property individual prisoners were allowed to keep. A list of items that may be held by a prisoner was issued at Parkhurst, along with guidance notes, on 1st April 1994. The salient paragraph, covering the maximum allowance, is produced below:

> *"The number of items permitted in a cell should not be so great that searching is unduly hindered; that a cell cannot be kept tidy; or that possessions cannot be carried by the prisoner on transfer. A prisoner should not be allowed in possession of more property than he can carry without assistance. This has become an increasing problem over the years and our policy is to encourage prisoners to hand in or send out excess property."*

2.67 The guidelines were commonly abused and, significantly, when the High Risk prisoners were moved out from D Wing after the escape, some had in excess of ten boxes of property. When four of these inmates were transferred, a Principal Officer described how:

> *"It took eight Officers four hours to pack the cell property of the* [inmates] *and take it from the Wing to the gate. That was so even though it was not listed. It would have taken a week to list all the property."*

2.68 There was no question of these prisoners being able to carry their possessions on transfer. In the case of two of the escapees, it cost the Prison Service (and therefore the taxpayer) £466, just to transport their personal property. Many prisoners had property in their possession which far exceeded the guidelines and which hindered the efficient searching of cells and Wings. Perversely, the most dangerous inmates had the most property and were therefore subject to the least effective searching. These circumstances mirrored the situation uncovered by Sir John Woodcock at Whitemoor Prison and emphasises the urgent need to implement volumetric control of prisoners' property. The volume allowed should be standard to all inmates, whatever their category. Prisoners should not be allowed to add to their property, if it would then exceed the allowance, until arrangements are made for excess property to be collected by relatives/friends or stored centrally.

Searching Communal Areas

2.69 The instructions on searching communal areas, such as association landings and inmates' kitchens, are contained in the Establishment Contract:

> *"All accommodation/workshops etc where prisoners have access will be searched monthly but checked daily by staff deployed in the area as fire checks."*

2.70 There was disparity between the Wings on this point. C and M Wings searched the communal Wing areas three times daily and kept records of each search. In the Segregation Unit, regular searches of the association area were carried out but no records were kept. On A and D Wings, there were no regular searching strategies and no records were kept.

2.71 The policy of an open regime allowed prisoners considerable freedom of association and use of communal areas, including the facility to store and cook their own food. Food was stored in the cupboards in the Wing kitchens, in the inmates' cells or in large chest freezers kept on each Wing. Members of the Inquiry were surprised at the volumes of frozen food. D Wing, housing approximately 60 inmates, had four large, family-sized chest freezers in the association rooms; all were full to the brim.

2.72 Similar freezers were kept on A Wing, one of which contained a locked metal box. However, the staff claimed to have a key and to have checked the contents regularly. As recently as March this year, a visit to D Wing resulted in a locked filing cabinet being found in an association room. The Wing staff did not have a key and could not say which inmate kept the key. On another occasion, Inquiry members were shown the freezers in A Wing, one of which clearly contained alcohol.

2.73 These examples highlight the amount and type of property kept on the Wings, sometimes even in locked cabinets. The potential to store illicit goods goes without saying, especially in view of the limited searching of these facilities on some Wings. There must be a coherent strategy for searching communal areas and appropriate records must be maintained.

RECOMMENDATIONS

1 Throughout the prison estate, establishments with workshops should set up daily audits of tools and materials. Workshops should be designed to ensure that prisoners can be observed at all times and, subject to health and safety regulations, safety screens should be made of transparent material.
(Paras. 2.21 and 2.29)

2 Such establishments should also ensure that Officers supervising workshops have basic knowledge and understanding of the work they are supervising, to ensure that they can identify security breaches and risks.
(Para. 2.23)

3 The Prison Service should review the type of work and training available to inmates in Dispersal Prisons, with emphasis on the central importance of security in all aspects of activity.
(Para. 2.29)

4 Sufficient accommodation and equipment should be provided, at the main gate of all prisons holding Category A inmates, to enable searching of all staff and visitors to take place at all times. This should be subject to CCTV observation. The main reception area should have direct communication with the visits reception area.
(Para. 2.31)
[See Woodcock recommendation 13]

5 Sufficient numbers of staff should be trained at each establishment to ensure that all X-ray and metal detection equipment, in particular at the gatehouse, is operated by qualified staff, who should be fully aware of searching procedures and relevant rules/ legislation. Searching procedures should be regularly supervised.
(Paras. 2.31 and 2.41)
[See recommendation 86 and Woodcock recommendation 12]

6 Visitors to prisons holding Category A inmates must be subject to a 'rub-down' search and X-ray check, in accordance with existing instructions. All hand baggage and loose items (eg coats) should be X-rayed. All baggage and property, except cash for canteens and vending machines, should be left in secure containers at the gatehouse or in a Visitors Centre situated outside the prison perimeter.
(Paras. 2.32 and 2.42)
[See recommendation 14 and Woodcock recommendation 14]

7 There should be full 360° fixed CCTV cover in visits rooms in secure establishments, with video recording facilities.
(Para. 2.34)
[See Woodcock recommendation 18]

8 Visits rooms in secure establishments should have fixed furniture with a formal and observable layout.
(Para. 2.35)
[See Woodcock recommendation 18]

9 Inmates on visits should wear some form of distinguishable clothing.
(Para. 2.35)

10 A visitor recognition system should be introduced.
(Paras. 2.36-37)

11 The closed visits room at Parkhurst should be reconstructed to an appropriate design and brought back into use for all prisoners suspected of receiving illegal items from visitors and for inmates on the escape list.
(Para. 2.40)

12 A clear written policy on searching procedures should be available to all staff, inmates and visitors and should be monitored and supervised to ensure implementation.
(Para. 2.41)
[See recommendation 87 and Woodcock recommendation 11]

13 Any prisoner or visitor needing to use the toilet facilities during a visit should be searched before and after visits to the toilet. In addition, all toilets should be searched before the end of a visits session and before inmates and visitors are allowed to leave.
(Para. 2.41)

14 Visitors should not make cash transactions in visits rooms except at canteens or vending machines.
(Para. 2.42)
[See recommendation 6]

15 Family visits are not appropriate for Dispersal Prisons and should cease.
(Para. 2.47)

16 In high security prisons, visiting children should be restricted to toys provided in the children's area. In other prisons, imitation weapons should be banned and other toys brought in by children should be checked.
(Para. 2.50)

17 All staff at Dispersal Prisons should be searched each time they enter the prison and there should be random searches of staff leaving these prisons.
(Para. 2.52)
[See recommendation 95 and Woodcock recommendation 27]

18 Facilities should be provided for all staff at Dispersal Prisons to leave civilian clothes and personal possessions outside the prison perimeter.
(Para. 2.52)
[See Woodcock recommendation 28]

19 Other than in exceptional circumstances, a prisoner's property should accompany its owner on transfer and should be checked against the inventory, searched and X-rayed by fully trained staff at each prison establishment.
(Paras. 2.54 and 2.68)
[See Woodcock recommendation 32]

20 'Rub-down' searches should be carried out consistently and to a standard specified in the annual security audit, agreed by the Area Manager.
(Para. 2.56)

21 Cell searches should be undertaken in accordance with the Manual on Security.
(Paras. 2.57-65)
[See recommendations 92 and 94 and Woodcock recommendation 8]

22 The Hadfield/Lakes proposal, for dedicated and specially equipped search teams in prisons holding Category A inmates, should be mandatory in Dispersal Prisons. Such teams should have available to them, on a regular basis, dogs trained to identify firearms, explosives and drugs.
(Para. 2.59)
[See recommendations 93 and 94 and Woodcock recommendation 9]

23 A volumetric control of all prisoners' possessions should be introduced forthwith, to reduce dramatically the amount of property in possession/storage and facilitate effective searching. The volume allowed should be standard to all inmates, whatever their category. Prisoners should be allowed only that amount of property which fits into a maximum of two transit boxes. Prisoners should not be allowed to add to their property, if it would then exceed the allowance, until arrangements are made for excess property to be collected by relatives/friends or stored centrally.
(Para. 2.68)
[See Woodcock recommendation 6]

24 There must be a coherent strategy for searching of communal areas and appropriate records must be maintained.
(Para. 2.73)
[See recommendation 92 and Woodcock recommendation 5]

How did they manage to breach the physical security measures and reach the outside of the perimeter wall?

2.74 The overriding principle of physical security in Dispersal Prisons is a very high standard of perimeter security. In 1988, the Working Group on Category A Security submitted a report which set out minimum security standards for high security prisons and listed the deficiencies which they had found at establishments. The two main criticisms of Parkhurst were that no detection device was fitted to the perimeter security fence and that CCTV cover of the fence and sterile area was incomplete. To reach the perimeter wall, the escapees had to surmount the locked doors and gates and cut through the inner perimeter fence. They also had to take account of the CCTV camera coverage. The Inquiry believes that mandatory minimum security standards must be set for all establishments.

(a) Locks

2.75 Locking schedules were dictated by the Locking Section at Headquarters. Decisions to upgrade locks could be made at a local level but decisions to downgrade could not be made without reference to that Section. The policy was that non-residential buildings were protected by one Class 2 and one Class 3 lock. Residential blocks were protected by a Class 1 ("doubles") lock, requiring two keys. However, it had been agreed, apparently orally, between Headquarters and Parkhurst, that the welding shop door did not require a second lock, the purpose of which would have been primarily to deny access to the workshop to unauthorised staff. The area around the sports hall therefore had gates requiring just one key and this meant that the gate protecting the rear door of the sports hall and both the door and gate into the welding workshop could be opened with the same key.

2.76 By exploiting this weak link, the three prisoners were able to leave the sports hall and enter the compound and the welding workshop. The rear door of the sports hall did have a second lock which was not in use. This lock had been primarily intended to keep prison staff out of what was originally a store-room in the sports hall but an extension of the weights room into the store-room area removed the need for this lock and it therefore fell into disuse. In conjunction with current moves to electronic/magnetic locks, locking schedules need to be reviewed to remove such anomalies.

(b) Inner perimeter fence

2.77 The fence was made of mild steel weld-mesh and was double-skinned to a height of about two metres. Above this height, it was a single layer and it was here that the escapees cut a hole through which to climb. In most high security prisons, this fence would be fitted with a vibration detection alarm system. No such device was fitted at Parkhurst.

2.78 There are various types of fence alarm, invariably known within the Prison Service as 'geophones'. A geophone is a specific type of fence alarm which detects vibrations. A string of geophones can be placed around a perimeter fence to form the first part of an alarm system. The system is connected to the ECR, where an alarm sounds when vibrations have been detected. The system can be sensitised to filter out background vibrations caused, for example, by birds landing on the fence. Complications can arise when sports activities or building works take place in the close proximity of the fence but these do not present insuperable problems (see para. 2.87).

2.79 Attempts were made to establish why there were no geophones fitted at Parkhurst. Reports and letters dating back as far as 1975 were examined. Some relevant correspondence had been routinely destroyed and some could not be traced. The examination revealed a confused story. The main thrust of the debate is set out in the following paragraphs. A full schedule of the correspondence examined appears at Appendix F, which reveals substantial weaknesses in the chain of command and decision-making process.

2.80 There has been considerable debate within the Prison Service about the issue of geophones at Parkhurst, fuelled by letters from the local Member of Parliament to Ministers expressing concern at the absence of fence alarms. The reasons for not installing geophones have included cost; technical arguments; problems caused by the building work programme; and the construction of the perimeter fence.

2.81 The local MP wrote to the then Home Secretary in October 1991 stating:

> *"... you may imagine my dismay that the geophones about which I wrote to* [the Minister of State], *and his reply is dated the 9th March 1989, are still waiting to be fitted!"*

2.82 A senior Governor Grade was consulted and wrote:

> *"There is no early plan to install geophones at Parkhurst ... DSP1* [Directorate of Services and Personnel] *have taken the view up to now that major rebuilding work needs to be completed before geophones can be installed. The earliest date quoted had been 1994-5 but there is no current planned date for their installation.*
>
> *I take the contrary view that geophones should be installed as early as possible to as much of the perimeter fence as practicable. If short gaps need to be left because of major redevelopment work that is a smaller price to pay than delaying the whole project for several more years. I believe the Governor takes a similar view."*

2.83 Indeed, the then Head of Custody had written to Prison Headquarters on 20th August 1991, emphasising that "Geophones and cameras go hand-in-glove and one without the other seriously compromises the security of the establishment." He thought that it would be technically possible to install geophones along most of the perimeter fence.

2.84 A senior Governor from the Custody Group wrote to the same Headquarters Department on 6th September 1991, recommending that the fitting of geophones along most of the fence lines be brought into the overall programme of work at the earliest possible time. The Governor himself wrote to the Area Manager on 14th January 1992, stating that, in his professional view, geophones should be put in place earlier than then envisaged and emphasising that Parkhurst was the only Dispersal Prison, holding high risk Category A prisoners, which did not have the protection of geophones.

2.85 This advice was apparently not provided to the then Home Secretary, who replied to the MP as follows:

> *"Geophones are already in place in the Special Secure Unit, which holds exceptionally high-risk prisoners. As you know it has been recommended to extend their use to the whole of the internal perimeter fence. However, our plans have had to be modified since* [the Minister of State] *wrote to you in 1989, because of the current extensive rebuilding programme which is taking place at Parkhurst. This will upgrade the accommodation and improve the overall security of the establishment, in the long run, but it is also very disruptive. Geophones are highly sensitive and their effectiveness depends upon the existence of a relatively stable physical environment. The difficulty with installing geophones while building work is being undertaken is that they might not provide substantial extra security, and the consequent danger exists that the building work itself would damage, or regularly immobilise the equipment. However, the Governor and the Area Manager responsible for Parkhurst Prison have asked for a feasibility study to be carried out which would look at ways of phasing in the geophones so that they would retain maximum effectiveness while the current refurbishment work is taking place."*

2.86 The Directorate of Works (DOW) has been unable to provide the technical evidence on which the reply was based and it has not been possible to ascertain whether the feasibility study was undertaken. However, it has provided an opinion from the then Senior Scientist in the Scientific Research Development Branch who, in a letter dated 6th April 1995, stated:

> *"At that time* [1987] *geophones were recognised as having an extremely high probability of detection, but also an unacceptably high false alarm rate ... which would be exacerbated by re-construction and building site vibrations."*

2.87 The Inquiry asked the Police Scientific Development Branch (PSDB), a Home Office Unit which also undertakes considerable work on behalf of the Prison Service, to visit Parkhurst on 15th February 1995 and, with the co-operation of the Works Department, to carry out a full on-site survey. Their findings, which were provided to the Prison Service, firmly rejected the notion that building works would have adversely affected geophones and showed that there were no technical reasons why geophones could not have been installed and tuned to work on the fence as then configured. PSDB contended that vibrations from nearby contractors' machinery were not likely to cause any damage to the geophones. Significantly, geophones at Wormwood Scrubs Prison had not been damaged during long-term building works, nor had those which were already located around the SSU at Parkhurst.

2.88 The MP restated his concerns in November 1992 and, on that occasion, the then Minister of State replied:

> *"... the installation of geophones will need to be carefully planned in conjunction with the other building work at the establishment. As you know, this year's public spending round was a particularly difficult one and it was not possible to make firm plans for building work at every establishment until we had a clearer idea of the resources which would be available. We are now in the process of finalising our plans for major building work in the light of the recent public expenditure settlement and we shall be examining how the installation of geophones might be phased in with this work."*

2.89 Throughout this period, pressure was maintained by the Governor and Area Manager; but, when the building programme for 1994/95 was presented to the Prison Service Executive Committee, the provision of geophones at Parkhurst had slipped again and was re-scheduled for no earlier than 1996. The Prisons Board has stated that this decision was the result of having to make urgent provision for extra blocks, to house the increasing prison population and implement recommendations of the Woolf Report (costing over £100 million). As a result, geophones at Parkhurst, and numerous other projects, had been deferred to 1995/96 or beyond. The Area Manager challenged the decision and, to overcome this further delay, he persuaded all the Governors in his Area to vire part of their own prison budgets, in order to pay for geophones to be fitted at Parkhurst, and the Directorate of Works was commissioned, in September 1994, to undertake the installation.

2.90 At that stage, the Directorate agreed to fund the work but decided that, in addition to fitting alarms, the fence itself would need to be replaced. It was suggested that the existing fence was constructed in such a way that excessive false alarms would have resulted. While improvements to the fence were desirable, the Governor and Prison Service Physical Security Adviser did not consider them essential for the operation of geophones. Indeed, the Physical Security Adviser, in his report of April 1994, had stated:

> *"... a programme of replacement of these panels is recommended but it is not vital to the installation of geophones ..."*

2.91 This view was endorsed by PSDB in February 1995. In the event, the replacement of fence panels, to be completed prior to the installation of geophones, had barely commenced at the time of the escape.

2.92 Geophones have been a standard requirement for Dispersal Prisons since implementation of the Mountbatten Report, in the early 1970s, and were fitted in most Dispersal Prisons even prior to confirmation of the requirement by the Working Group on Category A Security, in 1988. Senior, non-operational officials, however, were not persuaded of their prime importance at Parkhurst or Wakefield, establishments recognised as housing some of the most dangerous prisoners in the system. By the time the resources were found to install geophones, the escape had occurred. In the opinion of experienced members of PSDB, had geophones been fitted:

> *"... it is extremely likely that the 3 escaping inmates would have been detected at an early stage of cutting the fence ..."*

2.93 Indeed, two members of PSDB, who have studied this subject over many years, reported having never encountered a successful cutting attack against a correctly installed and working geophones system.

2.94 Many of the arguments over geophones at Parkhurst were based on financial and resource considerations but the Inquiry considered that the judgements made within the Prison Service took only a narrow view of costs. The estimate for geophone installation, which could have foiled the escape, was £250,000, far less than the cost of the Hampshire police operation to recapture the prisoners, estimated at £500,000.

(c) Closed Circuit Television

2.95 Although Parkhurst had widespread CCTV coverage, the cameras did not provide full surveillance of the compound, perimeter fence, sterile area and exterior of the perimeter wall. The escapees identified and exploited blind spots on the fence and compound. Some areas were not visible unless staff in the ECR decided to move the cameras. A large area of the compound leading to the workshop had no camera coverage and the effectiveness of other cameras along the escape route had been reduced by the erection of additional fences during the building work.

2.96 CCTV coverage at Parkhurst had been the subject of a number of reviews and adverse comments. Included among the recommendations following an escape in 1991 was:

> *"The CCTV system now in use appears to be the product of amalgamation of two systems - static cameras and mobile cameras - and consideration should be given to reviewing the efficiency of the CCTV cover."*

2.97 In January 1992, a Governor from the Directorate of Custody (DOC1 Division) reported on his examination into the efficiency of the CCTV system. He observed:

> *"... the confusion amongst controllers as to the purpose of particular cameras and that the system is not being used as designed. There are considerable dangers in this situation and it is recommended that action be taken to institute management controls over the system."*

2.98 Perimeter security and CCTV were reviewed in April 1994 by the Physical Security Adviser. The review highlighted weaknesses in the perimeter security and camera coverage and made recommendations as to camera datum settings (normal fixed positions) and re-positioning of fencing to allow for full CCTV cover. One recommendation was to fit a 'Spyhawk' camera in the compound, with 360° cover over a 100 yard radius. Recommendations were also made about camera datum settings, to prevent blind spots on the perimeter security fence.

2.99 While Parkhurst management implemented those recommendations within its control, eight months later CCTV cover was still not complete. Had all the recommendations been implemented, the escape should have been observed. On 14th February 1995, members of the Inquiry visited the ECR and noted that, although camera configurations had been set to reduce blind spots on the perimeter fence, datum settings had not been re-programmed. The object of camera datum settings is to ensure maximum camera efficiency while allowing for movement by the ECR staff, who can return cameras to their settings at the touch of a button.

2.100 The effectiveness of the CCTV system was tested one evening after dark when members of the Inquiry walked the escape route. The cameras could have covered the escape but, due to their siting, the size of the image would have been below the standard recommended by the Home Office, under which the image presented on monitors by a person of average height should fill at least 10 per cent of the screen height. Because this standard was not met, staff in the ECR would have had difficulty seeing any unusual movement, especially as they were frequently distracted from the screens by having to perform other duties. Home Office recommended standards should be applied at Parkhurst and throughout the prison estate.

2.101 To monitor a total of 53 security cameras, extraordinary powers of concentration and attention to detail are required. Modern screen technology and alarm-triggered systems would have offered some relief by ensuring that screens only became live when movement was detected, thus highlighting those areas requiring staff attention and reducing reliance on the human element. On the night of the escape, however, not only was there no alarm-triggered system but the staff were untrained and continually distracted by other duties.

RECOMMENDATIONS

25 Minimum physical security standards need to be set for all establishments and applied.
(Paras. 2.74-101)
[See recommendation 80]

26 Locking schedules for secure establishments need to be reviewed with modern electronic or magnetic systems in mind. Current policy in respect of locks for non-residential buildings should be urgently reviewed.
(Paras. 2.75-76)

27 Home Office recommended standards for CCTV systems should be applied throughout the Prison Service.
(Para. 2.100)
[See Woodcock recommendation 40]

Why did it take almost two hours to detect the escape?

2.102 It was about 6.15 pm when the escapees left the sports hall through its rear door. It was about two hours later, at 8.07 pm, that the dog handler found the hole in the fence. The escapees' identities were only confirmed at 8.40 pm.

2.103 The inordinate delay in the discovery of the escape highlights serious flaws in the most basic security procedures at the prison. The co-ordination of these procedures is the responsibility of the staff in the ECR.

(a) Emergency Control Room

2.104 The title 'Emergency Control Room' is misleading and implies an emergency function only. In fact, the ECR has many routine functions in addition to its emergency role. An appropriately staffed and properly equipped ECR should be at the heart of a prison's control systems and emergency procedures. The main functions of an ECR are set out in the Prison Service Manual on Security:

> *"(a) to monitor, through the use of CCTV and electronic locking where installed, the general physical security of the prison, and the movement of prisoners*
>
> *(b) to assess information received within the ECR so as to judge whether an emergency is imminent - and if so to initiate a response*
>
> *(c) to assume control of the prison immediately, if there is a serious threat to security or control, and to provide a venue for managing the incident if required.*
>
> *Emergency telephones and the internal radio net should terminate in the ECR. Alarms should either terminate in the ECR or be duplicated there."*

2.105 The ECR at Parkhurst was built as part of the gate lodge and administration complex, opened in 1988. At the time of the escape, the room was in a generally poor state with insufficient heating and ventilation and clear signs of wear and tear. One of the control desks was jacked up on pieces of wood and the plotting board, intended to display all movements within the prison, had an out-of-date plan and unusable magnetic markers. The relevance of the latter point was emphasised by one of the Senior Officers:

> *"A good controller should know where people are in the prison, assisted by the plotting board; in reality the majority of control was done in one's head."*

2.106 The scattered layout of Parkhurst Prison led to excessive prisoner movements, a situation exacerbated by the activities of building contractors and their vehicles. It was asking too much of ECR staff to monitor all prisoner movements effectively without accurate memory aids such as a plotting board.

2.107 The ECR fell far short of most of the basic requirements and, following the escape, the Director of Works described it as "woefully inadequate". He commissioned a review, the findings of which were submitted to the Inquiry The review stated:

> *"As requested the following are observations with reference to the inadequacies of the suite:*
>
> - *No overall management overview of the total prison security system.*
> - *Poor display of information received on site mimic* [alarm panel].
> - *Poor environmental conditions including lighting and air conditioning.*
> - *Monochrome monitors giving poor definition on some screens.*
> - *All perimeter alarm conditions could only be raised by the operator viewing* [the] *screens.*
> - *Generally the layout was poor ergonomically."*

2.108 There were also question marks over the professional competence of the ECR staff on duty on 3rd January. When the escape was discovered, there were five staff on duty, none of whom had received ECR training, not even the Acting Senior Officer in charge. Even worse, two Officers were recent recruits into the Prison Service and had virtually no knowledge of the prison and absolutely no experience of ECR procedures. It was the first time they had worked in the Control Room and they were made responsible for the two banks of camera monitors which represented the only perimeter alarm system available that night. All this was in direct contravention of instructions contained in the Manual on Security. The Manual requires ECR staff, amongst other things, to be familiar with the prison's contingency plans, take part in frequent exercises to test them and receive proper training in advance. Despite all these security instructions, it was common practice to post into the ECR newly employed Officers as well as Officers recently transferred from other prisons, irrespective of whether or not they had received any specific training. The Manual also recommends rotation of staff duties in an ECR at intervals of between 20 and 40 minutes, to increase the vigilance of individual observers. Given the inexperience of some of the staff on the night of the escape, rotation was seen as impractical. The Inquiry believes that, before Officers are deployed to an ECR, they must be fully trained to nationally agreed standards and familiar with the establishment.

2.109 The ECR was not up to standard. It was in need of overhaul and updating. It was frequently staffed by untrained and unpracticed operators who had resigned themselves to poor quality and inadequately maintained equipment. A supervisor commented:

> *"The ECR can be a temporary resting place for an incapacitated Officer but should not be a hiding place."*

2.110 One of the prime responsibilities of the ECR is to monitor and control prisoner movements. It failed on the night of the escape and could have failed on other nights. It must be upgraded in accordance with the findings of the review by the Director of Works.

(b) Movement Control System

2.111 All prisons containing Category A inmates were required to have a Movement Control System which could establish, at any time, the location of each inmate. The Manual on Security gives Governors discretion to:

> *"... adapt the set of measures covering the movement of Category A inmates around a prison according to local standards of physical security and other circumstances."*

2.112 In accordance with Headquarters policy, the practice at Parkhurst, after January 1993, was for all High Risk and Exceptional Risk Category A prisoners to have their movements recorded in Category A books and logged in the ECR. The movements of Standard Risk Category A inmates, including two of the escapees, and of lower category inmates, including the third escapee, were not recorded or logged. In March 1994, the Governor ordered that all Category A movement books for High and Exceptional Risk prisoners should be placed in red covers, that books should accompany prisoners at all times and that all movements should be recorded in the books by escorting and receiving Officers.

2.113 Movements of dangerous inmates require high standards of control and supervision and these should be enforced. This was not always the case at Parkhurst, as a member of Education Department staff told the Inquiry:

> *"On two or three occasions Category As arrived unescorted and banged on the door to get in. They said they wanted to get in early so as not to waste time registering with others and had tagged on the end of a work party and dropped off en route."*

2.114 On the evening of the escape, no early indication of the prisoners' intention to go to the sports hall had been required and staff had no prior knowledge of the security classifications of any who might attend the session. Among those who did attend were two High Risk inmates from A Wing. What happened to their movement books is not clear. It was suggested by one Officer that the books did not go with the prisoners to the sports hall but followed later. Another Officer recalled that the books had travelled with the prisoners. Such confusion is unsurprising, given the evidence that on many occasions the books did not accompany high security prisoners. The Area Manager commented after a visit to Parkhurst:

> *"You will remember on my last visit I discovered that high risk prisoners were taken to places of education without their Category A books."*

2.115 Many Officers referred to the high security Category A inmates as "HRVs", meaning "high risk visits" as their visits took place in a partitioned room off the main visits room. This appeared to be the only distinction made by some Officers between different categories of prisoners.

2.116 On 3rd January 1995, each inmate's departure from D Wing was recorded on a dry-wipe roll board maintained in the Wing Office. Ten inmates left the Wing and only seven returned; but a change of staff had taken place in the meantime and the accounting system was obviously not good enough to ensure that the absences were noticed. Whether this failure was the result of human error or prisoner complicity will never be known. It was not unusual for prisoners to enter the Wing Office. This practice should be discontinued. The Area Manager had commented, on a previous visit:

> *"I noticed that prisoners were intent on visiting the Wing Office to see what was taking place. Their resistance to being told to stay outside the Wing Office until given permission to enter was a clear sign of their willingness to be intrusive and intimidating."*

2.117 In Dispersal Prisons, an effective prisoner movement system must be introduced which provides a permanent record, is not accessible to inmates and requires prior notification by inmates of discretionary movements off their Wing. Had prisoners' activities been properly monitored, co-ordinated and controlled on 3rd January, staff would have questioned the attendance of one of the escapees on the sports hall movement, as he was due to attend a creative writing class from 6.00 pm to 8.00 pm that evening. This inmate was the only student on the course and the teacher reported his failure to attend class to a colleague. As it was not unusual for prisoners to miss classes, the absence was not reported to the Wing or elsewhere. The teacher left the prison as the escape was discovered, still unaware of the reason for the non-attendance of the pupil.

(c) Contingency planning

2.118 The aim of monitoring and controlling prisoner movements is to prevent escapes or incidents. Once that system fails, the prison must rely on contingency plans to retrieve the situation. At Parkhurst, the plans and their implementation were also found wanting. The chaos that followed the discovery of the escape gave rise to comment critical of the ECR.

2.119 New Officers were given the task of recalling staff into the prison. Not surprisingly, given their lack of knowledge and the unavailability of a call-out list, they did not prioritise and key people were not informed.

2.120 There were also delays in providing vital information to police, such as the identities of the escapees, details of their clothing, photographs and criminal records. Once staff were deployed, other problems emerged. The emergency packs issued from the gate lodge and given to Officers sent out to man fixed posts, such as ferry terminals, contained radios to link with the police network, torches and maps. Many of the radios and torches did not work, due to flat batteries and lack of maintenance, and the maps were poor quality, unreadable photocopies.

2.121 The contingency plans had been reviewed by a senior Governor Grade from Headquarters in December 1994, who concluded that:

> *"If there were an investigation into a major incident at Parkhurst, it would be difficult to defend the current position with regard to contingency planning."*

2.122 Another senior Governor Grade accepted that "the contingency plans were rubbish" but said that there were more than enough real incidents to obviate the need to hold exercises. ECR staff commented on several real incidents prior to the escape, such as fires on Wings, when, in the view of one Senior Officer, "chaos followed". The Inquiry believes that contingency plans should be reviewed at least annually, as part of a formal security audit. At Parkhurst, the contingency plans had last been re-written in 1992, were partially amended in 1993 and were being reviewed at the time of the escape. Senior staff at Parkhurst stated that the constant changes caused by the re-building work, with new fence lines, new routes for movements and new access points for emergency evacuation and the emergency services, presented almost insurmountable problems in maintaining up-to-date contingency plans. In such circumstances, the need to rehearse and test emergency procedures was even more pressing.

(d) The Duty Governor

2.123 The Manual on Security directs that:

> *"Governors of Dispersals, and any other establishments holding high risk Category A inmates, should ensure that the Duty Governor is in the establishment when it is unlocked and inmates in Category A are associated with others."*

2.124 An instruction issued at Parkhurst in March 1994, regarding Duty Governors, included no such requirement. It was considered that a requirement would be too time-consuming and would reduce the availability of Governor Grades during the working day. A further factor was the close proximity to the prison of the Governor Grades' homes. It was the practice for Duty Governors to leave the prison in the early evening and to be on call at their home address. One Governor Grade queried this disregard of the instructions contained in the Manual on Security. He was told to stop worrying and perform his duties as directed by the Governor.

2.125 Ironically, it was this individual who was Duty Governor on the night of the escape and he had left the prison at about 6.40 pm. A mitigating factor that night was that the governing Governor was still working in the prison and did not leave until 8.10 pm, just before the gate staff became aware of the emergency. The Duty Governor returned to the prison immediately he was called, together with other Governor Grades. He would have expected to take command in the ECR but was directed to take charge at the scene of the escape. Other Governor Grades went to the ECR but there was a delay in a senior manager assuming control, which must have placed further responsibility and pressures on the Acting Principal Officer (Orderly Officer) and Acting Senior Officer in the ECR.

2.126 Staff working in a Dispersal Prison need to be reassured that senior management support is immediately available and not just at the end of a telephone. Indeed, in November 1993, the POA at Parkhurst expressed their concern that Duty Governors were not staying in the prison until prisoners had been locked up at the end of the evening. The Inquiry believes that directions contained within the Manual on Security in respect of Duty Governors must be strictly followed.

(e) Duty to co-operate with police investigations

2.127 Hampshire Constabulary was anxious to interview, at the earliest possible time, all Prison Officers who might have been able to assist its enquiries into the escape and its efforts to recapture the escapees. Although many members of staff, of all grades, co-operated fully, some Officers sought legal advice from the POA before agreeing to be interviewed. This meant a delay of at least three days and denial of potentially vital information to the police, already fully extended by the hunt for the prisoners.

2.128 The Prison Service Code of Conduct and Discipline places no obligation on Officers to assist police investigations except if ordered to do so by the Governor of a prison, in which case non-co-operation could be grounds for a disciplinary offence.

2.129 The current uncertainties could have dire consequences for the administration of justice and, in circumstances such as an escape, could place the public at risk. The Inquiry recommends that a clear instruction be issued, directing that members of the Prison Service who witness or who may have relevant information regarding a crime that occurs in a prison establishment or on escort, must co-operate fully with the police and, if requested, make a verbal and/or written statement without delay. Such statements would not be disclosed to any Prison Service disciplinary inquiry without the consent of those who made them.

(f) Summary

2.130 It is not difficult to see how the absence of the three escapees went undetected for so long. Through a mixture of poor planning, below standard equipment, inadequate training and confused responses, procedures and systems for tracking inmate movements were ineffectual. At the heart of these systems and procedures should be an appropriately staffed and equipped ECR. The current state of ECRs Service-wide is apparent from a personal view contained within a memorandum issued by the Prison Service Security Directorate in February 1995:

> *"My belief is that the ECRs got lost in the mid-eighties and it is interesting that they are given half a page in the Security Manual. I am still uncertain whether or not there is any national training going on and how up to date any such training is."*

RECOMMENDATIONS

28 Before Officers are deployed to an ECR, they must be fully trained to nationally agreed standards and familiar with the establishment.
(Paras. 2.108-109)
[See recommendation 82]

29 The ECR at Parkhurst must be upgraded in accordance with the findings of the Director of Works.
(Para. 2.110)
[See recommendation 82]

30 Supervisors must ensure that high standards of control on the movement of dangerous inmates are enforced and that movement books always accompany Exceptional and High Risk prisoners.
(Paras. 2.111-114)

31 Inmates should not be allowed access to the Wing Office.
(Para. 2.116)

32 In Dispersal Prisons, a prisoner movement system must be introduced in a form which provides a permanent record and is not accessible to inmates. Inmates must be required to give advance notification of discretionary movements off the Wing. Such movements should be co-ordinated, monitored and properly controlled.
(Para. 2.117)

33 Contingency plans must be regularly tested and practised with all staff trained in realistic situations, in line with the instructions in the Manual on Security. Emergency packs must be subject to regular testing.
(Paras. 2.118-122)

34 Contingency plans must be reviewed annually, as part of the security audit.
(Para. 2.122)

35 Directions in the Manual on Security, in respect of Duty Governors, must be strictly followed.
(Paras. 2.123-126)

36 Clear instructions must be issued throughout the Service directing that staff must co-operate fully with any police investigation and, if requested, make a verbal and/or written statement without delay.
(Paras. 2.127-129)

Would improved intelligence handling have prevented the escape?

2.131 Two issues of intelligence arose in the context of this Inquiry: first, that the intelligence system within the prison should have led to perhaps two of the prisoners being targeted by the Security Department and, second, that a product of that targeting process should have been the rational consideration of all the available information with a view to appropriate action. Considerable amounts of information were available but never examined in a structured manner. If they had been, the escape might have been prevented.

(a) Intelligence

2.132 All prison establishments should have a system for handling security information and intelligence (Manual on Security, para. 13.1). Intelligence is information which has been collected, evaluated, developed, analysed, further developed, disseminated and acted upon.

2.133 Parkhurst did have the means to collect and record information, mainly through Security Information Reports (SIRs). The Manual on Security outlined how informants among the prison population should be handled and how their information should be processed. According to a Senior Officer, the four Security Managers knew which prisoners were giving information but no record was made. This was contrary to the instructions in the Manual on Security, which were designed to protect both staff and informants.

2.134 The Security Office was not equipped for its purpose. It was cramped, scruffy and out-dated; it projected an aura of inefficiency. The frustrations felt by security staff were best summed up by a Senior Officer who complained that he was forced to beg or borrow equipment and that his facilities compared unfavourably with those in the Administration Unit. This problem was compounded by the posting of staff to cover other duties such as prisoner escorts or work on the Wings. Even the collator, whose job was to receive SIRs and other information, record it on the inmate intelligence cards and security file opened for each inmate and evaluate it and take necessary further action, such as developing the information or disseminating it to others, was sometimes taken off these important tasks.

2.135 If the collation system had been operating efficiently, all the available information concerning the escapees would have appeared on their inmate intelligence cards. The nature and quantity of the information should have identified at least one and probably two of them, as prisoners to be targeted. The information should have been developed and the inmates' cells should have been regularly and meticulously searched. The proper use of collated information as intelligence might have prevented the escape, first, through the discovery of escape equipment and, second, through re-categorisation of the inmates. Details of the information available on each inmate was examined by the Inquiry and led to the conclusion that the assessment of at least two of them was anomalous within the present classification criteria.

2.136 Parkhurst did not have in place a fully efficient intelligence handling system. The Prison Service, in evidence to the Woolf Inquiry in 1990, said that there was a need for:

> *"... sound arrangements for gathering, collation and dissemination of intelligence."*

2.137 The matter was also recognised by Managers of Dispersal Prisons and summed up in a 1993 report of a meeting of representatives of Dispersal Prisons and Headquarters:

> *"Good intelligence is a vital part of control. Present arrangements for collating and monitoring data need improvement but the quality of information depends crucially on the relationships between staff and prisoners (dynamic security)."*

2.138 The importance of intelligence was further highlighted in a 1994 paper circulated by the Police Adviser, Custody Group, in which he stated:

> *"The importance of good intelligence must be recognised by management and staff at all levels who should be encouraged to devote the necessary time and resources to the task. It should be seen as high profile work."*

2.139 The need for good intelligence to assist in the control of difficult prisoners had been recognised by Governors, advisers and the Prison Service as a whole. Parkhurst and some other prisons have access to information on individual inmates. PROBE (Profiling Behaviour) is a system for handling up-to-date and historical data on individual prisoners, with a function to analyse the data and produce a rating. The rating for each inmate is a current and reliable indicator of the prisoner's behaviour, which allows intelligent predictions to be made of future behaviour. Over and above individual scores, mean scores can be calculated for groups, Wings and whole establishments.

2.140 PROBE was used by the Psychology Department at Parkhurst and maintained through the enthusiasm of the clerk and one psychologist. It had enormous potential, though it was not easy to operate and could not be described as user-friendly.

2.141 During the course of the Inquiry, a copy of the inmate intelligence card for one of the prisoners was received from another Dispersal Prison, to which he had been transferred after the escape. It had clearly been rewritten and, compared to the information available when the prisoner was at Parkhurst, was far superior. This prison was visited to examine the collation system.

2.142 It is not suggested that the intelligence system at the other Dispersal Prison has all the answers. What it does demonstrate is the value of some form of computer-based intelligence system within a Dispersal Prison. The frequent movement of prisoners within the Dispersal system and the need for establishments to share data underline the desirability of a national database.

2.143 An escape from Parkhurst was attempted in 1992 when five prisoners broke through the wall of M Wing. A Principal Officer said:

> *"There were a number of indications through Staff Information Reports and Wing Observation Books that the escape bid was going to happen, even identifying the cell from where it was going to be executed. The hole and the materials that were used in the escape bid should have been found much sooner."*

2.144 In general, escapes and prison disturbances do not occur spontaneously. The planning and preparation involved should allow the prisoners concerned to be identified and exposed through good information and intelligence handling.

2.145 The potential gains in constantly collecting and analysing information cannot be over-emphasised. Patterns of association, structures of criminal groups and the distribution of power among prisoners can be revealed through intelligence analysis and can give advance notice of escapes and disturbances. A working party should be set up to review intelligence and management information needs throughout the Prison Service, building on best practice, available IT systems and experience of other agencies.

(b) Categorisation

2.146 Categorisation of prisoners on security grounds originates from the Mountbatten Report (1966) which developed the concept of Category A, B, C and D inmates. These categories are defined as follows:

> *"Category A*
> *prisoners whose escape would be highly dangerous to the public or the police or the security of the state, no matter how unlikely the escape might be; and for whom the aim must be to make escape impossible.*
>
> *Category B*
> *prisoners for whom the very highest conditions of security are not necessary but for whom escape must be made very difficult.*
>
> *Category C*
> *prisoners who cannot be trusted in open conditions but who do not have the resources and will to make a determined escape attempt.*
>
> *Category D*
> *prisoners who can reasonably be trusted in open conditions."*

2.147 The helicopter escape from Gartree Prison led to the division of Category A into three sub-divisions; Standard Risk, High Risk and Exceptional Risk. In addition to the security categorisations, the Governor at Parkhurst could also place any prisoner on the list of potential escapees. The Standard Risk and High Risk definitions, reproduced below, underline the argument that two of the prisoners, who were both Standard Risk Category A, were not appropriately categorised:

"Standard Escape Risk

Most Category A inmates are classified as Standard Escape Risk.

They are not considered to have the determination or skill to overcome the range of security measures which apply to the custody and movement of Category A inmates.

There is no current information to suggest that they have associates or resources which could be used to plan and carry out an assisted escape attempt.

They have no history of escape or determined escape planning.

Even so, the Prison Service must assume that they would take any opportunity to escape and that, if unlawfully at large, they would pose a very serious threat to the public, the police or the security of the state.

High Escape Risk

A small proportion of Category A inmates are classified as High Escape Risk.

They have a history and background which suggests that they have both the ability to plan an escape and the determination to carry it out.

There is usually current information to suggest that they have associates or resources which could be used to plan and carry out an assisted escape attempt.

There is usually also information that the inmate or associates have access to firearms or explosives and have been willing to use them in committing crime or in avoiding capture.

Category A (High Escape Risk) inmates are likely to be major criminals. Examples include terrorists belonging to substantial organisations and armed robbers and major drug dealers who operate in powerful and violent gangs."

2.148 Two of the escapees had demonstrated on more than one occasion that they had both the ability to plan an escape and the determination to carry it out. Significantly, both had recently been recommended for downgrading to Category B by a Governor Grade at Parkhurst. The recommendation had been properly rejected but demonstrates the lack of understanding of the categorisation system as well as the absence of coherent intelligence at some levels.

2.149 After detailed examination of the background and prison histories of the two inmates (details of which appear at Appendix G), the Inquiry concluded that neither of them sat comfortably within either the Standard or the High Risk definition. Both inmates fully met the first criteria for High Escape Risk, in that they had a history of escape planning and the determination to carry out such plans. This should have placed them above the Standard Risk category. The reason they were not more highly classified was that, over the years, the Prison Service had come to regard the other three criteria as mandatory rather than discretionary. The escape from Parkhurst has highlighted anomalies within the categorisation system which underline the need to research and redefine the whole process (see also Section 5 of this Report).

RECOMMENDATIONS

37 A working party should be set up to review intelligence and management information needs throughout the Prison Service, building on best practice, available IT systems and experience of other agencies.
(Paras. 2.131-145)

38 Security categorisation should be reviewed and researched to remove dangerous anomalies produced by the current system.
(Paras. 2.146-149)
[See recommendations 102 and 103]

Did the building works contribute in any way to the escape?

2.150 Major building works at Parkhurst started in 1988. The construction of the gate lodge and visits area was followed by the construction of the sports hall, the refurbishment of what are now A and D Wings, which had lain empty since being rendered uninhabitable by riots in 1979, and the refitting of the old B Wing. The work was initially planned to be completed in 1993 but the programme of work now extends to at least 1999.

2.151 The building projects delayed the installation of geophones and, in consequence, physical security was jeopardised. There were other consequences of the building programme which contributed to a lowering of security, for example:

- Lengthy and varied movements of prisoners throughout the day, some in darkness.
- Diversion of management energy and resources.
- Huge commitment of staff.
- Reduction in staff morale brought about by dirt, dust, noise, constant change and general dissatisfaction over the requirement to run a maximum security establishment in a building site.
- Difficulty in maintaining up-to-date contingency plans.

2.152 The prison had somehow survived seven years of building disruption. At the height of the activity, there were almost 250 contractors on the site each day, with their plant and tools often close to windows of occupied cells. Several options had been open to the Prison Service:

- To close the prison, demolish it and build a modern maximum security establishment.
- To close the prison and refurbish it, either to Dispersal or lower category standards.
- To keep the prison open, without the Category A inmates, and refurbish it, either as a lower category prison or to Dispersal standards.
- To keep the prison open, and retain the Category A inmates, while refurbishing to Dispersal standards.

2.153 With the benefit of hindsight, it is easy to question the decision to keep the prison open, housing Category A prisoners. The decision was taken when 1,800 prisoners were in police cells and the Service was under intense pressure to remedy the situation. Nevertheless, the outcome was far from satisfactory and resulted in piecemeal work stretching over more than ten years, at considerable cost to staff morale, living conditions and security.

2.154 The decision dates back to the report by the Working Group on Category A Security in August 1988, following which the Prison Service Board agreed that provision should be made, in forward plans for the mid-1990s for six maximum security prisons. It was agreed that Parkhurst ought to be retained as one of these:

> *"... not least because of its location in the south, the hospital, the operating theatre, the psychiatric Wing ... and the SSU."*

2.155 A dissenting voice was heard at the then regional level, when a senior manager queried the practicality of keeping Parkhurst open, in a note dated June 1990:

> *"The amount of building work proposed for this prison during the first half of the 1990s is likely to keep the Works Department at Parkhurst at full stretch, indeed one suspects that one of the limitations in carrying out the programme is that department's ability to cope with a significant number of major projects at one time. As much of the work is to be carried out in the main Wing area, it must inevitably reduce the security of a Dispersal Prison which provides special facilities to the Prison Service. May I therefore raise a marker as to whether it is wise to plan to complete such work in Parkhurst while the majority of the prison remains open? If the prison could be partially or totally closed, not only could the work be completed much more speedily but possible security compromises would not have to be faced."*

2.156 Local views were clearly influenced by understandable self-interest and pressure from Headquarters to use every available cell, as expressed in two memoranda from the Governor at Parkhurst, in October 1991 and January 1992:

> *"You will be aware of my concerns about the reduction in our roll. I believe that if we do not keep our numbers as high as possible then there must be a possibility that Parkhurst will be closed in order to speed up the redevelopment."*

> *"The Service as a whole is dealing with more prisoners than was predicted and large numbers are being 'locked out', so anything we can do must be of help. Also we need to be conscious that if our roll falls too much then Headquarters will start examining whether it makes sense for us to remain open while major development work is in progress."*

2.157 The consequences for staff at Parkhurst, had it been closed, would have included long-term detached duties or relocation. If closure had been a precursor to permanent removal from the Dispersal system, considerable reductions in personnel would have followed. This was not an unrealistic assessment and served to cloud the issue of Parkhurst's future, impacting directly on security.

2.158 The building plans were complicated by other events, including the recommendations of the Woolf Report and the subsequent announcement in the House of Commons that all prison cells would have integral sanitation by 1994. In addition, the Food Safety Act, 1990, left prison establishments open to inspection by local authority and Environmental Health Officers. Consequently, the building programme was extended to include the installation of cell sanitation and a new kitchen block.

2.159 In March 1992, the issue of retaining high risk Category A prisoners was raised by a senior Governor in DOC1 Division at Prison Service Headquarters:

> *"I have to express doubts that, in spending large amounts of capital on refurbishing living accommodation, sight has been lost of the need to provide a secure perimeter. Each additional breach in the wall, or extra contractor's compound increases the possibility of an escape by a publicly sensitive high risk Category A prisoner ... It would be sensible therefore to plan for the removal of such prisoners ..."*

2.160 The response to this within DOC1 was to point out that:

> *"The recent loss of high risk places at Frankland placed considerable strain on the rest of the Dispersal estate. If Parkhurst were to be similarly restricted, at a time when Gartree and Albany have withdrawn and when Frankland was not yet up to complement, then I think it would be very difficult indeed to manage the high risk population ...*
>
> *If availability of funds or other factors get in the way of early installation of geophones at Parkhurst, then we need to look for alternative security measures which will enable the establishment to continue to hold high escape risk prisoners."*

2.161 The Governor of Parkhurst concurred with this view in a memorandum to DOC1:

> *"I agree that if we went down such a road it might expose weaknesses elsewhere in the system, and we should not be rail-roaded into making hasty decisions.*
>
> *There is no doubt that the building programme currently underway is a major security nightmare, and I would welcome any opportunity to discuss how we might best enhance our security arrangements so that all of us can be reasonably confident that adequate safeguards are in place."*

2.162 The outcome of all this discussion was that High Risk Category A prisoners stayed at Parkhurst while no additional security was provided from Headquarters. In other words, the discussions exposed genuine concern but no action was taken.

2.163 One example of the inaction was the debate over the provision of dogs. Documentation going back to 1990 shows repeated requests being made to increase the number of dog handlers from 18 to 20. The original request from the Governor referred specifically to the building work:

"You are aware that I require additional dog handlers, and dogs, to assist the security of the prison during this lengthy refurbishment."

2.164 Apart from two dog handlers being relocated from Albany Prison for a six month period, from October 1992, the request remained in abeyance until late 1994, when the Governor at Parkhurst wrote to the Area Manager stating that he could finance two additional dogs and handlers but asked for assistance with funding for four more. The result was that, at the time of the escape, the prison had no additional security to counter the recognised weaknesses brought about by building work. One immediate reaction to the escape was an increase in the number of dogs at Parkhurst from 18 to 28!

2.165 In February 1993, the Category A Policy Committee discussed the possibility of using HM Prison Bullingdon in Oxfordshire as an alternative to Parkhurst. From the outset objections were raised on the basis of Parkhurst's strengths:

"... security advantages in an island prison. The special facilities in terms of C Wing (Psychiatric) ... and the hospital facility ..."

2.166 A working party which was set up to take the proposal forward, concluded that it was not a viable proposition to close Parkhurst because of the staff expertise there for dealing with Dispersal prisoners, which was not available at Bullingdon.

2.167 The advisability of keeping 21 High Risk Category A prisoners at Parkhurst was again questioned in October 1994, when the Area Manager wrote:

"It is against the rising number of major capital works projects needed to maintain Parkhurst as a Dispersal Prison, and the rising level of alienation and tension displayed by prisoners (measured by adjudications, assaults, demands for medication) that I see the risk of escape by a Category A prisoner becoming unacceptable."

2.168 What had prompted the reassessment? Reasons for a change in attitude were mostly in place long before October 1994. The new ingredient was the escape from Whitemoor Prison. As stated in the same correspondence:

"The political problems for the Prison Service Agency and the Government arising out of a high risk prisoner escaping from Parkhurst during the next two or three years would be horrendous. If it were to happen I believe a subsequent enquiry would consider we had put too many pressures on local management."

2.169 The matter was taken further on 5th December 1994, by the Operational Director responsible for Parkhurst, who raised it for discussion by the Executive Committee:

"The case for removing Category A high risk prisoners from Parkhurst is a strong one. If we were not to accede to it, we would be open to substantial criticism should a high risk prisoner escape during the period that building works were taking place."

2.170 The Area Manager's worries did not persuade the Prison Service to move the High Risk prisoners from Parkhurst until 5th January 1995. In the opinion of the Inquiry, this was an inordinate length of time to take, over a straightforward operational decision. In the view of the Prisons Board, it was not a straightforward matter, as it involved an examination of the risk presented by retaining such prisoners at Parkhurst, with its recognised weaknesses in physical security, as against the risk posed to good order at other Dispersals which might be required to accommodate significant numbers of additional High Risk prisoners. The second Operational Director, concerned about the potential disorder in the Dispersal Prisons within his command, had suggested that additional security precautions might enable Parkhurst to retain the High Risk Category A prisoners. This suggestion was opposed by the Area Manager who had made the original request for their removal.

2.171 The Prisons Board contended, in its Salmon response, that the original request had not been presented as urgent and that the period during which the matter had been under consideration had been one of intense activity following the escape from Whitemoor. The Operational Director responsible for Parkhurst argued that this activity had inevitably affected a number of operational matters, including the question of retaining High Risk Category A inmates at Parkhurst.

2.172 While accepting that the Service was under pressure, the Inquiry maintains its view that the issue could and should have been resolved sooner. The urgency is very evident from the range of potential problems highlighted in the Area Manager's request:

"I have come to the conclusion that I must ask you and colleagues in Custody Services to consider the feasibility of removing high risk Category A prisoners as soon as possible and delaying the return of this category of prisoner until perimeter security has been completed in 1998."

"The major building projects will continue to the turn of the century unless Parkhurst can continue to receive priority status for funding. The present sports pitch is a very poor facility; the laundry equipment will be needed. The perimeter wall will be realigned when these projects are completed. These projects and all the others mentioned in this section bring contractors into close contact with prisoners and large numbers of vehicles will be removing rubble and returning with large quantities of building materials.

All this reminds me that when Wormwood Scrubs embarked upon the major re-building programme, high risk Category A prisoners were withdrawn and even some internal fences were alarmed in order to guard against escapes from within the prison."

"Whilst walking around Parkhurst on my last two visits, I was checking security routines, especially searches. However, wherever I went staff talked to me about the difficulties arising from prisoners seeking drugs. Visitors are thought to be the main route for drugs, including cannabis, heroin, cocaine and crack. It is believed that metal detector portals, handheld metal detectors, 'rub-down' searches and drug dogs will be ineffective because drugs are wrapped in cling-film secreted internally and passed onto prisoners who will swallow the articles."

"On the Wings I met prisoners who are openly intimidating staff. I find staff retreating to the Wing office and it feels as if they are seeking sanctuary. Parkhurst staff have a good reputation for handling difficult prisoners. Illicit alcohol has been driven further and further underground. The staff know they have a large percentage of prisoners who are violent, disordered if not psychopathic and increasingly on a knife edge because their craving for drugs blunts their controls and social skills.

I note that Parkhurst has a rising number of serious assaults upon staff and prisoner upon prisoner. The level of assaults have been low compared with other Dispersal Prisons."

"You will note that the level of disruptive prisoners in A, D and M Wings are higher than in other Dispersal Prisons."

2.173 None of the escapees was classified as High Risk, although two could have qualified as such (see paras. 2.147-149). Had the High Risk prisoners been removed, however, pressures on local managers would have been reduced and they could have concentrated on other security matters, in particular the Standard Risk Category A prisoners, which included two of the escapees.

2.174 The original decision to keep the prison open was influenced by the desire to maintain Parkhurst's traditional role in the Dispersal estate, because of its unique facilities, including the Psychotherapeutic Unit and hospital, albeit both resources had been under-utilised, with the newly-built operating theatre out of commission as a consequence of the building work. The Prison Service has left itself with a prison which is costly to run and maintain, has failed to provide the required security and will never meet the standards of modern prison architecture. Prior to the escape, Parkhurst was not due to be completely refurbished before 1998. After the escape, a security review was conducted by the Prison Service members of the Inquiry which highlighted further problems. They considered some features of the design of the refurbished A and D Wings ill-conceived, with numerous blind spots. Staff complained of poor sight lines and alarm buttons being badly located.

2.175 The SSU is perilously close to the outer perimeter wall of the establishment. The inherent dangers had been realised for a number of years, yet refurbishment of the Unit at a cost of almost £3 million was undertaken. The design brief now includes the creation of a dog-leg in the perimeter wall at a cost of a further £655,000. This is not only a highly expensive change to the programme; it has generated new security requirements to overcome the problem of obscuring previously satisfactory lines of sight.

2.176 Furthermore, the material used for the wall of the SSU exercise compound does not meet current security specifications and will have to be changed. Other changes will be required to prevent access to the roof. The juxtaposition of Wings which overlook the SSU also gives cause for concern.

2.177 As a consequence of the building works and the escape, opportunities for work for inmates were severely limited. The work available was menial and unchallenging and long-term plans for meaningful work were still at the preliminary stage. The situation is not peculiar to Parkhurst and is discussed more fully in Section 5.

2.178 The hospital did not feature in the escape but staff voiced concerns to the Inquiry regarding the security of the building and prisoner movements to and from the Wings. It is understood that a decision still has to be reached on whether a new prison hospital is sited on the Isle of Wight. Given that the new hospital would be a resource serving the prison population of England and Wales, escort costs and security implications should weigh in favour of a mainland site.

2.179 In summary, Parkhurst will have cost at least £56 million to upgrade but will still remain a Victorian establishment. The prison will always be expensive to run, requiring a high ratio of staff to prisoner numbers because of the inevitability of long and complex movements of prisoners outside the secure residential areas. Even at the conclusion of the present work, Parkhurst will not be an ideal site for a Dispersal Prison and certainly not a suitable location for an SSU. It should be downgraded as soon as possible and consideration given to its replacement by a more appropriate establishment. The relevance of current building work at Parkhurst should be re-examined immediately so that unnecessary work can be stopped.

RECOMMENDATIONS

39 The decision to retain a hospital at Parkhurst, as a Service-wide resource, should be reviewed.
(Para. 2.178)

40 Parkhurst should be downgraded as soon as possible and consideration given to its replacement as a Dispersal Prison by a more appropriate establishment. The relevance of current building work should be examined so that unnecessary work can be stopped.
(Para. 2.179)
[See recommendation 106]

41 The SSU at Parkhurst should not be reopened in that capacity. The accommodation should be put to other use.
(Para. 2.179)

Were there other factors in the management of the prison regime which affected the escape?

2.180 In the context of this Report, the term 'regime' is taken to cover the daily life of the prisoners and the management of their routine. It is worth referring to the Control Review Committee's (CRC) vision of an open regime (in its report of 1984):

> *"By an 'open regime' we certainly do not mean one that allows prisoners to decide what to do from day to day, but one that offers a range of constructive activities, the opportunity of association, and supervision by staff who have the time and training to take a personal interest in each inmate as an individual."*

2.181 Parkhurst was not untypical of other Dispersal Prisons in offering what it saw as an open regime. Unfortunately, it was the opposite of the CRC ideal, as the prisoners were allowed to decide what to do from day to day. One senior Governor Grade described the situation thus:

> *"At Parkhurst do we control the prisoners or do we allow them to do what they want? It is easier to allow them to do what they want to keep order."*

2.182 Life at Parkhurst must be viewed in full awareness of the types of prisoners with whom the staff had to deal. They were not short-term, petty criminals but men serving long sentences for crimes at the most serious end of the scale, men with very different personalities and ways of responding to the prison environment. Long-term imprisonment brings with it many social problems. Stability in this complex and somewhat artificial environment is desired by both prisoners and Officers, stability offering certainty and safety. A phoney stability was achieved at Parkhurst but only by surrender to the prisoners of control over their daily existence.

(a) Prisoner and staff relations

2.183 The problems associated with A and D Wings started when they opened in June 1993, with the initial allocation of inmates. Particular inmates were involved in the allocation of prisoners, with the result that D Wing housed, for the most part, white, mature and notorious prisoners, mainly organised London criminals. To A Wing went a number of drug addicts and younger inmates together with staff who, in the main, were young and inexperienced. It suffered control problems from the outset, according to one Senior Officer who said:

> *"On the first day that it opened A Wing was out of control by 6 pm."*

2.184 While A Wing remained disruptive despite concerted efforts by staff and management, D Wing quickly settled into a seemingly trouble-free existence; but control had been handed to the dominant, High Risk Category A inmates. The prisoners in control on D Wing were seen by the Governor as having a stabilising influence on the prison. This may have been the case but the power they held enabled them to condition staff to allow them to live a life of comparative freedom. Some of those employed as cleaners received full pay for doing nothing, the work being done by other prisoners on their behalf. A Governor Grade wrote:

> *"Wings are assigning Wing cleaners direct when it should go through the Labour Board, eg a Wing will ring up and state that an inmate will not volunteer for off-Wing work but is happy to be a Wing cleaner ... a large proportion of high security prisoners on D Wing have cleaning jobs."*

2.185 Despite 11 prisoners being allocated to cleaning duty, the Inquiry found D Wing to be grubby and untidy, a view acknowledged by some staff and commented on by an Officer:

> *"Each Wing has inmates on cleaning. They get paid for it, if it is not done efficiently little would happen to them. **** was the cleaner on top landing on D Wing but in reality he would get somebody to do it for him, they are paid £8 to £10 per week but pay is not docked for poor work and managers would not support this. Little enforcement to do a good job ..."*

2.186 The cleaner on the top landing of D Wing regularly received a weekly discretionary bonus of £2 for good work although he was never seen to do any cleaning. In reality, these inmates rarely did any work for themselves. They seldom fetched food; runners were sent to bring it up to their own association room where they had a television and cooking facilities. One Officer observed:

> *"The **** gang sent runners down to get food and then ate it with vegetables etc. which they had prepared themselves."*

2.187 One senior Governor Grade quoted an inmate who likened Parkhurst to "... a gentleman's prison", the implication being that inmates could lead a life free from supervision and discipline by staff. The few who dominated D Wing lived a life of leisure, with work and other tasks delegated to weaker prisoners.

2.188 Parkhurst prided itself on its non-confrontational stance towards prisoners and the open relationship between staff and inmates. In the words of a prison psychologist:

> *"There has been a tendency over many years for Officers to take the line of least resistance in response to demands from prisoners."*

2.189 The situation was confirmed by the reaction of experienced staff who had transferred to Parkhurst, some of whom requested transfer back to their original prisons because of the personal dissatisfaction they felt with the Parkhurst regime. One such Officer said that:

> *"The whole regime at Parkhurst was built around a policy of appeasement."*

2.190 Experienced Officers were surprised at the levels of verbal abuse tolerated and the general levels of freedom given to inmates to do as they pleased, a style more characteristic of a psychiatric hospital. According to a senior Governor Grade, this tolerance was described by long-serving Parkhurst staff as "the Parkhurst Way" and appears to have been widely accepted.

2.191 Considerable evidence was found of staff intimidation and conditioning by prisoners. Conditioning is discussed in the Woodcock Report on the escape from Whitemoor and was described by a psychologist who was able to observe and understand what was happening as:

> *"... more aligned to brainwashing. Prisoners deliberately set out to condition staff to behave the way they want them to."*

2.192 This was a disturbing yet common phenomenon entrenched in what the same psychologist called the "Dispersal syndrome":

> *"This comes out of the macho culture which pervades the Prison Service, effectively preventing Officers from acknowledging and discussing situations where inmates are attempting to make subtle inroads into their authority. Whilst not unique to the Dispersal Prisons, it is more prevalent there because of the sophistication of the inmates requiring Dispersal conditions."*

2.193 Staff did not regularly patrol the landings to supervise prisoners. Instead, they preferred to remain in the offices, an attitude attributed by one Governor Grade to either:

> *"... fear or laziness - this is difficult to judge, perhaps it comes down to personalities."*

When Officers did patrol, the prisoners commonly assumed that a Governor was on the way to visit the Unit. One Officer, temporarily working on D Wing, confirmed this view when he:

> *"... went into the censor's office where there were five basic grade Officers. These five Officers later disappeared, they were not on landings. When I later stood on the 3s* [third] *landing I was abused by inmates wanting to know what I was doing. I then received a phone call from the Senior Officer informing me a Governor was on the way. The other Officers then materialised on the landings. After the visit these Officers again disappeared."*

2.194 Wing Governors spent little time on the Wings, preferring to work from their offices in the administration block or 'the bunker' as it was called by the junior grade staff. There was no effective leadership or management of the Wings by the Wing Governors or Principal Officers. The calibre and experience of some Wing Governors was also the subject of criticism. In charge of some of the most difficult and dangerous prisoners in the Dispersal system, their ability was described by one senior manager thus:

> *"Parkhurst Governors are not all up to the quality demanded of a Dispersal Prison. The management structure is wrong and compounds the problems of poor communication."*

2.195 The regard for some Principal Officers was little better. One Officer reported that:

> *"When the sun shines the POs come out ... good POs are very few and far between and you rarely see one after 5 pm."*

Many staff complained of lack of support from their supervisors and, in particular, their Governors. They perceived this lack of support as undermining their ability to discipline inmates. These perceptions have been independently verified by the Area Manager since the escape. He described the situation as follows:

> *"It seemed that middle managers were either not up to the job or playing it so low-key as to be invisible. I thought I picked up ... that a number of Senior Officers were either sick or showing signs of stress and this was probably because Principal Officers were not carrying out their supervisory role."*

2.196 Prison Officers need effective leadership through the regular presence of senior supervisors, whose offices should be on the Wings. They must work together with staff in a team environment. Staff at Parkhurst tended to resist temporary postings to other areas of the prison and there was a lack of team spirit, which was not surprising, given that the unstructured, erratic and haphazardly compiled duty rotas gave staff no continuity.

2.197 Senior Officers and Officers had unco-ordinated shift patterns, confused further by the absence of any links to Principal Officers' and Wing Governors' duties. Wing POs and Governors did not even co-ordinate their own duties to cover each others' absences, so as to provide the best supervision of their Wings.

(b) Privileges for prisoners

2.198 It is clear that the way privileges developed, covering private cash, earnings, telephone calls and free association, had significant effects on the regime at Parkhurst.

2.199 Prisoners maintained two accounts, one for private cash and the other for money earned. Inmates were offered work but those who refused to work received no pay. Those wanting to work but for whom no work was available, received £2.50 per week. The minimum pay for work was £4 per week which could be increased through bonus payments. Some earned as much as £12 per week. In theory, food and tobacco could only be purchased from the earnings account, supplemented by up to £10 per month from private cash. In addition, items, such as phonecards, could be bought from private cash. In practice, there seemed to be few restrictions on what prisoners could order.

2.200 Prison Service policy regarding earnings and private cash is under review. It is characterised by differing instructions at different prisons. At Parkhurst, there was no effective limit to private cash holdings and the system supported the prisoners' hierarchy, creating, in the view of a member of the Board of Visitors, a situation of "haves and have nots". Access to money was not dependent on inmate behaviour. Some inmates were forced, through bullying and intimidation, to order extra goods to supply the leaders of the hierarchy. It is revealing that, when 20 High Risk prisoners were transferred from the prison after the escape, the total private cash balance held on behalf of inmates fell from around £20,500 to £6,200.

2.201 Cardphones were available on each Wing and inmates were issued with phonecards up to an incredible maximum of £40 per week, purchased from their own cash. Over £1,000 worth of cards were sold each week. An inmate's name, prison number and signature should appear on each phonecard in his possession but rarely did so. Moreover, each prisoner should have held a maximum of two £4 cards at any one time but often held more. The system of calls was widely abused.

2.202 In the lead-up to the introduction of cardphones to Dispersal Prisons in 1992, Governors had voiced concern that the procedures dictated from Headquarters were unworkable. Nevertheless, the Manual on Security (para. 38.7) lays down directions for the use of telephones by Category A prisoners:

> *"The use of telephones by Exceptional and High Risk inmates is subject to a number of restrictions. Exceptional Risk inmates should use official telephones and their conversations should be monitored and recorded. High Risk inmates may use cardphones, but their phonecards must be retained by staff; and calls must be pre-booked, made only to approved visitors (or to those exempted from the Approved Visits Scheme), and simultaneously monitored and recorded. Calls by Standard Risk inmates should be recorded but are not subject to other restrictions."*

2.203 At Parkhurst, the phonecards of High Risk inmates were not retained by staff but were kept by the prisoners, who were not required to pre-book calls. Calls were automatically recorded in the ECR but seldom, if ever, monitored. Monitoring equipment was also available on the Wings but it was rarely used. One Officer reported:

> *"There is monitoring equipment on D Wing, I've never used it although I do know how to. It's in the PO's office ... there is no monitoring even of high risk and other Category A phone calls."*

2.204 No record of, or check on, the numbers being dialled was made and prisoners were even known to ring the victims of their crimes. No effective facilities existed to monitor foreign language calls. Monitoring must be intelligence driven and include a capability to deal with foreign language calls.

2.205 Prisoners also had access to telephones in the Wing offices for official calls, for example to solicitors, and compassionate calls; such calls had to be authorised by a Wing Governor. Wings were issued with a limited number of phonecards for official and compassionate calls. Significantly, the weekly allocations of these cards was always fully used. In addition, inmates using the office telephones were sure of bypassing the monitoring systems on the cardphones. According to a senior Officer:

> *" Inmate **** has a regular phone call to Italy at public expense despite the fact that he has money in his private account. Another inmate up to recently was contacting Peru twice a week .... The biggest problem with these private calls is that they completely bypass the monitoring system."*

2.206 Phonecards have been a constant source of problems for prison staff as they are commonly used as currency. Recognition of the problem appeared in a notice from the Governor to prisoners in July 1993:

> *"In my recent note to you I mentioned particular concerns about heroin abuse. Since then we very nearly had a fatality as a consequence of a further overdose. We also found a large quantity of cannabis as well as about 20 'deals' of heroin, together with syringes.*
>
> *It is obvious that prisoners are using phonecards to purchase drugs, gamble and generally trade. One prisoner who hadn't purchased any cards at all was found to be holding rather a lot of them. Other prisoners are constantly seeking phonecards not for use on the telephones, but to pay off debts.*
>
> *I conclude that the present arrangements are being abused and I am therefore changing them with effect from week beginning Monday 9th August.*
>
> *The maximum amount of phonecards permitted in any week will be to the value of £20. This is in excess of all other Dispersal Prisons."*

2.207 This notice led to a discussion between the Governor and the prisoners with the result that a further notice was issued a week later:

> *"Most of you will be aware of my concerns about recent incidents of heroin abuse in Parkhurst. I have also been unhappy about the general level of disruption in recent weeks. I had resolved to do something about all this and was prepared to reduce private cash spends on phonecards to £20 per week.*
>
> *Having spoken with prisoner representatives one evening last week I think that we can expect some resolution of our present difficulties. I have therefore decided to increase the private cash allowance to £40 a week from 9th August. The maximum amount of phonecards permitted in any week will be to the value of £40."*

2.208 These two notices show the influence held by certain inmates and the apparent inability, or unwillingness, of prison management to confront them.

Whilst access to telephones plays an important role in helping prisoners to maintain family ties, the negative implications of abuse of the facilities are equally important. An example on D Wing was that prisoners in the lower hierarchy had to pay those at the top with phonecards, to gain access to the association landing. The phonecard system does little to help the weaker inmates, who are probably those most in need of family contact, but does more to reinforce the power bases of the stronger prisoners.

2.209 The fears expressed by Governors in 1992 appear to have been borne out in practice. Abuses of the system are widespread and recognised within Headquarters but the problem appears never to have proceeded beyond the 'too difficult tray'. The Inquiry believes that the £40 limit at Parkhurst, in respect of phonecards, should be reduced and that there should be a Service-wide review of the procedures in place.

2.210 Free association refers to specific times when no prisoners are at work and they are left to associate freely with others on their Wings. At Parkhurst, this arrangement was extended to include periods when inmates should have been engaged in work, education, the sports hall or the compound. The work ethic and attendance at Parkhurst were poor, leaving, according to the Area Manager:

> *"... an average of 50 unemployed or unallocated to work or education on a daily basis."*

2.211 The problems of persuading prisoners to become more actively involved in purposeful activities are not unique to Parkhurst. The danger is that prisoners not at work are left on the Wings at a time when most Wing staff are employed elsewhere, creating circumstances ripe for staff intimidation. The lack of supervision of the association areas, discussed earlier, compounds the problem and most staff acknowledge that they are not in a position to know what inmates are doing.

2.212 On one occasion at Parkhurst, a dog handler reported:

> *"In A Wing above the education block in a small room off the association area I found five prisoners watching a video. On the wall was a large electrical box which had been jemmied open, exposing the main electrical cable for the whole Wing. This could enable the prisoners to shut off all the lighting on the Wing. The inmates should not have been in that room."*

2.213 One solution regularly suggested by the Area Manager was to lock-up prisoners not gainfully employed, removing the threat they posed and at the same time providing an incentive to work. This option, with all its benefits, was rejected. Major factors were fear of prisoner reaction and the additional staff required to maintain the regime. Inmates must be offered genuine, meaningful work and education but those inmates who choose not to take these opportunities should be locked up in their cells.

2.214 Recreation facilities were offered through the free association areas on the Wings, including television and video rooms. Fully equipped kitchens were available on each Wing for the inmates, with chest freezers for food storage. Inmates had access to the sports hall and compound. Mini pool tables were set up on the association landings.

2.215 Access to cooking facilities was seen as providing a useful means of keeping prisoners occupied and in some control over their existence. The supply of kitchen knives, in the view of a senior Governor, presented a problem:

> *"If we give people cooking facilities they need knives to prepare food. At Dartmoor we did not have cooking facilities on the Wings but as part of the kitchen - a possible solution. Cooking on the Wings is popular and occupies them. I would have cooking facilities somewhere in the system and retain the control power that goes with it. Knives are issued for cooking and vegetable preparation. They maybe keep these knives in their cells but this should not be the case."*

2.216 It cannot be right that Category A and B prisoners had unlimited and unsupervised access to cooking facilities, with the possibility of hot fat being thrown at other prisoners and staff and with implements, including knives, at their disposal. The view that cooking facilities should be available but under proper supervision is supported by the Inquiry. Access to the facilities should be a privilege to be earned and not a right. At Parkhurst, cooking could only be undertaken by or on behalf of prisoners with sufficient cash to buy the ingredients. This accentuated the 'haves' and 'have nots' culture within the prison.

2.217 Free association was the least supervised activity. Certain landings were essentially no go areas and inmates were able to do what they pleased without fear of interference. This was the most dangerous time for the weaker, more vulnerable prisoners and the time when groups could gather for all types of unacceptable activities. On the rare occasions when staff did patrol the landings, they could not always see clearly what was happening because curtains were covering observation windows, poor design features created blind spots and sheets or blankets were hung by the inmates to break clear lines of sight. These obstructions to observation must be removed and Officers must be encouraged to patrol all areas of Wings unannounced and at frequent but irregular intervals.

(c) Personnel issues

2.218 At the meeting of representatives of Dispersal Prisons held in 1993, it was recorded that:

> *"We quickly agreed that unless we got it right for the Officer on the landing we might as well go home."*

2.219 This comment was made in the course of a discussion covering personnel issues, training, support and rewards. At Parkhurst, there was no coherent personnel policy or co-ordinated personnel management. The 1994/95 Establishment Business Plan paid very little attention to staff needs. As one senior Governor Grade put it:

> *"The business plan does not sufficiently cover staff welfare, it is aimed at prisoners."*

2.220 The Business Plan did mention welfare and occupational health but, in comparison with attention to prisoners' needs, those of staff were not sufficiently addressed. They should be addressed by the establishment and publication of a coherent personnel policy. Lack of training was identified earlier in this Report as a problem in the ECR but it turned out to be widespread. Even the training co-ordinator had received no training for the role. Training is vital but it received little attention and was treated as a dispensable task. The frustrations were best summed up by the training co-ordinator who said:

> *"Approximately 50 per cent of courses scheduled are cancelled at short notice."*

2.221 This problem is a consequence of the way staffing levels are calculated, allowing no more than 20 per cent of staff to be absent from operational duties at one time, 14 per cent for leave and 6 per cent for sickness **and** training. At Parkhurst, absence through sickness and leave invariably used up most of the 20 per cent allowance. Sickness rates for 1994 averaged 6.2 per cent, a situation exacerbated by the 4,500 or more hours 'time off in lieu' owed to Officers. With training considered a 'flexible task', the curtailment of training was inevitable.

2.222 Figures have been produced to the Inquiry showing an increase in hours taken up by training from 1.28 per cent in 1992/93 to 1.7 per cent in 1993/94 and 2.4 per cent in 1994/95, which exceeded the national target of 2.3 per cent. However, no account has been taken in these figures of the fact that Parkhurst has recruited 40 new entrants to the Service in the past year, all of whom would have attended the seven week initial training course. This would account for much of the improvement.

2.223 The unique nature of Dispersal Prisons prompted advice from a former Deputy Director General, as a result of the escape from Gartree prison in 1988, that:

> *"It would be timely to review the current arrangements for the selection and training of staff at all levels in Dispersal Prisons with particular attention being paid to how they might best be supported in their difficult and demanding work."*

2.224 However, the 1988 Working Group on Category A Security preferred to rely on identifying staff shortfalls in any post and addressing individual needs through existing or new training, with line managers discharging their responsibilities to provide support for their staff:

> *"The Working Group noted that there was possibly an argument in favour of providing specialised training for Dispersal Prison staff, albeit at the risk of creating an exclusive sub-group of prison staff, but was more attracted by the contrary argument that Officers in a Dispersal Prison have in the main to use the skills and functions demanded of all Officers."*

2.225 The issues of staff recruitment and postings across the whole Dispersal estate were referred by an Area Manager to the Category A Policy Committee in 1992. The response from the Personnel and Management Department was to bring forward the devolution of responsibility for staff provision to local managers, which effectively removed the problem from Prison Headquarters to individual establishments. This decision led to a local recruitment programme at Parkhurst which brought in the 40 new Officers. Many staff felt uncomfortable with inexperienced Officers in a Dispersal Prison. An example was a Senior Officer who said:

> *"... Officers should have two to three years experience prior to being posted to a Dispersal Prison."*

2.226 This view is strongly supported by the Inquiry. Intimidation by ruthless criminals does not provide a suitable learning environment for new staff, especially in the absence of training or guidance from experienced staff unaffected by "the Parkhurst Way".

2.227 Since the escape, an Operational Director has accepted that Officers working in Dispersal Prisons need additional training and the Inquiry believes the necessary resources should be made available. There is also a strong case for selecting staff specially for high security prisons and paying them more.

(d) Leadership

2.228 The Inquiry believes that Prison managers should set aside a minimum number of hours each day to walk around their establishments. There was a lack of visible leadership on the Wings and elsewhere at Parkhurst. Virtually all those interviewed complained of seldom seeing Governors or Principal Officers; and Wing Governors admitted that attendance on the Wings was invariably limited to hearing prisoner applications, a process that regularly took up to two hours to complete. They stated that, thereafter, they were fully employed dealing with paperwork which, because of its confidential nature, could not be undertaken in the Wing Office. A further and perhaps more substantial reason for their absence was that, on the Wings, they would be continually bothered by prisoners wanting to make repeat applications.

2.229 It is apparent that applications currently consume excessive management time, most of them reaching Wing Governors and many going even beyond the governing Governor to Area Managers and Directors. Others are referred by prisoners to MPs, which will often involve Governors in submitting reports to enable Ministers to reply to the MP. There is an urgent need for the system of applications to be reviewed so that minor matters are resolved at the appropriate level and only serious issues are referred to Governor Grades.

2.230 Another barrier to management and leadership at Parkhurst is the effect of protracted procedures to handle disputes with the Prison Officers Association (POA), which inhibit progressive and sound policy formulation. These procedures require review. Consultation with staff associations is an essential element of management and should prove of value; unfortunately, within the Prison Service, it too often leads to confrontation; but see also paragraph 3.50.

(e) Management structure

2.231 In addition to lack of leadership, many of the problems at Parkhurst stemmed from basic faults in the management structure. The current structure (see Appendix H) was introduced when "Fresh Start" was implemented in 1987 and no longer fits today's requirements. The Parkhurst Strategic Plan noted:

> *"There was a lack of clarity about what staff were expected to do at every level of the organisation, and too many matters are referred too far up the management chain resulting in duplication, overload at various levels and line managers being bypassed. All this reduces job satisfaction and stifles innovation and change. At present there is a very lengthy chain of management for most staff. Officers on the Wings for instance have Senior Officers, Principal Officer, Governor 5, Governor 4 Head of Residence, Governor 3 Head of Custody and then Governor in their line. This line needs to be shortened and clearer delegation of responsibilities defined."*

2.232 Prison managers should know their staff and their problems through regular contact and communication. Wing Governors must be free to spend most of their time on the Wings, closely supported by, and in return supporting, Officers of other grades. Without wishing to be too prescriptive, the Inquiry identified a number of principles which should form the basis of an effective structure.

2.233 Wings and Units are the basic building blocks of prisons and should only have one manager each; situations in which a Governor 5 and a Principal Officer, for example, can both claim management of a Wing, confuse the chain of command and are wasteful of resources. Wing Managers must be empowered. Their present isolation from the Senior Management Team (SMT) is exacerbated when Wing Governors report to the Head of Residence, who is not a member of SMT. Frustration was felt by operational staff at their inability to influence policy within the SMT. The SMT was dominated by the Heads of support services, with only one operational Governor to represent the core business of managing prisoners, a situation mirrored at Prisons Board level, as shown in Section 3.

2.234 The structure should be built from the bottom up. The Inquiry recommends a structure based on a maximum of five operational levels: Officer, Senior Officer, Unit/Wing Manager, Head of Operations and Security and Governor. The principles of this structure are illustrated in Figure 7.

Fig. 7 **Principles of Proposed Management Structure**

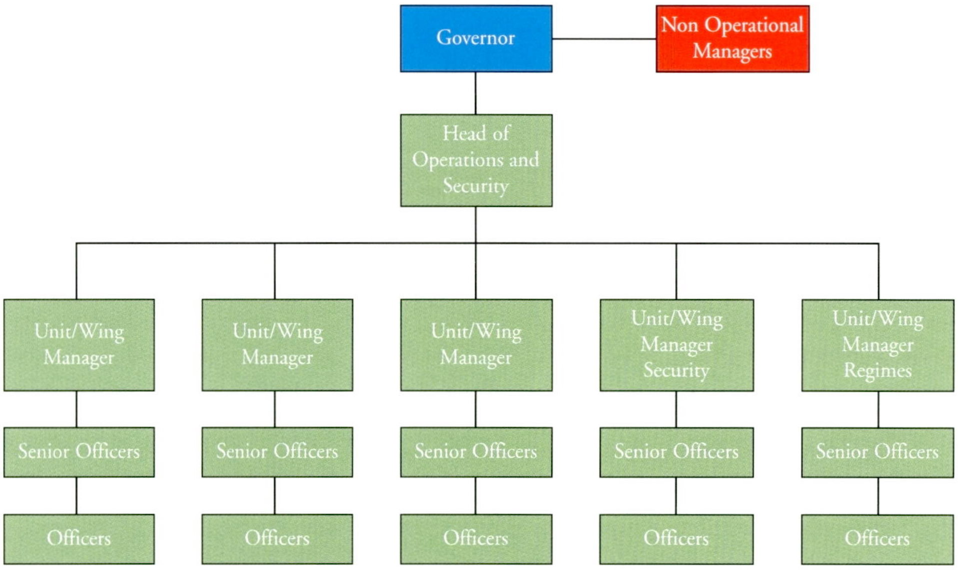

2.235 Prison Officers need to know to whom they report and should be team-based. The present system fails to ensure that staff are regularly on duty under a designated Senior Officer and needs to be replaced by a system of cohesive teams of the same Officers working together, led by a Senior Officer who is accountable for their tasking, development and performance.

2.236 Senior Officers, in turn, should be responsible to one Manager, flexibly graded according to the demands of the post. Unit/Wing Managers, of whatever grade, should report directly to a Head of Operations and Security who reports directly to the Governor. Both these should be supported by a Secretariat capable of relieving them of all routine paperwork.

2.237 The governing Governor has a particularly onerous job which warrants specific support. There is an urgent need for a Staff Officer to handle all routine administration and correspondence, as well as other tasks, at the Governor's discretion, releasing the Governor to spend more time walking the patch. The Staff Officer should be an up-and-coming, energetic member of staff, probably a Principal Officer or Governor 5.

2.238 These issues have been recently examined in depth in the Scottish Prison Service and the resulting recommendations provide a blueprint for addressing the same problems in England and Wales. A particular strength of the Scottish report is the range of alternative models offered for the management structures of prisons, dependent on the size and purpose of establishments. The model for a large establishment mirrored closely the Inquiry's recommendations for Parkhurst, which both validates that proposal and provides a basis for extending the principles Service-wide.

RECOMMENDATIONS

42 Visible leadership must be demonstrated by Wing Managers, who should work from an office located on their Wing.
(Paras. 2.194-196 and 2.228)

43 Telephone monitoring should be intelligence driven. Improved facilities need to be in place to monitor foreign language conversations.
(Paras. 2.201-205)

44 In the short term, the current £40 limit per week for phonecards at Parkhurst must be reviewed and set at a lower level. In the long-term, the issue of phonecards needs to be reassessed throughout the Service, to remove abuses of the system.
(Paras. 2.201-209)
[See Woodcock recommendation 53]

45 Prisoners should be offered sufficient, regular and meaningful employment or education facilities. Those not taking up work places should be locked in their cells during the day.
(Paras. 2.210-213)
[See recommendation 117]

46 Cooking facilities on Wings should be treated as a privilege and not a right. Access to stores of food must be supervised and regulated.
(Paras. 2.214-216)
[See Woodcock recommendation 51]

47 All curtains, blinds and obstructions should be removed from the association areas.
(Para. 2.217)
[See Woodcock recommendation 2]

48 Officers should patrol all areas of each Wing unannounced and at frequent but irregular intervals.
(Para. 2.217)
[See Woodcock recommendation 3]

49 A coherent personnel policy needs to be established and reflected in the Establishment Plan.
(Para. 2.220)

50 Training should not be regarded as a dispensable task.
(Paras. 2.220-222)

51 Additional training should be given to Dispersal Prison staff, to counter the extra problems inherent in dealing with the Dispersal population.
(Para. 2.227)
[See recommendation 99 and Woodcock recommendations 55 and 58]

52 Procedures need to be put in place to select, for Dispersal Prisons, staff with the necessary skills and experience for the work, with additional incentives to enhance the status of those selected.
(Paras. 2.225-227)
[See Woodcock recommendation 54]

53 Prison managers should set aside a minimum number of hours to walk around their establishments.
(Para. 2.228)

54 The applications system should be urgently reviewed so that minor matters are resolved at the appropriate level and only serious issues are referred to Governor Grades.
(Para. 2.229)

55 The procedures for handling disputes with the Prison Officers Association need to be reviewed.
(Para. 2.230)

56 Wings and Units should each have a single Manager, empowered through direct access to a Senior Management Team oriented towards operational needs. The management structure should be built from the bottom up and have only five levels.
(Paras. 2.231-238)

57 Officers should work in regular teams under a Senior Officer responsible to one Manager. Wing and Unit Managers should report directly to the Head of Operations and Security. The Head of Operations and Security and the governing Governor should both be supported by a Secretariat, including a Staff Officer for the Governor.
(Paras. 2.235-237)

Were there any previous warning signals?

2.239 There is a history of serious incidents at Parkhurst. They reveal security weaknesses on which action should have been taken and they should have provided clear danger signals; but they failed to ignite a sense of urgency for change and a proper regard for security.

(a) Attempted escape through the VTC welding workshop

2.240 In November 1990, a prisoner hid himself in the workshop (VTC) during afternoon work. Although he was one of only six prisoners, his absence was not noticed by the supervising Officer. He was reported missing from his Wing and a search was undertaken of the workshop, where he was found trying to cut his way out through the roof. He had broken into the tool store and taken tools. In addition, he was in possession of a grappling iron which he had manufactured in the VTC. The investigating Officer concluded:

> *"It is evident from my enquiries that the attempted escape could not have occurred if a proper count of the prisoners had been carried out as they left the workshop at 'cease labour'. Equally, if a proper check and search of the workshop had been carried out by the supervising Discipline Officer he would have been discovered immediately."*

(b) Escape by a Category A prisoner

2.241 On 22nd October 1991, a Category A prisoner escaped from Parkhurst Prison. The full circumstances were never established but it was believed that he hid himself on a vehicle that had gone into the prison to empty the waste bins. The subsequent enquiry concluded that:

> *"The escape was the result of failure to carry out basic Prison Officer security routines ... There were grievous shortcomings in procedures, notably the way in which roll checks of prisoners were conducted, the way in which Category A books were maintained and the way in which outgoing vehicles were examined."*

2.242 The recommendations of particular relevance to the present Inquiry were:

> *"Procedures for the movement of Category A prisoners within the prison be revised to conform with the* [then current] *instructions ...*
>
> *An up-to-date log should be kept in the ECR of the location of all Category A prisoners at all times of the day.*
>
> *The contingency plans for responding to a report of a prison break should be regularly exercised and a record kept of the date and any changes made to the plans as a result.*
>
> *The CCTV system now in use appears to be the product of amalgamation of two systems - static cameras and mobile cameras - and consideration should be given to reviewing the efficiency of the CCTV cover.*

The Training Officer should target inexperienced Officers (of whom there are many at Parkhurst) with a view to providing them with regular training/ advice in basic Prison Service jobs such as searching and escorting vehicles."

(c) Escape from M Wing

2.243 During the night of 19th/20th May 1992, five prisoners managed to escape from M Wing by breaking out through the wall of a cell into the building site created by the refurbishment of A and D Wings. They were all recaptured within the prison. The failure to take notice of a series of suspicious incidents leading up to the break-out were noted earlier in this Section. The main findings of the subsequent enquiry were:

> *"All internal perimeter fences to be fitted with geophones as a matter of urgency. The present programme must be brought forward. Any fences fitted as a result of the enabling work that are subsequently part of the inner security fence line must also be fitted with geophones before any work commences.*
>
> *The continued depletion of the Security Department particularly in the evening period to maintain the regime must be discussed following this incident. This policy contributed to the prisoners being able to breach the fabric of the jail. Similarly the MSL* [minimum staffing level] *should take into account that security is paramount in a Dispersal Prison."*

(d) Review of the Special Security Unit

2.244 A review of the Special Security Unit was conducted in June 1993, following interference with a tamper alarm. The SSU was found to be well below the required standards and the following problems were identified:

> *"There has clearly been a failure to meet basic security requirements of searching, locks bolts and bars and 'rub-down' searching. Equally disturbing is that percentage supervision and checking of these tasks has not been carried out by middle management as per the SSU operating instructions.*
>
> *There is no up-to-date inventory or record of tools and other items of equipment that appertain to the interests of security and staff/prisoner safety in the Unit. There is evidence of considerable amounts of prisoners' property that is in possession and should never have been allowed in the Unit.*
>
> *Many staff in all grades have allowed themselves over a period of time to have become conditioned by prisoners ... There are also signs that some staff in the Unit have become stale and complacent due to their time served on the Unit.*
>
> *There has been a failure to conform to the procedures as laid down for exceptional risk phone calls.*
>
> *Staff morale was found to be extremely low.* [The reasons given can be summarised as] ... *little or no management support, hastily made decisions*

by managers in order to appease prisoners' demands, failure to communicate between staff and managers, little or no staff training, late staff reports, staff constantly acting up without pay, the Unit being dirty and in need of redecoration."

(e) Fire in A Wing

2.245 On 11th August 1993, a fire was deliberately started by an inmate in a television room in A Wing. This was one of a series of incidents following the opening of A Wing in June 1993. In his enquiry, the Principal Officer wrote about the problems on the Wing:

> *"The most common reason given from staff was the mix of prisoners dispersed to A and D Wings when B Wing closed for refurbishment. The general consensus stated was that B Wing management selected the less troublesome prisoners and the more experienced staff for their own ends.*
>
> *There is a strong feeling among the Wing's Officer Grades of a neglect of quality first line and middle management support for them since the Wing opened.*
>
> *There is a general feeling among Wing staff that prisoners disregard and show contempt towards them. Intimidation and confrontation has undoubtedly led to conditioning. The result of this is that many areas in the Wing have become and been accepted by the Wing staff as 'no go areas'.*
>
> *There is an admission from the Wing staff that LBB* [Locks, Bolts and Bars] *checks, although being signed for, are not in fact being carried out."*

2.246 The Principal Officer went on:

> *"... There is a need to identify certain training needs for staff in all grades.*
>
> *Staff must have supervision ... support and guidance forthcoming from their line managers.*
>
> *To ensure that all managers clearly understand the dynamic security initiative and to encourage them to promote the staff they lead.*
>
> *The setting up of a well planned Personal Officer system should be expedited for A Wing."*

(f) Assault in A Wing

2.247 In early September 1994, an internal enquiry resulted from an assault on a prisoner in A Wing. The enquiry revolved around illicit dealing in methadone supplied to prisoners being treated for heroin addiction. The enquiry concluded that:

> *"Parkhurst clearly has a serious drug problem. The problem is greater than initially envisaged. The supply of drugs is spiralling out of control."*

2.248 Among the recommendations were:

> *"To make greater use of the closed visit facility which at present is seldom and reluctantly used. This facility should be high profile and known to be an automatic action for any prisoner convicted of an internal drug related charge under the prison code of discipline. A minimum period of six months closed visits should be actioned under all circumstances.*
>
> *All prisoners to be advised and be given the opportunity to use the toilet prior to their visit. No further use of the toilet should then be allowed until the visit is terminated. Obvious exceptions would need to be made for those with medical grounds."*

(g) Whitemoor escape

2.249 On 9th September 1994, six highly dangerous inmates escaped from the Special Security Unit at Whitemoor Prison. They successfully managed to breach all the security measures. They cut through the wire fencing of the exercise yard, scaled the inner wall, breached a further wire-mesh security fence and finally climbed over the gander. To assist the escape, they had taken with them a vast array of largely self-manufactured escape equipment as well as two pistols with ammunition. This escape signalled to the Prison Service that SSUs and Dispersal Prisons were not secure and foreshadowed many of the features of the Parkhurst escape.

(h) Letter from HM Chief Inspector of Prisons

2.250 In October 1994, HM Chief Inspector of Prisons took the unusual step of sending a letter to the Director General following an inspection visit to Parkhurst, showing obvious concern about security. Having stated that "The main trouble is inadequate searching", he identified the following problems:

> *"Evidence of staff's reluctance to confront prisoners shown by use of Security Information Reports for purely disciplinary matters instead of laying charges against the Prison Rules, and an almost complete absence of proper 'rub-down' searching whenever members of management are not present.*
>
> *The searching of Category B and C inmates and their cells hardly happened, that of Category A prisoners seriously behind target.*
>
> *Our experience was that triggering the metal detector portal did not result in a 'rub-down' search of visitors to the prison as it should have done.*
>
> *The X-ray machine in the gate lodge did not operate, because there were no staff to do so, at lunchtimes and in the evenings. It therefore fulfils no useful purpose because anyone intending to traffic knows this.*
>
> *High risk Category A inmates using the toilet during visits can mix (even briefly and with staff present) with non high risk or Category B men who have been 'rubbed-down' after their visits. Thus articles could be passed. This will be solved when the new high risk visits accommodation is brought into use.*

Management aware of most of these points (and should have done more to ensure that routine searching took place). Much of the rest depends on Prison Officers doing their work properly. If reluctance to confront inmates overcomes basic standards, management must encourage, exhort and admonish.

X-ray machine must be staffed so as to operate whenever people enter the prison. This is a resource point and may not lie within the Governor's immediate control."

(i) Area Manager's Visits

2.251 The Area Manager visited Parkhurst regularly and the thoroughness and structured style of his visits was complemented by full, written debriefs, sent to the Governor and Operational Director.

2.252 The Inquiry had the benefit of these notes, covering some four years, and it was evident the Area Manager regularly identified lax security procedures. As part of the annual security audit, Parkhurst had been visited twice in late 1994 and concerns had been raised regarding a number of issues, including cell searching, locks, bolts and bar checks, visits and examination of Category A books.

2.253 Extracts from the reports on two visits (published in October 1994) illustrate the depth of concern expressed by the Area Manager:

"Staff are buckling under the barrage of verbal and physical intimidation."

"On the Wings I met prisoners who are openly intimidating staff."

"I find staff retreating to the Wing Office and it feels as if they are seeking sanctuary."

"Curtains are there to restrict staff and give staff the impression that cells are 'no go areas'. What is the justification for curtains on the doors? I would urge you to consider the removal of this practice."

"I saw cells being searched with prisoners in the cells."

(j) Woodcock Report

2.254 The final and loudest warning came from the Woodcock Report into the Whitemoor escape, published in December 1994. This resulted in a hard hitting letter from the Director General to all governing Governors, dated 19th December 1994, in which he said:

"It is inevitable that the Woodcock Report will have far reaching consequences for the Prison Service. Sir John suggests that some of the problems identified at Whitemoor probably exist elsewhere in the Service. Our performance in security, while dramatically better, must improve further. The Enquiry has made 64 recommendations which have been accepted in full. They cover a wide range, including improvements in

physical security, changes in searching requirements, controls on privileges, property and private cash, and improvements in training. The recommendations will affect all prisons ... Many things contribute to effective security - secure buildings, effective detection systems, good intelligence, and rigorous procedures. All this is set out in the Manual on Security. Let me make it quite clear that the Manual is the definitive set of rules on security matters - it is not discretionary. It does not end there; many prisoners are cunning, manipulative and determined. There is no substitute for single minded attention to detail at all levels of the organisation.

Too many escapes have occurred because basic details have been overlooked and vigilance has been absent. There must be positive relationships with prisoners, so that staff know what is going on and are in control."

(k) Summary

2.255 The common threads between these earlier warnings and this Inquiry are obvious. These serious incidents sent out clear and undeniable warning signals about problems within Parkhurst. The Woodcock Report was the last in a series which accurately foreshadowed the events of 3rd January 1995. The escape from Parkhurst was not based on any new or ingenious plan but simply on the ability of prisoners to follow a well trodden path through loose and ineffective security. The alarm bells should have been constantly ringing throughout the Prison Service: some heard but did too little too late; others showed a reprehensible complacency and false sense of invulnerability.

CONCLUSIONS

2.256 *"The findings of the Enquiry describe an awful story where it appears that everything which could have gone wrong has in fact done so."*

This sentence starts the final paragraph of the Woodcock Report into the escape from Whitemoor Prison. Its applicability to the Parkhurst escape underlines the commonality between the two incidents and between the findings of the two separate Inquiries.

2.257 The Parkhurst escape revealed a chapter of errors at every level and a naivety that defies belief. Parkhurst should never have been retained as a high security prison, with so much construction work in progress and scheduled to extend over a considerable number of years. Although questions had been raised on a number of occasions as to the wisdom of such a course, there was a desire throughout to keep the status of the prison intact, for historical rather than for practical security reasons.

2.258 Not only was the prison totally unsuitable for housing some of the most difficult prisoners in the system but also the procedures employed were lax and unprofessional, making it relatively easy for the escapees to achieve their objective. In addition, the Service failed to provide the prison with the benefits of technology in relation to geophones on the fences, camera coverage and an effective, up-to-date, properly manned control room, despite persistent and legitimate requests from local management. These deficiencies were bad enough but mere pin pricks compared to the disastrous indecision and apathy which pervaded so many working practices. It is quite extraordinary that so much effort was invested in persuading the Parkhurst management to continue to accept Category A prisoners, including those in the High Risk category, whilst so little was done to ensure that tried and tested security technology was installed.

2.259 It is difficult to come to terms with the expenditure of so much money on renovations which added little to the capability of the establishment to contain high security prisoners. Immediately following the escape, additional security measures were implemented which, in addition to the increase of dogs from 18 to 28, included:

- Immediate halt to the building programme, pending installation of physical perimeter security devices.
- Increase in number of cameras.
- Improvement of lighting.
- Immediate removal of High Risk Category A prisoners, followed by Standard Risk Category A inmates.
- Fitting of sensory devices and movement alarms to vulnerable areas.
- Change of locking schedule.

2.260 Further security works have been identified, in addition to those required to meet the recommendations of the Woodcock Report, but, when all the work is completed, Parkhurst will still be a Victorian prison with significant security weaknesses. It should be removed from the Dispersal estate and alternatives, such as Belmarsh Prison, should be considered.

2.261 The Inquiry has pinpointed a multitude of security lapses and unacceptable practices. It is easy to condemn those on duty at the time of the escape but the break-out could have been launched at any time with the same chances of success. There is little to commend in the way things were done, despite the conscientiousness of many individuals. The hopelessness of the situation is perhaps best illustrated by the comments of many honest Prison Officers who, during interviews, made the plea:

> *"Please come back and check that your recommendations have been implemented."*

2.262 These comments reveal a sense of frustration over the failure of the Service to respond to and learn the lessons of previous incidents.

2.263 The Inquiry recognises the commitment and bravery of many individual members of staff but the quality of leadership, from all levels of management at the prison, has to be questioned. There must be something radically wrong with an organisation in which the Governor has regularly to work in excess of 50 hours a week coping with a blizzard of paper, leaving him only two to three hours per week to carry out the essential function of walking around the prison meeting staff and inmates.

2.264 The escape from Parkhurst will haunt the Service for many years to come. The escape was not due to one person's folly, because many of its ingredients can be traced along the lines of communication to Prison Service Headquarters. The numerous failings identified in this Report indicate that there were many 'hands on the tiller' on this voyage to disaster.

SECTION 3: CENTRAL ISSUES AFFECTING SECURITY

INTRODUCTION

3.1 Hadfield/Lakes (in their Report following the escapes from Brixton Prison in 1991) wrote:

> *"Virtually every area of Prison Service policy and operations can impact on security ... the policy making and developing process should ensure that implications for security procedures and resourcing are identified."*

3.2 In the final analysis, the top management of any organisation must be responsible for its performance. This Inquiry has found a great deal that needs to be put right within the Prison Service, spanning leadership, structure, the management chain, and the ethos of the Service.

3.3 It would be wrong, however, not to recognise some positive aspects of the Service, not least the much improved general conditions within prisons in recent years, the successful handling of increased prison populations and greatly improved financial planning. There is also evidence of some high quality staff at all levels. The importance of able and dedicated staff in the Prison Service cannot be over-emphasised. Whilst technology and physical barriers are an essential part of security, they will be of little use without the active commitment of fully motivated staff. Technology should be an aid to staff, not a substitute for them.

3.4 The Prisons Board, in its Salmon response, indicated that it did not consider that paragraph 3.3 adequately reflected its achievements over the last two and a half years. The Board's response on this matter is reproduced in full at Appendix I. The Inquiry noted with concern that only five points out of more than one hundred in the Board's paper related to security and two of these were responses to the Woodcock Report.

3.5 A Board member has stated that:

> *"The resultant managerial challenge has, I suspect, been dangerously under-estimated in years past - a situation exacerbated more recently by pressures of population numbers, more difficult prisoner profiles, finance increasingly constrained, rapid changes and developments dictated by the political agenda, and a thoroughly unhelpful and pervasive industrial relations climate."*

The Inquiry took note of these points but had already discovered a fundamental mismatch between the perception of the Board and what was happening on the ground. The dichotomy is described in some detail in this Report and forms the basis of many of the Inquiry's findings, particularly in this Section.

3.6 In recent speeches and during interviews, the Director General and his Board have highlighted a number of areas of success within the Service. According to Prison Service Briefing Number 78, dated 8th December 1994, the Director General set out the achievements of the Prison Service, over the previous 18 months, at a conference at Solihull which had taken place from 31st October to 2nd November. Whitemoor was a very recent memory and the Director General first reminded delegates that the Service continues to be a tough and demanding environment for managers. He said that recent events, especially those at Whitemoor, were very serious matters to the Prison Service; that he did not underestimate their significance; that there would be no sweeping under the carpet; that the Service was already learning lessons; that security and control were inevitably a continuing battle of wits and wills; and that the Service must do everything in its power to stay one step ahead of prisoners.

3.7 The Director General stressed, however, that it would be wrong for the public to judge the Service on the basis of individual incidents and said that it was up to the Service to tell the public about its achievements and to explain more clearly what it does. He told delegates that escapes had been reduced by a third. As a result of better management, greater vigilance, new approaches, new technology and well targeted capital investment, the Service had coped with a prison population increase of 10,000, nearly 25 per cent, while meeting its commitment to decent conditions and positive regimes. This had been achieved with an average of only 150 prisoners in police cells in that financial year and the elimination of trebling (ie three prisoners in a cell). The numbers of prisoners with access to integral sanitation had been increased to 94 per cent. More prisoners had been doing more work, training and education; more prisoners had been given opportunities to change their offending behaviour.

3.8 In his closing address to the Conference, the Director General gave his overall view of the progress of the Service:

> *"There have been many references during this Conference to fighting battles and winning - and in some cases losing - wars. There is no doubt this Service is winning the war. This is a fine organisation and this Conference has shown plenty of evidence of it."*

3.9 These were grand sentiments and formed part of an understandable rallying call at the end of a conference attended by many of the senior managers of the Service. The Inquiry's research painted a different picture, revealing widespread frustration over the lack of decisive leadership in the Service, with morale frequently described as being extremely low. Although the Board, in its Salmon response, has submitted a selection of comments from Board of Visitor Reports which indicate a different view of morale, these do not accord with opinions expressed by staff on many visits by the Inquiry. Neither do they accord with the views outlined by the Chairman of the Board of Visitors Co-ordinating Committee (see para. 3.144) nor with the Prison Service's own attitude survey (see para. 3.24).

3.10 Low morale was described by one Board member as part of the public sector psyche. This view was taken into account by the Inquiry but there was ample evidence to suggest that the problem was real, not imaginary. In addition to the concern over leadership at all levels, the uncertainties surrounding private sector involvement in the Prison Service and the Service's poor public image, resulting from recent escapes, were consistently identified as contributory factors. Staff also displayed irritation at the way the Service was becoming strangled by bureaucracy and few of those interviewed would agree with the Director General's assessment that the 'war' was being won. It is a sad irony that, within two months of his address, three more extremely dangerous prisoners escaped from a second high security prison.

3.11 The depth of frustration is perhaps best illustrated in the following comments from a senior Governor Grade, who felt so strongly about the state of the Service that he made a submission to the Inquiry:

> *"I feel that the present Headquarters structure reinforces bad behaviour in managers rather than good and is incompetent at offering direction, advice and/or leadership. Whilst I have often not represented the common view, I have never experienced such common agreement amongst colleagues that directives, advice and leadership are all absent.*
>
> *The various management changes after the Mountbatten Report, the May Report, the introduction of Fresh Start and the Headquarters Review latterly have merely served to add layers of bureaucracy to an overloaded structure. As a result Headquarters, now grossly oversized, creates nothing but work, issues absurd directives to local prison management and sees prison management as serving it rather than the other way round."*

3.12 The same Governor Grade continued by examining the 'new, improved' structure of the Service:

> *"The new organisational structure was sold on the grounds that the line would be clear and policy initiatives discussed with the field. The latter does not happen and with regard to the former things are so bad that some speak with fondness of the old regional structure. In short it is difficult to know who is doing what and to what purpose."*

3.13 The views expressed by this Governor Grade were verified and reiterated by other operational staff. These contrasting views typify the yawning gap between the perception of senior management and that of their operational staff. The divide was so great that it created severe doubts in the minds of the Inquiry about the intermediate linkages in the chain of command.

VISIBLE LEADERSHIP

3.14 Admiral Lygo, in his Report on the Management of The Prison Service (1991), described the issue of leadership as "first and fundamental". This was not a new sentiment. As far back as the Mountbatten Report, observers of the Prison Service had recommended professional, high profile, visible leadership. Mountbatten declared:

> *"It is the professional Head of the Service who must be free to spend a good deal of his time visiting the outstations. Only in this way can he truly establish his personal leadership of the Service."*

3.15 Lord Justice Woolf, in his Report on the prison disturbances of 1990, developed this theme further by saying:

> *"The Director General must also give the leadership which is expected of the Head of an Operational Service ... he needs to play the part his title of Director General suggests. An operational service such as the Prison Service requires a leader who is not merely the Chairman of the Management Committee."*

3.16 The Director General and Board should have regular contact with those who have operational responsibility, so that security weaknesses do not go unnoticed. In addition to visits to establishments by Board members, the present Director General has taken a high profile in very trying times, visiting all 130 establishments in two years, undertaking 175 visits since 1st January 1993 (at an average of seven per month). It is to his credit that he has coped with the personal pressures which the competing demands of politicians, the media and successive operational incidents must have inflicted upon him. It is, however, surprising that neither he nor his Board recognised the signs and symptoms of failure and inefficiency that were so obvious and so dramatically illustrated by the escapes from Parkhurst and Whitemoor. This is confirmed by the Board's Salmon response, which stated:

> *"Although it is evident that there were weaknesses at Whitemoor and Parkhurst, these specific weaknesses were not visible to the Director General or the Board."*

3.17 The Director General and Board members claim that the problems which have emerged were not drawn to their attention. The value of visits is diminished if the inherent problems remain undiscovered. In its own visits to prison establishments, the Inquiry has identified these problems simply by talking to Governors, staff and prisoners and by observing failures in 'basic' security procedures. Since the Inquiry was set up, the Prison Service's own professional Audit Team has identified similar failures and reported a wide range of security flaws in the Dispersal estate.

3.18 At present, the Prison Service is led by a Director General recruited from industry, supported by main-stream Civil Servants and a few Governors promoted into the Civil Service structure. The management style and culture at the top of the Prison Service, not surprisingly, reflects that of the senior Civil Service, which is trained to support Ministers rather than to manage a people-orientated organisation. This has unfortunate consequences. Any prison Governor aspiring to the most senior posts in the Service sees the current requirements for those posts as the skills and approach of senior Civil Servants. The high degree of mobility of senior Civil Servants makes for a lack of continuity in senior management and the management style is not conducive to obtaining the best from the Service. Headquarters and other senior appointments need to be filled largely by Prison Service professionals who have practical prison experience.

3.19 An independent consultant, commenting recently on the balance between management and leadership in the Service, made the following distinction:

> *"Management is about planning, organising and controlling; it is about producing predictable results; it tends to produce only incremental change. The kind of paradigm shift for which people are craving calls for leadership - the ability to create a vision of how things could be, producing alignment, generating energy and inspiring people to achieve the overall aims and objectives of the Service."*

3.20 He went on to comment about the culture of the Service, in the following terms:

> *"The Service has had entrenched cultures and further radical change of thinking at all levels is required. There needs to be a change in attitudes, and new patterns of behaviour need to be developed based on co-responsibility and trust.*
>
> *Without the kind of leadership which generates enthusiastic commitment to the purpose, direction, values and beliefs of the organisation, we will get, at best, only compliance from prison staff."*

3.21 He related the issue of leadership directly to security:

> *"Effective security will be delivered only when all the staff in the establishment feel in tune with the values demonstrated by the Leadership, are clear about and have commitment to the goals, and feel personally accountable for implementing procedures."*

3.22 An important leadership function is recognition of good service. Only the leader can credibly represent the whole organisation in conferring credit on an individual. The Prison Service seems to have underestimated the significance of such recognition. In the last ten years, national awards have never been more than 20 (for over 30,000 staff) and have diminished in the last few years. No gallantry awards have been made. No use seems to have been made of awards such as the Queen's Commendation for Bravery. There is no medal for long service and good conduct. Excellent means of recognition, such as Director General's, Area Managers' or Governors' Commendations, are under-used. There seems to be little understanding of the value of creating occasions when individuals can be singled out for recognition.

3.23 The Prison Service must address these issues. Commendations can be produced on vellum, signed, framed and presented in public with a few well-chosen words. Families and friends can and should have the opportunity to share in the occasion. Commendations can also be published in the Service media. Such gestures cost nothing but they mean an enormous amount to people and cement a sense of pride in an organisation. The Prison Service fails even to make adequate gestures to recognise major changes in the lives of staff, with congratulations from senior line managers on promotion or thanks on retirement. The lack of grasp among top management of the importance of such minor ceremonies and acclamations is regrettable.

3.24 Prison staff do not feel that their Headquarters cares. That is confirmed by the Prison Service's own staff attitude survey of 1994 (reported in Service Briefing Number 74), which showed a demoralised workforce. Only 19 per cent of staff felt that they worked for a well-managed organisation. Ninety-two per cent of Prison Officers agreed or strongly agreed that:

> *"People who run the Prison Service don't care enough about the people who have to deal with prisoners face-to-face."*

3.25 The Service must move very rapidly from being a paper-orientated organisation to becoming a more people-orientated one, if it is to have any hope of solving some of its present difficulties. This will require a complete change of ethos and a shift of personnel policy.

3.26 Personnel policy is discussed in more detail in paragraphs 3.70-72 but it must cater for career planning in such a way that fast-stream individuals are given the experience and training to develop a rounded personality with the confidence and knowledge to tackle senior posts. An effective understanding of the working of the operational chain and the proper role of support staff in a disciplined service is gained only through experience at an operational level.

3.27 Positive and visible leadership at all levels is required to move the Service forward. The Inquiry identified two particular areas of concern. First, there were elements within the fundamental management philosophy and practice which appeared wholly inappropriate and, second, there were severe problems within the management structure of the Service.

MANAGEMENT PHILOSOPHY AND PRACTICE

3.28 The management of the Service was a constant topic of debate during the Inquiry, with differing views being expressed at different levels of the organisation. The majority were strongly critical and the consensus was that management did not meet the needs of the Service.

Confusion over the primary purpose

3.29 There was widespread confusion over the present Statement of Purpose of the Service. This was discussed with a cross-section of senior management in the prisons visited. The present Statement of Purpose is:

> *"Her Majesty's Prison Service serves the public by keeping in custody those committed by the courts.*
>
> *Our duty is to look after them with humanity and help them lead law-abiding and useful lives in custody and after release."*

3.30 These two objectives provide a constant and inevitable tension between levels of security and degrees of trust. As one interviewee described it:

> *"A major difficulty is ambiguity. Governors have bought into the humane approach advocated by Woolf and others but are now confused by the switch to a more austere approach. There are two strong but different philosophies shown in the Statement of Purpose. The purpose of the Service is not to pursue two different aims but to achieve balance."*

3.31 The competing objectives are normally termed 'Custody' and 'Care'. The Prison Service, and their counterparts overseas, have long debated how the correct balance can be achieved between them. The following passages, taken from a booklet issued by another European Prison Service, describe the contrasting perceptions. Where the **care** elements are foremost, the image can be one of lax security:

> *"Prisons are luxury hotels at the state's expense. Vicious criminals are pampered with the taxpayer's money. They have televisions, they can get hold of all the drugs they want, and when they come out on leave they commit serious crimes. The "punishment" is much too short, because the criminal justice system ... is a joke. The Prisons have got as many holes as a sieve - anyone can escape from them. And when the criminals are finally released they are horribly spoiled and go straight back to their criminal ways."*

Conversely, where **custody** measures appear to dominate:

> *"The prison is a place that is cut off from the outside world. Everything you do is watched. The staff are trained to harass you as much as possible. The food is bad and there is nothing to do all day. When you get out you are so full of hate for the free society. So you want to get your revenge on the society that did this to you. Because you haven't learned anything while you were*

inside, you have to go back to a life of crime. Prison sentences are pointless: people who have accidentally made a little mistake are turned into hardened criminals."

3.32 The inter-relationship can be thought of as a set of scales, with one side representing Care (or humanitarianism), and the other representing Custody (or security). They are kept in balance by Control. Control is not simply physical restraint. It involves non-physical measures such as incentives, sanctions and prisoner programmes. The art lies in having Custody, Care and Control in harmony, to provide a balanced regime.

3.33 The tension between care and custody was a central factor in the divergence of practice noted by the Inquiry on its visits to prison establishments. Depending on the interpretation of control by Governors, management teams and even individual Prison Officers, the approach to prisoners differed enormously. One significant effect was to allow inmates who move between establishments to exploit the system, by obtaining concessions through highly selective comparisons.

3.34 The Lygo Report found:

"... confusion on the part of staff about their own purpose and, more significantly, wide variations of approach between establishments depending, so it seems, on local culture rather than management decision. In the short term, the need to clarify the Service's sense of purpose is one of the critical tasks for management. All this has led to an absence of discipline in the strict sense of the word. Very few seemed to know whether they were members of a disciplined service or not although nearly all thought they should be. Moreover, all too often members of the Service, some in relatively senior positions, are prepared to disown Headquarters instructions. In these circumstances, it is not surprising that, in turn, staff are inclined to treat instructions as mere suggestions."

3.35 The Inquiry found the same situation and supports the frequently expressed view of senior management at the prisons visited that there is an urgent need for clarification of the Service Statement of Purpose. Without a clear purpose, staff will continue to provide a disjointed and unco-ordinated service, which will continue to be exploited by the prisoners.

3.36 The Scottish Prison Service (SPS), also an Agency, has a model 'mission statement'. The four aims are easily remembered by use of the mnemonic 'COCO', as follows:

C *to keep in **custody** those committed by the courts,*

O *to maintain good **order** in each prison,*

C *to **care** for prisoners with humanity, and*

O *to provide prisoners with a range of **opportunities** to exercise personal responsibility and to prepare for release.*

3.37 The Statement appears similar to that of HM Prison Service but the Scottish Prison Service is clear that custody comes first. Their Corporate Plan has a 'Key Performance Measure and Target':

> *"An 'escapes' measure reflects the primary responsibility of the SPS: to keep prisoners in secure custody."*

3.38 One HM Prison Service Governor, recognising the need to provide greater clarity for his staff, has identified four main groups to which prison management has responsibility, namely the courts, the public, prisoners and prison staff.

3.39 The Inquiry has considered forms of words for a mission statement which might be more useful to the Service than the present text and have built on the thoughts of that Governor. After wide consultation, the following wording is recommended:

The Prison Service is responsible for providing:

Custody -

- on behalf of the courts, by keeping in custody those committed by them and
- on behalf of the public, protecting them from those committed by the courts and also deterring potential criminals;

Care -

- on behalf of the prisoners, by offering opportunities to learn from their mistakes, make amends for the harm done, maintain links with families and acquire skills and knowledge to plan for the future;

Control -

- of the prisoners, by inducing improvements in behaviour and attitude, through an appropriate mix of incentives and sanctions and
- by equipping staff with the skills and knowledge needed to accomplish difficult and demanding tasks.

Although all these elements must be in balance, the primary responsibility of the Service is custody.

3.40 If it is felt that a radical change in the Statement of Purpose would cause too much confusion in the Service then, at the very least, the primary purpose should be made clear as follows:

The primary purpose of Her Majesty's Prison Service is to serve the public by keeping in custody those committed by the courts.

It is also our duty to look after them with humanity and help them lead law-abiding and useful lives in custody and after release.

Disunity within the Service

3.41 Although a clarification of the Statement of Purpose will remove a great deal of the present uncertainty within the Service, the Inquiry found, as others have done, that there is a deeply rooted disunity within the Service which needs to be addressed before all personnel can function in a harmonious and co-ordinated fashion.

3.42 The most obvious and damaging disunity is between establishments and Headquarters. This goes far beyond what might be expected in a large organisation of this type. It is discussed more fully under 'Structure', later in this Section. A second disunity exists, within some establishments, between management (Governor Grades) and staff (Prison Officers).

3.43 The Prison Service has a unique place in society and comparisons with other Services are not straightforward. Nevertheless, it is hard to escape the conclusion that the Service has marked similarities to the armed forces and police. It has a coercive as well as a rehabilitating role and is prepared ultimately to use physical force to maintain order and ensure compliance. Matters such as security and intelligence loom large in its thinking. Contingency plans exist to co-operate with armed police or the armed forces in emergency situations. The Service speaks of 'operations', 'exercises' and 'command'. Prison Officers (but not Governors) wear uniform.

3.44 Other disciplined services have found it useful to insist on measures such as uniform, not simply for the sake of appearance but as part of a special code of conduct and discipline, to reinforce their culture and team efforts. Great attention is paid to ensuring that all ranks know exactly what is required of them and where they fit into the team.

3.45 At present, the custom in the Prison Service is that only Prison Officers below Governor Grade wear uniform and the Governors wear civilian suits. The result is often a 'them' and 'us' culture, which brands those in uniform as of inferior status. Ambitious Prison Officers aspire to wear a suit to work and it becomes a badge of rank. The attachment of the 'Governor' title to all grades above Principal Officer serves to accentuate the gap between uniformed and non-uniformed staff. Prisoners, who may also wear their own clothes, are thus encouraged to look down on the 'lesser mortals' in uniform and, as time goes by, they insist more and more on dealing only with Governors.

3.46 Prison Officers, and indeed prisoners, seem to yearn for a more disciplined environment. The Lygo Report recommended that all staff wear uniform and this was initially accepted by the Service. At the last moment, the decision was reversed. The Inquiry feels that Admiral Lygo was right and that all staff in prisons, including Governors, should normally wear uniform. This would help to ease the divisions that can exist between Governor Grades and junior ranks and to remove a weapon of mischief from the prisoners' armoury. There is considerable support for this view within the Service. It is also important that civilian members of staff are clearly identified, to distinguish them from inmates.

3.47 Following the Woolf Report, the Prison Service in England and Wales stopped wearing uniform caps, because it was felt that they created the wrong image of the work Prison Officers were endeavouring to do. The Scottish Prison Service has retained headgear. Whilst no recommendation is made on this issue, Scottish Prison Officers do look smart and business-like and it is easy to accept their claim that the practice helps to unite them as a disciplined service and aids identification of Officers when large numbers of inmates are being moved through an establishment.

3.48 There has been a long-running debate over the wearing of name badges by prison staff. Although it is a requirement arising from the Citizens' Charter and has been promulgated in a notice to staff, it has been resisted by some staff associations and only a small minority of staff wear badges. Name badges are important because they enable prisoners, visitors and colleagues to identify with whom they are dealing. The Prison Service decided that name badges should be worn and it is disturbing to find that many staff have chosen to disobey the direction. It shows that the discipline of the Service leaves much to be desired. The top management did not think it advisable to enforce the wearing of name badges but now says that it will be reviewing its decision shortly.

3.49 It is of interest to examine the position taken on these points by the new contracted out prisons. Some private companies have appointed just one 'Director', equating to the governing Governor, and have put all staff, including the Governor Grade equivalents, into uniform (blazers), with name badges.

3.50 Throughout the Inquiry, it was apparent that difficulties had been experienced in the past, with the different staff associations, on various issues, including the introduction of new and improved practices. Paradoxically, the staff associations could not have been more helpful to the Inquiry. They are anxious to co-operate in every way to take the Service forward and out of its present malaise. The Board should build on the spirit of goodwill which clearly underlies the attitude of the associations and turn it into a real instrument for increasing harmony. There has never been a better time to rid the Service of practices that delay progress. It yearns to be a united Service, with everyone pulling together 'on the same rope'. The Prisons Board has expressed a desire to work constructively with the Prison Service Trade Unions to promote positive industrial relations and this should start forthwith.

Key performance indicators (KPIs)

3.51 Although the measures discussed so far will assist in producing a greater clarity of purpose and team effort, another essential element is an accurate and reliable way to measure the performance of the Service and identify improvements and problem areas.

3.52 Confusion of purpose within the Service is apparent in the area of performance standards and measures. The Corporate Plan, 1994-97, includes the Statement of Purpose, a Vision, five Values, six Goals, seven Strategic Priorities and eight KPIs. Although the Inquiry made some effort to draw all these into a self-evident inter-relationship, it proved impossible to do so. For example, although commitment to staff is a value and although staff motivation and training are strategic priorities, there is no goal associated with staff and no KPI against which performance can be judged. It is little wonder that staff in establishments are equally confused and this may have some bearing on why so few hopes have been fulfilled.

3.53 It is a well-accepted principle that the success of an organisation should be judged by results but it is crucial that the areas chosen for measurement reflect the main objectives. The measures should be capable of meaningful and valid interpretation. Goals are aspirations whereas KPIs are drivers for action on the ground. As such, they are powerful tools against which to monitor standards but they can also be very misleading.

3.54 The current set of eight KPIs (analysed in detail in Appendix J) was introduced at the time the Agency was formed and represented the first attempt to assess the 'business performance' of the Prison Service in a quantitative way. It was a laudable and important first step. KPIs are, however, management tools that need regular review. They send messages to the workforce about what is important. There were grounds for concern in a number of areas. First, the KPIs showed a strong bias towards care issues (five KPIs), to the potential detriment of custody (one KPI) and control (one KPI). Second, there were significant omissions in the areas of Headquarters staff reductions; staff development and commitment; recidivism; physical security; discipline; drugs; and suicides. The third major concern related to the way in which statistics were being collected and used. In particular, staff perceived KPIs, rightly or wrongly, as a benchmark for judgements about privatisation and were tempted to be economical with the truth when submitting returns. The Inquiry believes that KPIs must be revised as indicated in Appendix J.

3.55 Performance indicators, as the name implies, only indicate and can never be a complete measure of the success or failure of an organisation. In principle, the establishment of performance indicators within the Prison Service is wholeheartedly supported by the Inquiry but it is clear that at least some of those presently in use are not achieving their objective. Indeed, they may even be counter-productive, in respect of both security and conditions for inmates. The Prisons Board must not fall into the trap of managing the indicators rather than managing the organisation.

3.56 Although the Prisons Board has accepted that KPIs need to be constantly reviewed, the Inquiry has observed that the latest Business Plan, 1995/96, shows no change to the KPIs discussed in this Report. In the latest plan, the Board proposes to develop new indicators for 1996/97 covering areas such as drug misuse, serious assault and re-conviction rates. The timescale for these changes causes the Inquiry concern.

Devolution

3.57 The Service has made devolution part of the "Strategic Priorities for 1994-1997". The current management structure of the Service is set out at Appendix K. The Corporate Plan puts the philosophy thus:

> *"Governors will be the focal point in delivering the Service's objectives. They will have wide delegated authority to innovate and to manage effectively within the national policy framework and specified local plans. They will be expected to use their initiative and will be accountable for the performance of their establishments."*

3.58 It is certainly good practice in any organisation to devolve responsibility as far down the chain of command as possible; but devolution should not be confused with surrendering responsibility. In the United States, 'headquarters develops policy, regional management enforces it and Wardens (Governors) implement it'. In England and Wales, the intention has been to establish a very similar structure but the Inquiry found that there was a confusion amongst some Area Managers as to whether their role was advisory or executive.

3.59 The Corporate Plan describes the role of Headquarters as being: "... to determine policy and priorities, set objectives and targets and monitor performance." If the monitoring of performance had been effectively carried out at all levels, some of the security failures, identified by this Inquiry, could have been avoided. This view has been reinforced since the Inquiry opened by some of the Prison Service's own Security Audits.

3.60 Genuine involvement of managers at all levels will only be achieved by a clear commitment to devolution. One Director gave his rationale for devolution in the Service as follows:

> *"In our case* [the Prison Service] *we have four contradictory characteristics to consider:*
>
> *1. We are in a highly political environment with constant recourse to central scrutiny. This would push us towards centralisation.*
>
> *2. We have only one core activity, the custody and rehabilitation of prisoners. This would permit a centralised management style.*

> 3. *We have an estate of highly individual establishments none of which are absolutely identical to each other and which have both physical and historical characteristics which lead to an exceptional diversity. This militates against centralised management.*
>
> 4. *We are characterised by the need to make a large number of rapid individual decisions on many of which it would be impossible to provide precise guidelines.* ***This makes devolved management inevitable."***

3.61 He went on to list three prerequisites for devolution. They were: effective line management; checks and audits; and standardised procedures. He identified line management as the most important and stressed the need to empower Governors in a number of ways, not least by more budgetary devolution.

3.62 The Inquiry found that both the traditional centralisation and the more recent devolved arrangements have marginalised Area Managers. Devolution has given more power to Governors but reduced the effectiveness of the Area Managers which has weakened line management. If the Service is to establish a workable management chain, Area Managers must be given complete responsibility for their areas and become full budget holders, rather than being required only to review their area's monthly budget analysis. The question is examined in more detail in paragraphs 3.133-136.

Training and career development

3.63 The majority of staff encountered in prisons have impressed the Inquiry with their eagerness to do a good job and their desire to have their professional abilities recognised. The adverse publicity which the Prison Service often attracts unsettles them, lowering their self-respect and their self-confidence. External criticism is bad enough but, when staff also feel that the Prison Service cares little for them, morale sinks further. There is much the Service could and should do to demonstrate the value it claims to place on staff. Proper training and career development would help to promote identification with the organisation.

(a) Training

3.64 The Prison Service sets out its stall with regard to personnel management in one of its strategic priorities for 1994-97:

> *"Developing a well trained, well motivated staff with a shared commitment to the Service's goals and values ..."*

3.65 Nationally, the provision of training is the responsibility of the Director of Personnel, through the Head of Training Services. A Training Policy and Planning Unit identifies new training needs for the Service as a whole, draws up plans to meet them and evaluates their effectiveness. The Prison Service College offers an impressive range of courses and a consultancy service to

Governors. At establishment level, Governors are expected to ensure that their staff are trained and they receive guidance from Headquarters about the training which should be provided. They have freedom to organise local training to meet the particular needs of their establishment and most produce a training programme.

3.66 In visits to establishments, however, the Inquiry found that the aspirations of those who plan training are not always translated into action. Many staff reported that they were doing jobs for which they had not been trained and described training as a low priority. In some cases, staff seemed unaware of basic security procedures, suggesting that those searching visitors had not always been trained for the work. An inconsistent approach to training was found in ECRs, where some staff had learned the job by watching others and picking it up as best they could. Expensive and relatively sophisticated equipment was rendered useless because operators did not know how to use it properly. The Whitemoor and Parkhurst escapes show that deficiencies in training contribute to lapses in security and they must be rectified without delay.

3.67 Around 100 Governor Grades nation-wide, any one of whom might temporarily be in command of a prison as Duty Governor, had not been trained in the management of serious incidents. The Duty Governor is expected to take charge of an incident until a more experienced commander arrives, which can be some time. As the decisions taken during the initial stages of an incident often have a close bearing on the final outcome, this is clearly an unsatisfactory situation, although the Prison Service now states that all Governor Grades who have not been trained will have attended a course by the end of the year.

3.68 For Prison Officers and some other grades, work has begun to identify core competencies. These are the basic skills and knowledge required to perform duties satisfactorily. This work is an excellent foundation for management training. It should be extended to all grades and ranks and used to assist in the planning of training. A primary requirement for the selection of line managers at all levels should be their ability to lead and inspire people. Before line managers take up a new post, they should receive suitable leadership and management training.

3.69 For all its stated commitment to staff, the Service has failed to deliver adequate training in respect of security, its core business. Even where courses are identified as mandatory, such as the 'Command of Serious Incidents' course, line managers seem unable or unwilling to compel attendance. Training is regularly dropped when other pressures increase. The Prison Service has set a target of six days training for each member of staff for the year 1995/96. Whilst this is an improvement, it is unlikely to be enough to raise professional competence and skills to the levels required. Discussions during this Inquiry have indicated that a target of 14 days annual training, for all staff working in establishments, would be a more desirable objective. This would put the Prison Service at the leading edge of international comparisons. The Prison Service should reach this higher training target over the next five years by annual increments.

(b) Career development

3.70 At the end of 1994, two Dispersal Prisons were allowed to run for two months without Governors. One Governor had left on normal retirement after more than 30 years service, the other had been transferred to a job in Headquarters. To leave two key posts unoccupied, especially at a time when much attention was focused on Dispersal Prisons, reveals inadequacies in personnel planning.

3.71 The Service should show how it values its staff through positive personnel management systems. Much personnel work has been correctly devolved to Governors. It is, however, important to recognise that staff are members of a national Service, with career and promotion opportunities often lying outside their current establishments. Systems are therefore necessary to ensure equal opportunities and common standards by which staff can be judged. Maintaining unity and cohesion in the Service is vital if consistency of standards is to be achieved and mobility of staff maintained. Future changes in the personnel area must take this into account. Some fashionable approaches, such as indiscriminate use of performance pay and local pay negotiation, would seriously undermine cohesion and inhibit mobility. A mechanism which identifies talent at an early stage and ensures that it is properly developed is an essential part of any personnel system. Whilst the Prison Service can claim to have an accelerated promotion scheme, it otherwise shows little evidence of proactive career management.

3.72 It has been suggested that the dearth of Board Directors with operational experience as a Governor is in some way due to a lack of talent in the Service. If this is true, the fault lies with those who, over many years, have failed to prepare prison staff properly for higher positions. The top managers of tomorrow must be tested in responsible positions today and broaden their outlook through rounded experience in appointments outside their specialisation. All this needs to be carefully thought through as a deliberate policy. The fact that no Director General has ever been appointed from within the Service is a damning indictment of career development policy in the past.

STRUCTURE OF THE ORGANISATION

3.73 Organisation is not an end in itself but a means to the end of good performance and results.

> *"Organisational structure is an indispensable means; and the wrong structure will seriously impair business performance and may even destroy it."*
>
> *'The Practice of Management' Peter Drucker*

> *"We cannot escape the conclusion that many of those employed in the Service feel a deep sense of dissatisfaction with the organisation and management of it as a whole and that a gulf has grown up between the establishments in the field and the staff who work in them on the one hand and headquarters at the Home Office in London on the other."*
>
> *'The May Report on the UK Prison Services' 1979*

3.74 Peter Drucker's observation would have struck a chord with the May Inquiry and, despite many subsequent organisational changes in the Prison Service, including Agency status, it resonates still.

3.75 Before discussing the Service structure, it is worth making a few general points of principle. A fundamental requirement is that the operational chain of command should be the core of the business; functional activities, though important, should play a supporting role. The number of layers should be minimised to aid rapid, undistorted transmission of instructions or information up and down the chain.

3.76 The structure of the Prison Service falls into three principle layers. The top layer consists of those above the level of the Director General and the Prisons Board. The next layer is the Prison Service Headquarters, from the Director General down to and including Area Managers. The third layer is the organisational framework within prison establishments themselves, from the governing Governor down, already discussed in section 2 (paras. 2.231-238).

Relationship with the Home Office

3.77 The current management style of the Prison Service appears to owe much to an historically close involvement of the Home Office, particularly in major operational matters. The question of the Service's dependence on the Home Office has surfaced in a number of Inquiries. In 1991, the Lygo Report commented:

> *"... each of the major reports on the Service since the absorption of the Prison Commission by the Home Office have called for a greater degree of managerial independence for the Prison Service from day to day Home Office control. Again it has not happened to anything like the extent necessary."*

3.78 A covering letter to the then Home Secretary stressed the importance of independence for the Service:

> *"As we discussed at our first meeting ... it was very clear that unless there was a preparedness on the part of the Home Office to take its hands off the management of the Prison Service in its day to day business and allow itself to be constrained by matters of policy only, then it would not be possible to effect the changes which you deemed desirable and which have become very clear to me as being necessary during the talks I have had and the visits I have made."*

3.79 That report went on to recommend formal 'Agency status', with a strengthened Management Board. The intention was to distance Ministers from operational matters. Since 1993, the Prison Service has been a 'Next Steps Agency' with its own budget and a Director General appointed by open competition.

3.80 The Inquiry sought clarification of the 1987 Government Next Steps concept from the then adviser to the Prime Minister, Sir Robin Ibbs. He confirmed that there was no conflict between Agency status and the proposition that the Chief Executive should report to an "owner" in the Home Office. The "owner" would be responsible for guarding the independence of the Agency and:

"■ *Clearing or changing the Agency framework document.*

■ *Acting as a 'champion' for the Agency.*

■ *Setting a policy framework within which the Chief Executive and the Agency are obliged to operate.*

■ *Appointing and appraising the performance of the Chief Executive or removing him if circumstances warrant such an exceptional step.*

■ *Helping, advising and supporting the Chief Executive.*

■ *Deciding the budget allocation, delegations, freedoms and flexibilities.*

■ *Setting objectives and targets.*

■ *Approving corporate and business plans, monitoring achievement and outturn."*

3.81 In the current situation, Sir Robin Ibbs envisaged that the "owner" would need to be supported by a small policy unit outside the Agency, which would need to include staff with Prison Service experience to provide operational expertise. In its present relationship with the Home Office, the Prison Service suffers from two particular disadvantages:

■ The absence of any individual nominated as its "owner".

■ The absence of a Home Office corporate plan, setting out strategy and relating objectives to the resources allocated.

3.82 As there is no "owner", the Director General is put into the position of trying to generate Prison Service policy internally, influenced, predictably, by conflicting pressures from the media, prison reformers and politicians. Whilst he has a fundamental responsibility to provide leadership for the Service, he also needs guidance and support from within the Home Office. An "owner" should be specifically nominated for the Service, to act as its champion, set policy and goals, monitor results and fill the role of line manager for the Director General. The "owner" should be supported by a small, high quality staff, which should include Prison Service professionals with an operational background.

3.83 The Director General also needs minimum political involvement in the day-to-day operation of the Service. In order to gauge the extent of involvement with the Home Office, the Inquiry asked Prison Service Headquarters to produce copies of all correspondence with Ministers in the previous four months, from October 1994 to January 1995, comprising 83 working days. Just over 1,000 documents had been submitted, relating to life sentence prisoners, appointment of members of Boards of Visitors, parliamentary questions, ministerial cases, briefing on incidents, reports on media stories with 'lines to take', briefing for visits and meetings and briefing on specific prisoners or prisons. One hundred and thirty-seven were 'full submissions', containing substantive advice about policy or operational matters. The Prison Service is a politically sensitive area and ministerial involvement is bound to be relatively high. This was also an exceptional period, given the number of escapes, riots and other incidents. Nevertheless, it is at just such times that top management attention needs to be firmly fixed on solving the problem, not merely explaining it. Such a level of upwards-focused activity needs to be carefully managed if it is not to interfere with the Headquarter's proper downwards supervision and control of the organisation.

3.84 The Director General is required to deal with a great number of ministerial queries, letters from MPs and parliamentary questions. These are now running at a total of 600 questions per year, many of which require discussion with Ministers to achieve a mutually acceptable answer, and 4,000 MPs' letters. The Director General has not assumed the task voluntarily: it is assigned to him, as to Chief Executives of all Agencies. It occupies too much of his time, to the potential detriment of the efficient running of the Prison Service. Ways and means must be found to overcome the problem.

3.85 As an example of the Director General's over-commitment to these matters, a full day's interview with the Inquiry was disturbed on a number of occasions because Ministers required his advice. At a lower level, one of the Operational Directors said that the size of the daily press cuttings on the Prison Service was an informal 'performance indicator' for the Service, not least because defensive briefings had to be provided for Ministers on every press story.

3.86 The Inquiry believes that the Headquarters has developed an ethos which regards upwards communication not just as one of a number of important functions but as its main raison d'etre. If the organisation is to work effectively and command operations at establishment level, the Director General must find a way to balance the need to keep Ministers informed with that of providing leadership and management. The current approach has created a reactive rather than proactive approach at Board level. It is all too apparent that operational considerations have received insufficient priority, with the results that led to this Inquiry (see also paras. 3.93 et seq).

3.87 The Inquiry has only had time to take a preliminary look at the relationship between the Home Office and the Prison Service Agency. However, in view of the foregoing paragraphs and the fact the Agency has now been in existence for two and a half years, it is recommended that someone with wide experience of the workings of Agencies should be identified to undertake an in-depth study of this relationship with a view to giving the Prison Service the greater operational independence that Agency status was meant to confer.

Prison Service Headquarters

3.88 The second and certainly most widely criticised layer of the Service's structure is its Headquarters. This layer contains the Director General; other Directors; a host of functional departments and groups; and Area Managers.

3.89 As with much of the Service, this element of the structure has been the subject of many reviews. Changes occurred in 1990 as a result of a consultant's report. Admiral Lygo re-examined the situation in 1991; further 'fine-tuning' was carried out in 1992/93; and a Taskforce was established in 1993 specifically to look again at how best to reorganise this part of the Service.

3.90 The general effect of such frequent review and change led one senior manager to quote Gaius Petronius (AD 66):

> *"We trained very hard, but it seemed that every time we were beginning to form into teams we would be re-organised. I was to learn later in life that we tend to meet any new situation by re-organising, and a wonderful method it can be for creating the illusion of progress, while producing confusion, inefficiency and demoralisation."*

3.91 The frustration of Petronius has been reflected consistently in comments made by senior members of the Prison Service to the Inquiry. One of the Directors was cynical about reorganisation and felt it was a favourite management trick when faced with criticism. Many staff expressed profound fear of further reorganisation whilst others have attempted to deflect any recommendations by suggesting that structure is unimportant and that anything can be made to work, given the will. Such a response, though understandable, fails to recognise how structure influences effectiveness. It is perhaps indicative of the attitudes which have caused previous failures in this area.

3.92 Whilst the present structure of the Prison Service (as set out in the chart at Appendix K) is widely acknowledged as an improvement on its predecessor, it is still confused and over-complicated. Structure charts, like KPIs, send implicit messages to an organisation and should clearly indicate the areas which the Director General (in the case of the Prison Service) thinks are important. The chart should therefore be carefully constructed to deliver the right messages. The present structure chart raises questions over the role and relative importance of three main areas of management: the Board of Directors, Headquarters staff and Area Managers.

(a) Board of Directors

3.93 Prior to the 1989/90 reorganisation of the Service, the structure included four Regional Directors reporting to a Deputy Director General. That structure had two major weaknesses, in that the span of control of a Regional Director was too big (up to 37 prisons) and, even more significantly, the Deputy Director General was interposed between the Regional Directors and the Director General, which created an undesirable 'one-over-one' relationship between the Director General and his Deputy.

3.94 The changes introduced in 1990 removed from the Board the Deputy Director General and the four Regional Directors, all of whom were ex-Governors. They were replaced by three Operational Directors, subsequently reduced to two. Although the 1990 changes also introduced 15 Area Managers, who each had responsibility for between 8 and 11 prisons, the reduction to two Operational Directors increased spans of control which, arguably, were already unmanageable. The effect of the change was that the number of establishments for which Operational Directors were responsible increased from over 40 to over 60 and the amount of travelling time increased by over 50 per cent. This produced a tension between the need to be on the road and the need to be at Headquarters.

3.95 With such an inordinate workload and with a number of important issues arising at the same time, it is little wonder that the delays outlined in paragraphs 2.150-179 occurred.

3.96 The Board structure presently consists of the Director General, four non-executive Directors and six executive Directors. Only two of the executive Directors are operational line managers, the remaining four having functional responsibilities (see Appendix K). The Board structure is therefore weighted against those with direct operational responsibilities. Until recently, Board discussions were informed by only two Directors with operational experience as Governors, only one of whom was an Operational Director.

3.97 Throughout most of the period of the Inquiry, the two Operational Directors also had significant policy responsibilities and there was a strong inference, both within the structure diagram and from discussion with Service personnel, that these took primacy over operational responsibilities. As one of the incumbents explained, the combination of policy and operational responsibilities was:

> *"... a deliberate factor brought about by the organisational review in 1990, which was aimed at increasing the cohesion between policy and operational issues."*

3.98 Whilst the combination of policy and operational roles may indeed have been intended to achieve cohesion, it has actually produced confusion. Admiral Lygo said, in his 1991 Report:

> *"I found the concept of "operational directors" with their mix of functional and line responsibilities curious."*

3.99 He did not recommend immediate change, because he wanted to give the new organisation a chance to prove itself. Experience now suggests that the configuration failed and was partly responsible for the neglect of operational supervision, lack of visible and positive leadership and surrender of operational accountability at Board level. This problem was recognised by the Prison Service and, on 12th May 1995, policy responsibilities were removed from the two Operational Directors with line management responsibilities.

3.100 Operational Directors were unable to give establishments the attention they deserved, partly because they were distracted by their additional policy responsibilities and partly because their span of control was too large. Even when they were aware of a problem and were able to assess its importance correctly, they did not always have the authority to act because too much power still lay in the hands of the heads of functional areas. An example of this is illustrated at Appendix F. Of even greater concern are the present arrangements for emergency command procedures. Written instructions do not include the Operational Directors in the chain of command in the event of a major incident. This omission is an unwarranted departure from the normal chain of command and potentially excludes Operational Directors from emergency situations. Whilst there is nothing to prevent an Operational Director from being in attendance and giving advice, there is no substitute for an Operational Director being firmly in the chain of command and thereby taking responsibility for incidents on the ground. The position with regard to emergencies in private prisons is potentially even more unsatisfactory, since Prison Service Headquarters only acts in an advisory capacity in such cases, unless Ministers decide to use the provisions of Section 88 of the Criminal Justice Act, 1991, for the Prison Service to take over command of the prison.

3.101 During the Salmon procedures, a paper was produced, entitled "The Management Structure of the Prison Service", which dealt with the roles of the Director General, the Prisons Board, the Executive Committee, the Area Manager and the Governor. Whilst details of this document have not yet been promulgated, the Inquiry was disappointed by the limited role proposed for the Board in the core prison business of running 130 establishments in England and Wales. The Director General, in a separate submission, summed up the Board's proposed responsibilities thus:

> *"The Board is required to give* [strategic] *direction through the Corporate and Business Plans and* [take] *decisions on all major matters of strategy and policy, including recommendations to Ministers. It is not intended as a forum for monitoring performance in detail, although it does so at an overall level, nor for taking decisions on detailed operational matters."*

3.102 This arrangement is heralded as a change but there is a strong possibility that, by leaving operational matters to the Executive Committee, the Board will become even more divorced from its main raison d'etre.

3.103 In summary, the Inquiry found the existing Board structure highly flawed with a number of major, mainly operational, weaknesses. The most serious were the under-representation of line management and the predominance of functional interests. Evidence was produced to the Inquiry that the Board rarely discussed top level operational matters adequately. The Prisons Board has made a submission, as a result of the Salmon procedures, disagreeing with this assertion but the Inquiry has no reason to doubt the initial evidence of five Board members to the effect that operational matters were not often raised at Board level. An additional weakness was that non-executive directors, while able to make a significant contribution in many areas, were light on Prison Service operational experience and possibly over-represented.

3.104 The Inquiry has not conducted an in-depth study, either of the Prison Service Headquarters in general or of the Prisons Board in particular, but it has familiarised itself with the 1994 Review of the Headquarters and has discussed Board structure with Board members and others. It was not thought necessary to interview middle-ranking and junior Headquarters staff since the Inquiry had no reason to believe that they were not properly carrying out the directions of senior management. The Inquiry has, however, considered a number of options to address what it believes are the shortcomings of the present Board structure and recommends the outline model in Figure 8:

Fig. 8 **Outline Board Structure**

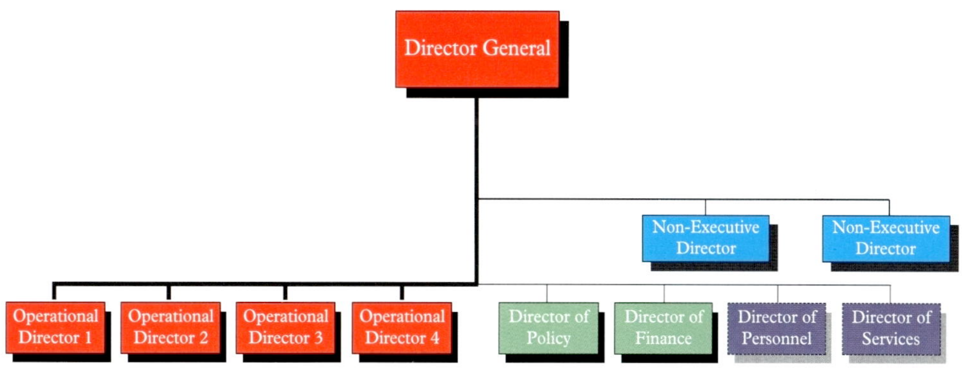

3.105 Operational Directors should have previous experience as governing Governors. The number of Operational Directors would be increased from two to four in order to reduce their spans of command, strengthen their control of establishments and put substantial extra prison experience on the Board. The proposed line management roles of the Operational Directors are detailed in Section 5 of this Report and none has accountability for general functional or policy matters. This structure would ensure both that the Director General could not be isolated from vital operational matters and that Functional Directors would not have undue influence in Board deliberations.

3.106 If the Service is adequately to address security issues in the future, the operational strength of the new Board must be paramount. The Inquiry does not wish to be prescriptive about the number of Functional and non-executive Directors or their responsibilities but believes that these matters should always be considered with a view to maintaining the primacy of operations. The Inquiry sees the role of Functional and non-executive Directors as outlined below.

3.107 **Policy.** There is concern that the handling of policy at Board level is fragmented. The responsibility for policy should be vested in one Director with Board status. The Director's duties should cover:

- Security.
- Operational Audit.
- Health (see para. 3.110).
- Press and public relations.
- Custody.
- Programmes.

3.108 The Policy Director would need to consider policy issues coming from or generated by the Prisons Board. In general terms, it would be the responsibility of staff in the Policy Directorate to consider the issues, with input from the operational side, and of the Policy Director to present them at Board level. This would ensure that operational policy had been fully considered at the key levels of Governor, Area Manager and Operational Director.

3.109 The Policy Director post should be filled by someone with operational experience, gained ideally from within the Prison Service. The person would be regarded, for all intents and purposes, as the designated deputy to the Director General and a potential candidate (from within the Service) for the top job.

3.110 **Health.** In 1979, the May Committee endorsed the view of the then Director of Prison Medical Services that, given the specialised job which he had to do, he did not need to be a member of the Board, provided he always attended when any issue involving medical questions was on the agenda. The Director of Medical Services has, however, remained a member of the Board. It is vital that the Prisons Board has a credible adviser on health issues, whose voice has recognised authority, nationally and internationally, and who can respond rapidly to any challenge. The Inquiry has no wish to devalue the importance of health in prisons but believes that policy objectives can be achieved by following the May recommendations. They would permit the Head of Health Care to concentrate on professional matters and relieve the incumbent of responsibility for issues outside the medical field. Accordingly, it is recommended that the Head of Health Care report, in future, to the Director of Policy but attend Board meetings when medical matters are discussed. This would not preclude the Head of Health Care from being a member of the Executive Committee, at the discretion of the Director General.

3.111 **Finance.** It is self-evident that an organisation of the size of the Prison Service, involving a substantial budget, needs a Director of Finance at Board level. The proposed main policy areas to be covered would be:

- Financial planning and control.
- Accounts and systems.
- Financial Audit.

The post should be filled by a professional, as at present.

3.112 **Personnel.** No change to the appointment of Director of Personnel is proposed. However, it is an appointment which should be reviewed within the next three years. The need, in the short-term, would be to ensure the proper devolution, to area and establishment level, of most personnel matters. At Board level, responsibility for personnel matters would fall largely to the four Operational Directors, the ultimate line managers for the personnel in their Directorates. If devolution of personnel matters across the Prison Service can be achieved without reducing the attention paid to them, responsibility for personnel policy at Board level, including training, might fall to the Director of Policy, supported by a Head of Personnel. The latter appointment should be filled by a professionally trained personnel manager, as at present.

3.113 **Services.** The range of non-core services presently covered by the Director of Services include supply, transport, construction and industries. These functions place too great a burden on top management's time. Services should be contractorised by competitive tendering, with contracts renewable only if standards are met. This will give the tax-payer better value for money. Once this exercise has been completed, the need to retain a post of Director of Services might be reviewed.

3.114 **Non-executive Directors.** The main thrust of the proposed changes to the Prisons Board would be a better balance between the operational and non-operational functions, to ensure that operational matters are properly voiced at Board level. Non-executive Directors bring to the Board skills, competencies and experience acquired outside the Prison and Civil Services; act as a sounding board for the Director General; provide voices on the Board fully independent of Government; represent public opinion; and undertake specific tasks. Their input can be invaluable but their number should be dictated by the need for balance on the Board, the need of the Board for outside experience and the availability of suitable people. Currently there are four non-executive Directors which may be too many. The proposals to increase the number of Operational Directors and appoint a Director of Policy who has had operational experience in the Prison Service may lessen the need for the present number of non-executive Directors. The case for reverting to two should be considered.

(b) Headquarters staff

3.115 Apart from reservations over the present structure of the Prison Service Board of Directors, the most widespread criticism of the Service structure has related to the sheer size of the Service's Headquarters. Admiral Lygo had this to say on the size and role of Headquarters:

> *"Headquarters is at present too large: this seems to me to reflect an over-centralised approach to management and, with the move to Agency status, and a distancing from day to day Ministerial involvement, should be susceptible to substantial reduction and reallocation. The Prisons Board should review each function on the basis of need rather than practice."*

3.116 In one submission to the Inquiry, the mismatch between establishments and Headquarters was described thus:

> *"The Agency has been described as centrifugal. We have over 130 establishments with a tendency to fly off in different directions and the response has been to place a large weight in the centre to hold the whole together."*

3.117 Complaints about Headquarters abound and, despite numerous attempts to address them, little evidence was found of improvement. In looking for the reasons for such apparent failure, it was useful to examine the latest review, the 1994 Prison Service Headquarters Taskforce Report.

3.118 The review of Headquarters was part of the Service's first Corporate and Business Plan, issued in 1993/94. The main object was to delegate more responsibility to Governors and transform the relationship between Headquarters and establishments. The Taskforce was instructed to report by January 1994.

3.119 The review first sought to identify what work was performed at the centre on behalf of three main 'customers', namely Ministers, Parliament and the wider Government machine; Headquarters; and establishments. It identified the key roles and made proposals on the number of staff required to fulfil these roles.

3.120 A number of key points were presented which the Taskforce believed should feature in any new structure. These included improved and clearer relationships between the Service and its primary customers in establishments and a greater emphasis on personnel strategy.

The top two requirements were:

> "*a.* *a smaller headquarters of at most 400 staff, located in one building, with scope for (further) reduction over time;*
>
> *b.* *greater clarity of the operational line.*"

3.121 Neither of these points has been met in the reorganisation eventually recommended and accepted. The Taskforce reported:

> *"Part of our work ... involved the consideration of options for the Prison Service Headquarters with 500 and 1,000 staff. It should be noted ... that some of the potential models which the Taskforce outlined to the Board would have led to the creation of a Headquarters with markedly lower staff numbers than either of these options. These models were rejected by the Board."* (Para. 81)
>
> *"The revised structure ... involves no immediate change in numbers of staff, of itself. However we are clear that the implementation will result in staff reductions (which may be substantial) over the next two to three years."* (Para. 82)

3.122 In the 1994 Annual Report of the Service, there is mention of the Headquarters being divided into "Core Headquarters" and "Central Services". The Report explains that Core Headquarters will be reduced to around 400. There is no figure relating to the size of the Central Services, which are still co-located in the same Headquarters building. However, the Director General in his response to his Salmon letter stated that:

> *"... there is a phased plan for the reduction in the size of Central Services from approximately 1,600 to approximately 1,100 staff by 1998".*

3.123 The Taskforce Report gave the overall figure for Headquarters staff (Core and Central Services), in December 1993, as 1,938. The Taskforce suggested that there might be scope for cutting Headquarters further by a significant amount. At the time of the Inquiry, the number of staff in the Core Headquarters and Central Services was 1,817. On the evidence of the Salmon letter, there is a clear intention to reduce Core Headquarters and Central Services staff by at least 500 posts by 1998. The Inquiry was concerned to note, however, that the current Business Plan (1995/96) no longer refers to a reduction in Headquarters (Core and Central Services). The Inquiry believes that the momentum to downsize both Core Headquarters and Central Services must be maintained.

3.124 Three groups, with a total strength of 123, should be moved out of Prison Service Headquarters. The Lifer Group (excluding the operational management of lifers through the Allocation Unit) carries out quasi-judicial work, with the bulk of decision-making at ministerial level. The Parole Unit considers recommendations from the Parole Board and the decision is usually taken by the Unit, with a few cases referred to Ministers. The Unit also deals with deportation cases and substantial operational policy work. The Superannuation Section, which calculates and administers superannuation for both the Prison Service and the Home Office, has been transferred to the Prison Service from 1st April 1995. Any activities taking place within Prison Service Headquarters which are not essential to the operational management of the Service are a distraction to top management and should be moved forthwith.

3.125 One effect of an over-large Headquarters is that it tends to generate a blizzard of paper and there is plenty of evidence of this within the Prison Service, especially when viewed from the operational level.

3.126 The Lygo Report recognised the paper problem and commented on:

> *"... the background and training of Headquarters staff, who are largely administrators drawn from the rest of the Home Office, with no operational management experience. By instinct and training they look 'up' to Ministers rather than 'down' to establishments and their performance tends to be judged on the formidable volume of initiatives launched rather than on the extent to which they are given effect in establishments."*

3.127 Although some might cite the paper mountain as evidence that they are indeed looking down as well as up, this argument merely demonstrates a belief that written instructions constitute adequate and effective 'communication'. That view is natural, and possibly correct, for administrative Civil Servants, trained to meet the needs of Ministers, but it is out of place in an operational Headquarters. The point was made forcibly in the May Report, in 1979:

> *"It was argued (by witnesses) that the organisation and ethos of a Civil Service department was inappropriate for the management of an operational organisation dealing 24 hours a day with the difficult human problems of both staff and inmates alike . ... Prison Officers in the field, it was said, find it frustrating and maddening to be told how to handle prisoners in a particular situation by someone who has never had that experience himself. Whether rightly or wrongly ... the Prison Officer unlocking 40 criminals on a Wing in an establishment two or three hundred miles from London saw the headquarters of his Service as a faceless monolith caring not for human beings but merely for efficient administration."*

3.128 The situation today is identical. Governors in charge of prisons commented that the paper load they bear prevented them taking more of a personal interest in the running of their establishments. Infrequent visiting and inspecting by Governor Grades conveyed the message to staff and inmates that paperwork had a higher priority than operational activities and that work on prison Wings was not important.

3.129 The paper load arises from the way in which the Prison Service Headquarters operates and it has a detrimental effect on prisons. There appears to be little understanding in Headquarters that unworkable initiatives, issued without consultation to a hard-pressed workforce and without an effective system of checking compliance, weaken the whole edifice of management.

3.130 A list of 38 current initiatives by Prison Service Headquarters (not necessarily exhaustive) is at Appendix L and it is not difficult to see how confusion and resentment could emerge if these were thoughtlessly handled. During the course of the Inquiry, the Director General wrote to all Governors to postpone or re-phase about half of them "... in areas which will not directly contribute to the new top priorities ...". Ironically, as part of the review following the Woodcock Report, a series of courses on 'Command of Serious Incidents' was cancelled.

3.131 A typical prison was asked to record all correspondence received for a period of one month (20 working days). The prison logged an average of 230 letters, 65 faxes and 24 E-mails (electronic mail messages) **per day** during that period. Other Governors confirmed that this was a fair reflection of their own experience, although there is some variation between different types of establishment. If this was extrapolated to all 130 prisons, then during the same four months for which the Inquiry logged 'upwards' mail (see para. 3.83), establishments would have received an estimated 47 tons of paper, equating to a pile nearly a mile high or more than 800 feet higher than Ben Nevis as shown in Figure 9:

Fig. 9 **The Paper Mountain**

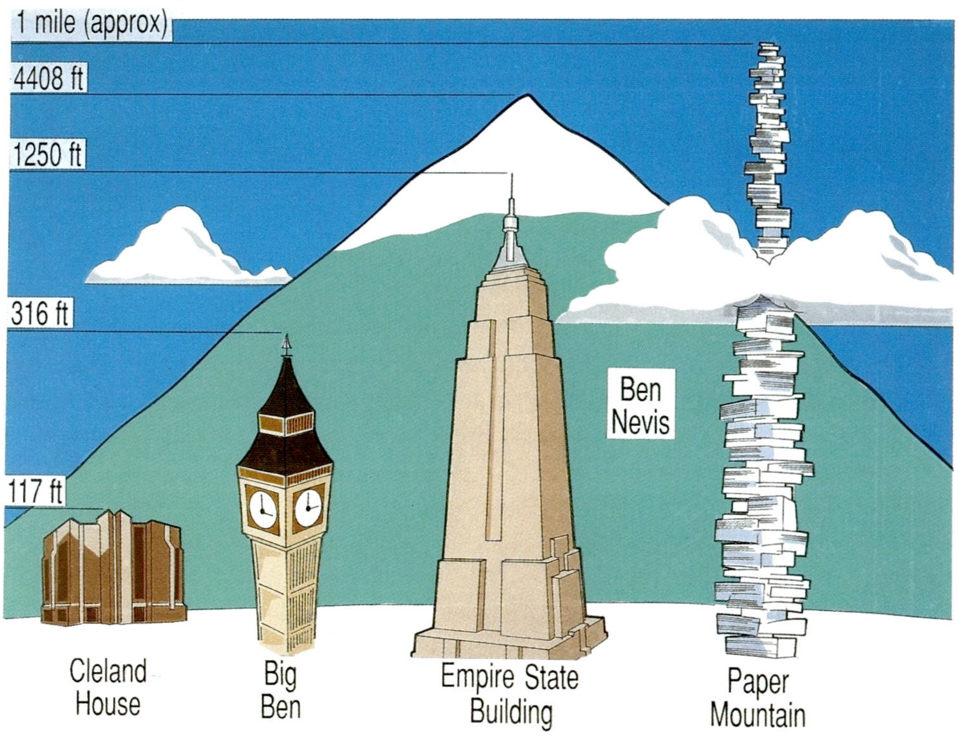

3.132 The calculations for the figures used for the above diagram appear at Appendix M. The papers covered mainly casework, personnel matters, procurement, correspondence from Headquarters/Central Services and operational issues. Although the Prison Service claims that only 12 per cent of these papers originated from Headquarters/Central Services, the cumulative effect was to sap management strength and take the eye off the security ball. Governors and their staff are hard-pressed merely to respond to correspondence, let alone raise problems, even when they genuinely need help or support. The Service must not only look for better ways to deal with the proliferation of paperwork but also take urgent and positive action to reduce it significantly. Nothing must prevent the Governor from discharging the primary role of hands-on management of the establishment.

(c) Area Managers

3.133 The Inquiry noted that some Area Managers and Governors were confused as to whether or not the Area Manager was in a command position. The confusion was exacerbated by the fact that correspondence between Headquarters and Governors frequently by-passed the Area Manager, sending an implicit message that the Area Manager was not an integral part of the line management chain.

3.134 The Area Managers are the line managers of Governors and should be part of the corporate planning process, receiving objectives and performance targets from Operational Directors and in turn setting them for Governors. This would involve co-ordinating the efforts of the various establishments into an overall plan. While Governors must have day to day responsibility, Area Managers should ensure consistency between establishments and monitor service delivery through regular visits to establishments and comprehensive management information systems. They also have an important role in the appointment and management of senior staff in establishments, especially Governors. They must manage the area's resources effectively and this can only be achieved through a proper alignment between the budgetary and line management chains.

3.135 Area Managers and their staffs have to be communicators both upwards and downwards, not only explaining and interpreting Prisons Board policy to establishments but also representing their interests, influencing the policy agenda and contributing to the organisational development of the Service. They have a role in protecting establishments from unnecessary paperwork, by insisting that all operational tasking comes through them and acting as a filter.

3.136 Admiral Lygo expressed surprise that Area Managers were located at Headquarters. The Headquarters Review Taskforce commented that the Area Managers' role might alter as devolution increased and management information systems improved, the implication being that they would be more usefully deployed away from Headquarters. It is clear that, although Area Managers have legitimate business at Headquarters, the proper place for them and their staffs is in their areas, where they would be closer to establishments and could spend less time on the road. They must become budget holders with devolved authority and powers over expenditure; divest themselves of much of the routine administration associated with casework and exercise responsibility for the operational management of establishments; make their voices heard at Board level, through the Operational Directors; and be appropriately resourced, to allow them to assume a pivotal position in the chain of command. It will be essential to move them to their areas if this Inquiry's recommendations with regard to reorganisation of the Service are accepted (see Section 5).

CONTRACTED OUT PRISONS (PRIVATE PRISONS)

3.137 Potential involvement of the private sector and the prospect of competition promotes internal re-examination. It stimulates the adoption of modern best practice and business methods. Experience has also shown that competition is likely to cut the cost of services and increase their efficiency. Of particular advantage for the Prison Service is the potential introduction of prisoners to activities run by the private sector, including profit-making enterprises serving the marketplace. Employment of prisoners can also be targeted to meet internal requirements of the Prison Service or other government departments and can be funded by charging. The danger is that pursuit of cost control, either to maximise profit or to win a market test, could lead to ill-judged economies that threaten physical or dynamic security.

3.138 Three private prisons were visited. Conditions were clean, the chain of command in each was taut and all staff wore uniforms, albeit some uniforms consisted of blazers rather than traditional Prison Service dress, as recommended in the Woolf Report. The management obviously saw its role as to manage; and the value of the front line operational staff was recognised through higher pay for those who worked in daily contact with the inmates. One Warden (Governor) extolled the benefits of this policy and pointed out that there was a waiting list of Officers seeking to work in contact with prisoners. On the other hand, concern about manning levels in private prisons has been expressed from time to time. The numbers of staff on duty tend to be lower than in public sector prisons and raise serious questions about their ability to cope with major incidents. Prisoners have complained that low staffing levels lead to violence, exploitation and insecurity when they are out of cells. The Prison Service must incorporate, in the invitation to tender for private prisons, a minimum staffing that guarantees the correct level of security. Staffing levels should be decided on the basis of staff and prisoner safety and the protection of the public.

3.139 The Directors of the contracted out prisons are accountable to their parent companies. Delivery of performance, measured against the specification in the contract, is monitored by a Controller, who is an experienced Governor, with a small support staff provided by the Prison Service and located at the prison. The Controller is also required to carry out all adjudications on prisoners and to advise the Area Manager on all matters regarding the running of the prison. The Area Manager is expected to ensure compliance with the contract, to identify any variations necessary and generally to be satisfied with the way the prison is working. Such arrangements raise the question as to whether the problems at Whitemoor and Parkhurst would ever have arisen if the Prison Service had the same monitoring and audit arrangements which are compulsory for the private sector. Through this mechanism, performance standards in private prisons are kept under review, with the result they are maintained at a high level. In comparison with public sector prisons, private prisons demonstrate the advantages of a tauter management chain, greater freedom for Governors to manage and continuous audit on site.

3.140 Government policy is that 10 per cent of prisons (13 establishments) will be operated by the private sector in the initial phase of the privatisation programme. Four prisons are already under private management and tendering is nearing completion for the first two of the six entirely new prisons to be designed, constructed, managed and financed by the private sector. The Inquiry considered whether security could be improved by privatisation of the entire Service. One argument in favour of the retention of a public sector Service came from Lord Woolf, who felt that, as the State committed the inmates to prison, it was the responsibility of the State to provide the accommodation and guarantee their security.

3.141 The Inquiry concluded that the continued existence of a substantial public sector is vital for the stability of the Service as a whole. It provides a safeguard against private sector bankruptcies, withdrawals or monopolies. However, there were lessons to be learned from the private prisons which should be applied across the Service.

BOARDS OF VISITORS

no evidence!

3.142 The Inquiry met representatives of the Board of Visitors at most of the prisons visited. There is no doubt that the Board's role, as an informed watchdog acting on behalf of the Secretary of State and independently of the management of the prison, is necessary and that the system is functioning well. Boards of Visitors should be properly resourced and the Liaison Section should be moved out of the Prison Service Headquarters, to ensure full independence.

3.143 The Boards have a valuable role to play in ensuring that advice on urgent operational matters can be forwarded direct to Ministers. This is a most important safeguard and should be preserved.

3.144 Towards the end of the Inquiry, discussions were held with the Board of Visitors' Co-ordinating Committee. The following observations on the Prison Service today were made by the Chairman of the Committee:

- "*Morale amongst staff is very low.*
- *The chain of command is not sufficiently rigid and communication is not good.*
- *The Operational Directors should concentrate on their establishments and less on policy.*
- *With the possible exception of the Director General, all staff at Area Manager level and above should have run a Governor 1 prison."*
- "*There is a shortage of Senior and Principal Officers. There should be a review of which staff wear uniform, all should wear name badges and all Governor Grades need to be seen on the Wings frequently."*

3.145 The views of the Board of Visitors' Coordinating Committee provide collateral for many of the points made in this Section.

CONCLUSIONS

3.146 The thrust of this Section is the difference between the perception of the Prisons Board and the reality at prison establishment level. The management ethos does not reflect the sense of devastation and failure at Parkhurst when an escape was mounted so soon after the escape from Whitemoor. The fear experienced by people on the Isle of Wight, while the inmates were at large, became national and even international news, giving rise to statements in Parliament and much debate.

3.147 In the Salmon response from the Board, a draft document was submitted, entitled "The Management Structure of the Prison Service" (see para. 3.101). In this document, the role of the Prisons Board is described as follows:

- "*Take decisions on major strategic and policy issues concerning the Service, including, for example, approval of the annual Corporate and Business Plans, personnel and industrial relations strategy and major policy recommendations to the Home Secretary*
- *Take major expenditure decisions including approval of the PES* [Public Expenditure Survey] *submission, 3 year capital plan and final approval of budgets, and major individual spending commitments (currently defined as building projects over £5 million, service contracts over £10 million, and IT contracts over £3 million)*
- *Monitor operational performance, including monthly finance and performance reports*

- *Approve quarterly reports to the Home Secretary, the Prison Service's Annual Report and the communications strategy for the Service."*

3.148 As pointed out in paragraph 3.2 of this Section, the top management of any organisation must be responsible for its performance. It cannot surrender or delegate this task. In the view of the Inquiry, the Board's stated role pays insufficient attention to operational matters and will deflect it from the essential task of dealing with the consequences of failures like the escape from Parkhurst. One Board member, in a Salmon response, said astonishingly:

> *"It would be a tragedy if an "accident"* [the escape from Parkhurst], *because of the way it is treated, is allowed to result in the Service having a permanent deformity."*

3.149 Board members, in their Salmon responses, argued that the Inquiry had given them insufficient credit for the efforts made since the establishment of the Agency was set up (see Appendix I and para. 3.4). Notwithstanding this view, the Inquiry believes that the criticisms outlined in this Section are valid. They are substantiated in some degree by one Board Director's Salmon response, which set out the balance sheet on the current state of the Service as follows:

PLUS	MINUS
- Vision, policies and priorities established and promulgated	- Policy and operations confused but should not be separated
- Visibility of Director General transformed	- Ministerial involvement too detailed
- Performance monitoring against the corporate plan systematic & relevant	- Mixed messages around custody or care; should be a balance
- Finances management/ reporting transformed	- Line management chain weak and dysfunctional, particularly at Area Manager level
- Consultation with field in place and improving in quality	- Headquarters too large with a pervasive administrative (non-managerial) culture
- Value For Money vigorously pursued	- Personnel function very weak
- Operational decisions of the Executive Committee (Board members receive minutes and pursue concerns) focused and action-oriented	- Industrial Relations problems very large
	- Management development and succession planning very weak

3.150 The Inquiry is concerned about the last point on the positive side of the balance sheet, which confirms that operational matters are predominantly left to the Executive Committee. Operational matters have taken a low priority with the Board, as individual interviews with five Board members confirmed. The Board should be much more involved in operations if it is to play a real part in managing the Service (see para. 3.103).

3.151 The Inquiry does not take serious issue with the other 'plus' points. The 'minus' points, however, reflect some of the realities and provide considerable support for many of the judgements reached in this Section.

RECOMMENDATIONS (CENTRAL ISSUES AFFECTING SECURITY)

58 The Director General and Board should have regular contact with those who have operational responsibilities so that security weaknesses do not go unnoticed.
(Para. 3.16)

59 Headquarters and other senior appointments should be filled largely by Prison Service professionals.
(Para. 3.18)

60 The Service must rapidly become a more caring and people-oriented organisation. Gallantry and good service should be recognised.
(Paras. 3.22-23 and 3.25)

61 Positive and visible leadership must be shown at all levels.
(Para. 3.27)

62 The Service Statement of Purpose should be clarified, to make custody the primary purpose.
(Paras. 3.35-40)

63 All staff, including Governors, should normally wear uniform, with name badges. Civilian members of staff should be clearly identifiable from inmates.
(Paras. 3.46 and 3.48)

64 The Board should build on the willingness of staff associations to co-operate in taking the Service forward.
(Para. 3.50)

65 The Board should review its approach to Key Performance Indicators, to reinforce the main objectives of the Service and to ensure meaningful and valid interpretation:

(a) "Escapes" is too negative an indicator on its own and should be supplemented by indicators that show progress towards preventing escapes.

(b) Figures for assaults should show percentage changes separately for assualts on staff, inmates and others.

(c) Greater care should be taken to monitor the way "purposeful activity" data is captured, to prevent exaggeration and ensure credibility.

(d) The Service should develop new KPIs to indicate:

(i) the extent to which staff training fulfils a clear staff development policy (the Service having first introduced a clear development policy).

(ii) staff morale. Three obvious indicators are turnover, sickness and absence. Complaints by staff are also an indicator if a sufficiently well-developed scheme is in place.

(iii) recidivism rates. Examples might be the percentage of new inmates who have a previous conviction, the percentage of inmates released during the past two, five and ten years who have been re-convicted and the average number of years before released inmates re-offend. There are difficulties in expressing these figures meaningfully but there are ways of handling them.

(iv) the degree of success in dealing with the drug problem in prisons.

(v) inmate behaviour, eg disciplinary cases and suicides.

(vi) standards of physical security.

(vii) reduction in Headquarters personnel.

(viii) reduction in the percentage of total Prison Service budget absorbed by Headquarters and support (ie non-operational) activities.

(Paras. 3.54-56 and Appendix J)

66 Deficiencies in training must be rectified without delay. The identification of core competencies, for training purposes, should be extended to all grades. Before line managers take up new posts, they should receive leadership and management training. Over the next five years, annual training for all staff should rise to 14 days.
(Paras. 3.66-69)

67 Personnel management systems should be introduced to ensure equal opportunities and common standards, to identify talent for fast-streaming and to develop top managers.
(Paras. 3.71-72)

68 The operational chain of command should be the core of the business. Functional activities should play a supporting role. The number of layers in the structure should be minimised.
(Para. 3.75)

69 An "owner" should be nominated for the Service, to fulfil the role of line manager for the Director General. A small, professional unit should be formed to support the "owner".
(Para. 3.82)

70 The problem of the Director General's pre-occupation with Parliamentary matters must be overcome. He must redress the balance between keeping Ministers informed and running the Service.
(Paras. 3.83-86)

71 The Home Office should undertake an in-depth study of the relationship between itself and the Prison Service.
(Para. 3.87)

72 Service structure should deliver the right messages to the organisation and the Board should be restructured to strengthen operations:

(a) Operational Directors should have previous experience as a governing Governor and should be increased from two to four as outlined in Section 5. They should be in the chain of command in emergency situations.

(b) Responsibility for policy at Board level should be vested in one Policy Director, with operational experience gained, ideally, from within the Prison Service.

(c) The Head of Health Care should report to the Policy Director and need attend Board meetings only when medical matters are discussed.

(d) The Finance Director should be a professional, with financial experience gained in an operational environment.

(e) The Director of Personnel appointment should be reviewed within the next three years, after devolution of personnel matters to operational directorates, areas and establishments, when responsibility for personnel policy at Board level could pass to the Policy Director, supported by a professional personnel manager.

(f) Services should be contractorised by competitive tendering, with contracts renewable only if standards are met. The Director post might then be reviewed.

(g) The number of non-Executive Directors should be reviewed.

(Paras. 3.92 and 3.100-114)

73 The momentum to downsize Headquarters and Central Services, by at least 500 posts by 1998, must be maintained. Activities not essential to operational management, such as the Lifer Group (excluding the operational management of lifers through the Allocation Unit), Parole Unit and Superannuation Section, should be moved out of Headquarters.

(Paras. 3.123-124)

74 The Service must look for better ways of dealing with the proliferation of paperwork and take urgent action to reduce it.

(Paras. 3.129-132 and Appendix M)

75 Area Managers should be an integral part of the corporate planning process, monitor service delivery and manage the area's resources. They should be located in their areas and hold their own budgets. They must concentrate on operational management of establishments and make their voices heard at Board level through the Operational Directors.

(Paras. 3.133-136)

76 The Service should ensure that, when contracts are drawn up for private prisons, staffing levels are set on the basis of staff and prisoner safety and the protection of the public.

(Paras. 3.137-138)

77 A substantial public Prison Service should be retained but the advantages arising from competition and private sector involvement should be applied across the Service.

(Paras. 3.140-141)

78 Boards of Visitors should be properly resourced and the Liaison Section should be moved out of Headquarters.

(Paras. 3.142-143)

SECTION 4: SECURITY - GETTING THE BASICS RIGHT

4.1 Security should be the prime responsibility of the Prison Service. It is influenced by a great many factors, from building design to purposeful activity. There are, however, a number of 'basic' requirements. These include physical security measures, security procedures, emergency procedures and staff skills and motivation.

PHYSICAL SECURITY

Structures

4.2 The prison estate comprises a wide variety of buildings. Some date from Victorian times and earlier, others are redundant military camps and a few are converted country mansions. There was virtually no new prison-building during the first half of this century but, during the 1960s, more than 20 were constructed. There was another boost to the estate during the 1980s but some of the designs used were out-of-date. The use of old plans was widely criticised and, in 1984, a Prison Department Committee instituted a study into designs for a new generation of prisons. A report was published in 1985 which recommended the adoption of some aspects of new designs used by the US Federal Bureau of Prisons. From these, the then Prison Department produced standard drawings for the future use of the Service, including anti-helicopter devices. Four years later, the Prison Design Briefing System was published, providing specifications and detailed guidance for the construction of buildings and for physical security. Unfortunately, during the gestation period of the briefing system, more establishments were built, based on pre-1988 models.

4.3 Although, since 1988, the briefing system has formed the basis of prison design, the need for speedily erected buildings, and other political and financial considerations, have moved the Prison Service away from the specifications contained in the briefs. The Service is now adopting a more commercial approach to prison construction and some projects will be market-tested on a design, build and run basis. It is a laudable aim to keep down the costs to the public but security is so important that there must be national agreement on designs to which all prisons comply.

4.4 During visits to prisons, the Inquiry noted that the fabric of some of the older prisons had been neglected for years and poor features were evident in some of the newer ones. In two prisons, the modern Units holding high security risk prisoners offered very poor visibility. Lines of sight were blocked every few yards by corners, staircases and other obstructions. In these Units, staff said they felt threatened and afraid because they could not see each other and prisoners could indulge in mischief unobserved. The reinforcement of the internal structure of several establishments were not to the latest standards. Generally, entrance buildings and gate lodges were found to be cramped and some offered poor visibility. The decision to install X-ray and metal detecting equipment has created demands for space which current entrances cannot provide, leading to inadequate searching systems and frustrating delays. Such searching aids are essential at Dispersal Prisons and the appropriate facilities must be provided at the entrances to these establishments. CCTV observation, to enhance security and safety, is essential. In recent years, the Prison Service has taken steps to improve the security of establishments but much remains to be done. The estate must conform to up-to-date security standards.

Electronic security

4.5 In addition to standard physical barriers, electronic devices are also deployed in some prisons to assist in the maintenance of security. These devices include CCTV, electronic movement detectors and electronic locks.

4.6 The Prison Service began to install electronic security aids during the 1960s, when concern was growing at the number of determined and dangerous potential escapees in custody. After inquiring into several notorious escapes in 1966, the Mountbatten Report commended use of such aids as one means of enhancing security. Despite the passage of 30 years and the proven value of these aids, no cohesive policy for their installation has been formulated within the Prison Service. The absence of policy has resulted in wide variations in both the quality and deployment of electronic devices.

4.7 A survey, by Prison Service Headquarters, has identified serious deficiencies in electronic security defences. This unsatisfactory situation was confirmed by the Inquiry. The deficiencies in relation to fence alarms, movement detectors, camera coverage and locks outlined in Section 2 of this Report, in relation to Parkhurst, were not confined to that particular prison. Similar problems were identified in other parts of the prison estate. At the time establishments were visited, internal cameras were too few to ensure proper safety or security and, in the main, equipment was found to be old and subject to frequent breakdown, with long delays in repair or replacement.

4.8 Accountability for the correct use of technology has been devolved to Governors but some Governors reported difficulties in obtaining expert advice on the latest systems. One Governor, on his own initiative, sought advice from private contractors. This approach can scarcely be the best way of ensuring high standards overall. It must be wrong for the Prison Service, with 130 establishments, to rely on local management to resolve technical problems requiring national solutions.

Security audits

4.9 Since 1st January 1995, the Prison Service has created a team, within the Security Directorate, which is examining the physical and electronic security of establishments. This initiative is supported by the Inquiry. From it should emerge a strategy to improve general security. Audits already completed on all Dispersal Prisons have verified that deficiencies exist in both physical and electronic security. The findings of these, and subsequent, audits must be given urgent consideration and the necessary action taken to correct the deficiencies which are identified. Remedial work should start at maximum security prisons, with every effort made to ensure that expenditure is properly targeted. This work is crucial and should be a high priority for funding.

Emergency Control Room (ECR)

4.10 Each Dispersal Prison has an ECR which is the hub of its security system, controlling movement, monitoring prisoners, watching for security breaches and responding to alarms. A number of ECRs were poorly organised and ill-equipped and the staff were inadequately trained. One ECR appeared particularly dirty, neglected and in poor decorative order. The signal this sends to staff about the need for high levels of security could hardly be weaker.

4.11 In addition to a properly equipped ECR, every Governor of a Dispersal Prison, when acting as local commander in emergencies (Silver Commander), must have a suite of rooms dedicated for the purpose, properly equipped and held in constant readiness. Here again, considerable variations were found: the best establishments provided adequate accommodation for the whole command team; the worst comprised a single room off the ECR which, when used, would become hot, noisy and overcrowded.

4.12 Staff should be properly trained for the work of the ECR and practised in both the routine tasks and emergency procedures.

SECURITY PROCEDURES

4.13 Good physical and electronic security is essential to the containment of determined and dangerous potential escapees. They are not, however, sufficient in themselves. Security also requires effective systems and procedures, co-ordinated both nationally and locally, to cover application of the procedures manual, policies for visits (open and closed), searching and prisoner escorts.

Procedures manual

4.14 The Prison Service has invested a great deal of effort in the production of a document, entitled the "Manual on Security", which outlines national policy on custody. The content of this Manual is good but only a very few copies are retained in each establishment and access to the document is limited. Both the Hadfield/Lakes and Woodcock Reports recommended that the Manual be made widely available and that staff familiarise themselves with its contents. To ensure this familiarity, Hadfield/Lakes went further and recommended that concise versions of the Manual should be made available to operational staff. Four years later, this has not been done. The Manual should be a basic document for training purposes.

4.15 The Woodcock Report also highlighted the confusion which exists at all levels as to whether the Manual should be considered mandatory or advisory. Many Governors stated that they treated it as advisory and the use of words such as 'may' and 'could' in some passages have helped to reinforce this perception. It was heartening that, late in December 1994, the Director General circulated an instruction to establishments confirming the mandatory status of the Manual (see para. 2.254). Less heartening was the discovery that news of this decision had taken a considerable time to reach some operational levels. The Manual must be treated as mandatory; its wording should be reviewed accordingly and copies should be widely distributed in all establishments.

Visits

4.16 The majority of illicit items infiltrated into prisons probably arrive through social visits. It is also no secret that drugs are smuggled in during such visits. The increasing availability of drugs was of particular concern to prison staff and was highlighted as a problem by many prisoners during discussions with the Inquiry. The establishment of drugs-free Wings at some prisons and the introduction of drugs testing are positive steps forward which should be taken where appropriate.

4.17 Such measures could give some protection to inmates who are fearful of becoming victims of the drug culture, whilst isolating those within the system who gain power from drug trafficking. The danger from shared needles, either during use or when unexpectedly discovered during cleaning or searching, was a major concern. In one prison, prisoners stated they had seen upwards of 40 people share the same needle. The scope for infection and HIV is obvious.

4.18 Stringent efforts are needed to encourage addicts to reform and to ensure support for those who need it. Every prison must have drug abuse programmes which inform, educate and help prisoners combat the drugs habit. These programmes must include medical treatment based on the best of international practice. Prisoners who succeed on such programmes should be rewarded through the incentives system. In these ways, the Prison Service can make a positive contribution to the health of the nation as well as to that of individual prisoners. This matter is so important that a KPI should be developed to ensure that the Service's performance is adequately measured (see para. 3.54).

4.19 Procedures for searching visitors are laid down in the Manual on Security and staff are supposed to be properly trained and proficient in the use of X-ray and metal detecting equipment. Many of the procedures are routinely ignored, often because of other pressures but sometimes to meet statistical targets.

4.20 Despite the Whitemoor and Parkhurst escapes, the criticisms in recent reports and the public outcry over lax security in prisons, considerable variations in practice at the prisons visited were noted. Staff at some were found to be ill-prepared and were expected to achieve an almost impossible task with insufficient resources or space. Local instructions also varied widely. In one establishment, staff reported they were not allowed to remove visitors' shoes whereas, in another prison, staff insisted on removal and X-rayed every pair.

4.21 The initial searching of visitors on arrival is the main safeguard against smuggling. If searching is not carried out efficiently, this safeguard is lost. It is essential that the Prison Service reviews its policy for searching visitors, develops searching standards for each type of prison and maintains a system for auditing performance.

4.22 Design of and procedures within visiting rooms also varied widely. In terms of design, rooms at Cardiff and Belmarsh Prisons were among the best visited. Some establishments insisted that prisoners sat on designated chairs on the opposite side of a table to their visitors. Others allowed them to sit side by side and embrace. Staff at one establishment told of their embarrassment and that of other visitors when, on one occasion, the full sex act was performed between a prisoner and a visitor and they felt unable to prevent it. In another visits room, clothing was draped over chairs to obscure the view of staff.

4.23 In some visits areas seen by the Inquiry, staff were either seated or standing around the walls, well away from the prisoners and visitors. Some staff reported that they felt reluctant to walk around between tables because prisoners did not like it. Staff working in visits rooms are clearly intimidated by prisoners and visitors and lose control. Any small item, and especially drugs, can be passed unnoticed between visitors and prisoners. To help combat this, the Prison Service must develop standard designs for visits rooms, commensurate with the levels of security and facilities required for differing establishments or circumstances. Existing rooms should be surveyed and, where practicable, brought up to these standards.

4.24 CCTV cameras in visits areas are of enormous value, as illustrated by the pictures in Figure 10:

Fig. 10 **Photographs of Smuggling in Visits Area**

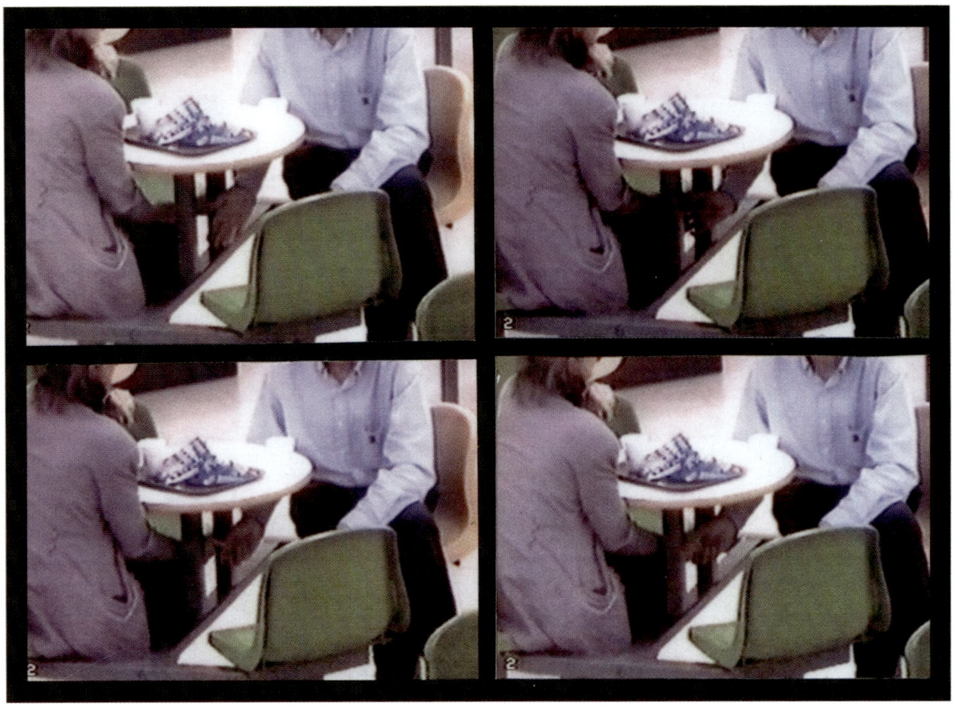

4.25 This series of pictures was recorded on video in 1995, in the visits area of a prison visited by the Inquiry. They show drugs being passed from a visitor to an inmate. The capture of this act on CCTV cameras allowed immediate action to be taken and prevented these drugs entering the system. In addition to detecting smuggling, the cameras can act as a deterrent, if they are appropriately located and utilised. They should be covered for protection against tampering and to disguise movement. Full video recording facilities must be available. The consequences of illicit items being passed to prisoners are extremely serious and systems and procedures must be followed to minimise the risk. Whether visits are open or closed, staff should have the latest searching and surveillance equipment.

4.26 The Inquiry's terms of reference required a specific examination of closed visits in respect of Special Security Units (SSUs). The only way to eradicate infiltration of goods during visits is to instigate closed visits and the searching of all visitors, prisoners and prison staff. Having given very careful consideration to the views expressed by Lord Woolf, by HM Chief Inspector of Prisons, by Prison Reform Groups and by others, the Inquiry is clear that, in most cases, some physical contact should be allowed between inmates and family, in particular where children are involved.

4.27 Mandatory closed visits are therefore recommended only for Exceptional Risk Category A prisoners. By removing all physical contact between prisoners of this category and their visitors, the opportunity for passing illicit items should be eliminated. The Inquiry feels that the absence of such measures of control poses a significant and unacceptable risk.

4.28 In all other cases, the option of closed visits should be available in all secure prison establishments, to be used at the Governor's discretion for those prisoners suspected of or found misbehaving. If there are reasonable grounds to believe an individual has been or is likely to be involved in trafficking, subsequent visits should automatically be closed. There is a disparity between establishments on this point; at some, closed visits are never imposed whilst, at others, they are imposed when necessary. There seems to be a greater propensity to exercise this option in the private prisons than in the public sector. Governors generally should make more use of closed visits and should be supported by Headquarters when they do so.

Searching

4.29 Once items have infiltrated the prison, the only defence against their illicit use is a thorough search programme. Every establishment should have a search programme, in accordance with the Manual on Security, agreed between the Governor and Area Manager. Whilst these are mostly in place, Governors spoke of difficulties due to the time-consuming nature and resource implications of searching.

4.30 Both the Hadfield/Lakes and Woodcock Reports recommended the introduction of specialist search teams. Current procedures in the Prison Service in Northern Ireland, where dedicated search teams exist, are most impressive. At Maghaberry Prison, the search team has specialised equipment and is trained to very high standards in the detection of illegal substances and items. It also has access to training facilities which accurately represent cells and landings. The team has a secondary specialist role in control and restraint, which serves to provide a variety of work without reducing availability for the prime role.

4.31 The presence of such specialists is vital in maintaining a constant awareness of security and a thorough programme of searches. All establishments accommodating significant numbers of Category A inmates should have such teams. The Prison Service must therefore establish dedicated search teams at all Dispersal Prisons (a recommendation made in the Woodcock Report on the escape from Whitemoor) and at the two new prisons recommended later in this Report. Across the rest of the prison estate, better use must be made of search teams, supported by appropriate equipment and the wider deployment of trained dogs to search for drugs, guns and explosives. A thorough reappraisal of the requirement for and deployment of 'sniffer' dogs should quickly be carried out, with a view to making them generally available and their use normal rather than exceptional. The Inquiry understands that such a review is underway. Everywhere in the prison estate, the procedures for searching prisoners should accord with the Manual on Security.

4.32 Prison staff should also be searched, to protect them from intimidation by prisoners and prisoners' associates. A search of all staff entering Dispersal Prisons (a recommendation made in the Woodcock Report on Whitemoor), and the two new establishments should be mandatory; and there should be random searches of staff leaving these prisons. Staff interviewed in both the Whitemoor and Parkhurst Inquiries have indicated that they would welcome such a regime. It is the only defence against allegations and innuendo so often made through the media after an escape. Elsewhere in the prison estate, programmes for searching staff should be agreed between the Governors and Area Managers and based on the security requirements of the establishment.

4.33 At some of the prisons visited, contractors and their vehicles, on occasion in very large numbers, were entering and leaving every day. There was evidence that such movements were not fully supervised and that, over time, staff became less vigilant. This lack of control represents a serious threat to security and the Prison Service must pay special attention to the procedures for checking goods, vehicles and contractors entering and leaving establishments.

Prisoner escorts

4.34 The bulk of prisoner escorts, outside the establishments, involve transporting remand prisoners between prisons and Courts. This activity is extremely resource-intensive and poses a significant security threat. At the start of the Inquiry, nearly 200 Category A remand prisoners were being held in 24 'local' prisons, many of which did not have accommodation purpose-built to hold Category A prisoners. During visits to establishments, it was noted that manning levels were often reduced to a minimum, due to the deployment of staff to escort remand prisoners. All too often, such commitments last all day for just a few minutes in Court and, although there are already arrangements which permit remand prisoners to appear only once monthly, many elect to attend weekly, for the excursion and opportunity to escape. Prisoners have also been known to engineer lengthy postponements of their trial date specifically to spend as much as possible of their sentence period under the more attractive conditions for a remand prisoner. These include being located close to home, use of their own clothing, no requirement to work and a greater frequency of visits.

4.35 The dispersal of high risk, remand prisoners throughout the country has two major implications. First, security is jeopardised. Second, the presence of such inmates in local prisons increases the potential for difficulties and discontent at those establishments. The security implications are illustrated by recent escapes of prisoners whilst under escort. Since 1990, there has been an average of one Category A prisoner escape from escort per year, the most recent during the period of the Inquiry, when a prisoner on remand, charged with attempted murder, escaped from a London Magistrates' Court. Although numerically small, this rate of loss is unacceptable, given the dangerous nature of the individuals involved. An alternative to the system is required. Whenever possible, remand Category A prisoners should be held in the Dispersal Prisons, for security reasons, but it will be necessary for many of them to be held in other strategically placed prisons which have accommodation to Category A standard.

4.36 Due to the large number of Category A remand prisoners in the system and the need to ensure access to the Courts, the Service will continue to require a significant number of places in which to hold Category A prisoners awaiting trial, unless alternative systems can be agreed. For reasons of security and cost, there is an urgent need to reduce the number of prisons used for this purpose and the Service must examine the options of holding court at the high security prisons or of establishing TV links between the Magistrates' Courts and the prisons. Whereas the construction of Courts at prisons might require major capital expenditure, current technology is such that TV links between prisons and Courts are feasible.

4.37 Despite the procedural and jurisdictional implications, full support for the idea has been received from many sources, including the Association of Chief Police Officers and Lord Woolf, who also commented on the potential savings that might be made nationally in the legal aid budget. The overall savings could pay for provision, installation and maintenance of the necessary equipment.

4.38 TV links would dramatically reduce the number of prisoner escorts and, by reducing dependence on location, would allow greater concentration of Category A remand prisoners in far fewer, more secure establishments (see also para. 5.19). Whilst TV links would appear ideal for remand hearings, it is accepted that the personal appearance of the accused prisoner at the eventual trial cannot be avoided. In such cases, the need for secure accommodation locally will remain.

STAFF SKILLS AND MOTIVATION

4.39 Whatever steps are taken to implement the physical security recommendations of this Report, security will remain absolutely dependent on the personal efforts of prison staff. They have a very difficult job which can be lonely, frightening and boring. Most have entered the Service from some feeling of vocation but it is unrealistic to expect them to tackle the challenges without proper preparation and support. The quality of the present staff is such that there is no reason why they should not succeed, providing the Service takes every opportunity to ensure that they are well trained, well motivated and well led.

4.40 The recruiting process has to ensure that those selected have the capacity to cope with the requirements of the job. As discussed in Section 3 of the Report, personnel systems must ensure that training and career structures are in place, resourced and monitored. Equally and importantly, line managers have to take personal responsibility for ensuring that their staff are properly trained to cover both long-term needs and current tasks.

4.41 More important still is visible leadership which recognises the human dimension, shows enthusiasm for people's efforts and promotes feelings of self-respect and self-confidence. That is the only way to fortify staff against the worries and temptations of the landings.

Intimidation

4.42 It became clear to the Inquiry that prison staff are subject to a level of intimidation by prisoners well beyond the appreciation of either senior management or the general public. Assaults on staff have doubled in the last five years. The Prison Service Business Plan, 1994/95, suggests that these figures should be treated with caution because they may reflect strenuous efforts to deter and punish perpetrators. That was not, however, the message from Whitemoor or Parkhurst and anecdotal evidence from visits certainly supported a sense of rising tension.

4.43 The problem of intimidation impacts on security, particularly in high security prisons. If prisoners are able, by means of threats, intimidation, coercion or other forms of pressure, to affect the way prison staff behave and respond, then no physical constraints, sophisticated electronic surveillance or security procedures and systems will be effective. If prisoners feel safe indulging in intimidatory behaviour, they obviously do not fear the consequences. Typical examples of intimidatory behaviour are:

- Threats against family members, in which knowledge of their addresses, routines or other personal details is revealed.
- Strong verbal confrontation or physical violence.
- The generation of a climate of fear, in which violence is never far below the surface.
- Regular challenges to instructions from staff.
- Constant concoction of complaints to senior staff about treatment.

4.44 In such circumstances, there is a risk that some Prison Officers will respond by retreating into a passive role, in which they do little to enforce rules or correct prisoners' behaviour. Officers have no disciplinary powers beyond placing a prisoner on report. The Inquiry seeks no change on this point but recognises that some Officers are discouraged by intimidation from using the disciplinary procedures. This danger has to be acknowledged and full use must be made of sound procedures, good intelligence and appropriate surveillance aids. The problem has also to be thoroughly addressed during initial and refresher training and continuously monitored by line managers.

Psychological manipulation

4.45 A feature of prison life is that prisoners endeavour to manipulate staff. They may do this for malicious reasons or as a game played for psychological domination. Whatever the motivation, the consequences are always serious. In manipulating staff, prisoners seek to take control from them and this threatens safe custody, leaving staff anxious and uncertain.

4.46 Psychological manipulation can take many forms, from distraction to exploitation of relationships and conditioning. Staff can be deceived into thinking that particular forms of behaviour are commonplace and innocent when, in reality, they serve a sinister purpose. The effects of conditioning can be particularly serious in Special Security Units and were demonstrated in the Whitemoor escape. The Prison Service recognises that staff training, backed up by attentive and supportive leadership, is the only effective counter to this security threat.

Boredom

4.47 Good security depends as much on routine tasks being performed well as it does on sophisticated equipment. Even well motivated staff can become bored and their efficiency reduced if the tedium of important but routine tasks is not relieved. This can be achieved through a range of measures, including job rotation, job enrichment and the use of technology. During the course of the Inquiry, it was found that regular visits from supervisory grades do much to relieve boredom and to support staff. The Prison Service is aware of the problem and some of the remedies for it.

4.48 The Prison Service produced, on 23rd March 1995, a paper about the relief of boredom amongst staff. It identified the factors contributing to boredom and listed staff concerns. In proposing ways of tackling the problem, the paper suggested a range of options, including job enrichment, rotation, better management, the use of technology and improved training. All have considerable merit and deserve proper consideration. The problem of boredom should, therefore, continue to be studied carefully by the Prison Service and an action plan should be developed to deal with it. The implications for security are so serious, particularly in relation to searching, escort procedures and the close supervision of prisoners, that the work should be put in hand immediately and completed quickly.

Motivation of civilian staff

4.49 A large and important section of the day-to-day work of establishments is carried out by non-Prison Officer grades. They are drawn from diverse groups, including education officers, workshop and trade training instructors, administrative staff, psychologists, chaplains and medical staff. A number are in contact with prisoners throughout the working day. The successful running of all establishments is dependent to a large extent upon the expertise of these specialist groups of staff.

4.50 The Inquiry met a number of representatives of these groups who said they felt undervalued and regarded as second-class citizens in the Service. These staff perform an important function and it is vital that their contribution is properly recognised. Many felt that some visible sign of corporate identity would reduce their vulnerability, distinguish them from inmates and encourage their acceptance as part of the staff team.

EMERGENCY PROCEDURES

4.51 Each establishment has contingency plans for handling emergencies and Headquarters has plans for providing support. In addition, support from the police is often necessary and arrangements are in place to provide manpower and specialist equipment to assist Governors during emergencies.

4.52 The Silver Commander will have available highly trained and well equipped Prison Officers capable of dealing with the majority of hostile and dangerous situations. The Control and Restraint techniques, taught to Prison Officers on joining and refreshed thereafter, are extremely effective in dealing with a wide variety of problems, using minimum force. These techniques are internationally respected and mark the Prison Service out as a humanitarian service which does not have to rely on force to control emergencies.

Use of incapacitants

4.53 In the US and some other countries, pepper mace is used in prisons to control inmates in difficult situations. Its prompt deployment can prevent incidents from escalating and minimises the risk of injury to staff. In prisons in England and Wales, CS gas has been used only rarely and only by the police. Within the Prison Service, serious questions have been raised about the effects of incapacitants on health, especially when used in confined spaces. The fact that it can drift unpredictably, poses a potential threat to innocent people inside and outside the prison.

4.54 These reservations are understood but incapacitants could provide Governors with a valuable tool for the control of prisoners. The justification might be that other techniques are less likely to succeed or might delay the resolution of the incident. Work is currently under way in the Police Service to evaluate the use of chemical incapacitants and the Prison Service should remain informed of these developments. The advantages for the Prison Service of deploying incapacitants, with the right safeguards, must be reconsidered on the basis of up-to-date research and the experience gained in other Services.

Use of firearms

4.55 The use of firearms to assist in preserving security at selected prisons has been considered in the past and rejected. The Service should re-examine this issue because the numbers of dangerous prisoners and the availability of firearms to their criminal associates has increased in recent years. There is no intention to suggest the routine arming of Prison Officers but rather an acknowledgement that the secure prisons should have the capacity to provide an armed response promptly when necessary. The means by which this response is made available is a matter for discussion between the Prison Service and other parts of the criminal justice system.

CONCLUSIONS

4.56 Security covers a wide spectrum of measures. However, within that spectrum are certain fundamental requirements which must be met before further action is considered. First and foremost, prisons must be built to a nationally agreed design and a nationally agreed standard. Sadly, neither of these requirements are being met in the major part of the prison estate in England and Wales and, until action is taken to correct this, the Prison Service remains vulnerable to further escapes.

4.57 Not only must the outer perimeter and buildings reach a satisfactory standard but also up-to-date electronic devices, such as closed circuit television systems, electronic movement detectors and electronic locks, must be installed, to complement the perimeter security. Again, the Inquiry found that the Prison Service has fallen behind acceptable standards.

4.58 Each Dispersal Prison is equipped with an Emergency Control Room which controls surveillance, movement, security breaches and response to alarms. A number of the ECRs were poorly equipped. Staff at Parkhurst, on the night of the escape, were untrained. These were elementary failures by the Prison Service and must be corrected forthwith.

4.59 In any disciplined Service, operational directives and instructions must be obeyed. Within the Prison Service, the Manual on Security outlines national policy. In specific areas investigated by the Inquiry, including procedures at visits, searching and prisoner escorts, current instructions were ignored. The Director General has recently issued instructions that the Manual on Security should be considered mandatory and it is essential that top management audits all establishments to ensure that the correct drills are being carried out.

4.60 As indicated in Appendix J, the US Federal Bureau of Prisons has eight core values, of which four relate directly to staff, and six strategic long-term goals, of which human resource management appears as the second highest. The goal is supported by a commitment to effective recruitment, selection, training and development strategies. It is obvious that the Prison Service in England and Wales has not devoted enough care and time to recruiting, training or looking after its staff. Unless the staff are properly motivated, properly trained, properly equipped and properly led, carefully drafted instructions and directives will be ineffective. Staff must possess the basic skills to enable them to undertake an unsung and dangerous task on behalf of the general public. This has special meaning in an emergency situation.

RECOMMENDATIONS (SECURITY - GETTING THE BASICS RIGHT)

79 Designs for all prisons must be agreed nationally.
(Para. 4.3)

80 Appropriate facilities, including CCTV, must be provided at the entrances to Dispersal Prisons. The prison estate must conform to up-to-date security standards.
(Para. 4.4)
[See recommendation 25]

81 The Prison Service Headquarters Security Survey, on electronic security defences, should be actioned without delay. The Service must provide national solutions to technical problems. Remedial work identified by security audits should be a high priority.
(Paras. 4.7-9)

82 Each Dispersal Prison must have a properly equipped ECR. All staff must be properly trained for their various tasks and every Governor of a Dispersal Prison must have a Command Suite for use in emergencies
(Paras. 4.10-12)
[See recommendations 28 and 29]

83 The Manual on Security should be mandatory and used as the basic document for training purposes. Copies should be widely distributed in all establishments and concise versions should be available to operational staff.
(Paras. 4.14-15)

84 The concepts of drugs-free Wings and of drugs testing should be implemented where appropriate.
(Para. 4.16)

85 To deal with drug abuse, all prisons must have programmes which inform, educate and help prisoners combat the drug habit. Success on such programmes should be rewarded through the incentive scheme.
(Para 4.18)

86 Procedures for searching visitors are laid down in the Manual on Security and must be obeyed, to minimise the risk of smuggling. Staff must have the latest equipment and be properly trained and proficient in the use of X-ray and metal detecting machinery.
(Paras. 4.19 and 4.25)
[See recommendation 5 and Woodcock recommendation 12]

87 The Prison Service must develop visitor searching standards for each type of prison and maintain a system for auditing performance.
(Para. 4.21)
[See recommendation 12]

88 The Prison Service must develop standard designs for visits rooms, commensurate with the levels of security and facilities required for differing establishments or circumstances. Existing rooms should be surveyed and, where practicable, brought up to these standards.
(Para. 4.23)

89 CCTV cameras should be covered for protection against tampering and to disguise movement. Full video recording facilities must be available.
(Para. 4.25)

90 In most cases, some physical contact should be allowed between inmates and family. Mandatory closed visits are recommended only for Exceptional Risk Category A prisoners.
(Paras. 4.26-27)

91 For other than Exceptional Risk Category A prisoners, the option of imposing closed visits should be available in all secure establishments, to be used at the Governor's discretion. Governors should make more use of the option, when they have reasonable grounds for suspicion, and Headquarters should support them.
(Para. 4.28)

92 All prison establishments must implement a searching programme in accordance with the Manual on Security.
(Paras. 4.29 and 4.31)
[See recommendations 21, 24, and 94 and Woodcock recommendations 5 and 8]

93 The Prison Service should establish dedicated search teams at all Dispersal Prisons and at the two new prisons recommended in Section 5.
(Para. 4.31)
[See recommendations 22 and 94 and Woodcock recommendation 9]

94 Across the rest of the estate, better use must be made of search teams, supported by appropriate equipment and the wider deployment of trained dogs to search for drugs, guns and explosives.
(Para. 4.31)
[See recommendations 21, 22, 92 and 93]

95 All staff entering Dispersal Prisons, and the two new establishments, should be searched and there should be random searches of staff leaving these prisons. Elsewhere, programmes for searching staff should be agreed between Governors and Area Managers.
(Para. 4.32)
[See recommendation 17 and Woodcock recommendation 27]

96 Prison establishments must properly supervise on-site contractors and their vehicles particularly when entering and leaving establishments.
(Para. 4.33)

97 In the short term, whenever possible, remand Category A prisoners should be held in Dispersal Prisons but it will be necessary for many of them to be held in other strategically placed prisons with accommodation to Category A standard.
(Para. 4.35)

98 The practicality of installing TV links between prisons holding remand prisoners and Magistrates' Courts should be explored.
(Paras. 4.36-38)

99 The problems of intimidation, manipulation and boredom must be thoroughly addressed during recruitment and training, continuously monitored by line managers and carefully studied by the Service with a view to appropriate action. More important still is visible leadership which recognises the human dimension, shows enthusiasm for people's efforts and promotes feelings of self-respect and self-confidence.
(Paras. 4.39-48)
[See recommendation 51 and Woodcock recommendations 55 and 58]

100 The Prison Service should ensure that the contribution of civilian staff is properly recognised.
(Paras. 4.49-50)

101 The Service must keep abreast of work on chemical incapacitants and consider the use of CS gas to quell riotous behaviour. There is a need also for the Service to re-examine the argument for an armed response capability.
(Paras. 4.53-55)

SECTION 5: SECURITY - THE WAY FORWARD

5.1 The basic security requirements outlined in Section 4 must be met. In addition, in order to tackle effectively the security problems identified in this Report, the Prison Service must take a number of steps forward. These include a change in the system of categorisation of prisoners, the accreditation of establishments, the development of special facilities for particularly high risk and difficult inmates, improved management of prisoners and more effective use of the prison estate. The effective management of prisoners requires incentives for good behaviour such as early release, TV in cells, home leave, visits, telephone privileges, work and wages, the concept of Industrial Prisons, and last, but not least, prisoner programmes. This Section makes specific recommendations with regard to women prisoners.

CATEGORISATION OF PRISONERS

5.2 Prisoners are currently placed into one of four security categories, according to the threat posed to the community and the likelihood of escape. This system has its origins in the 1966 Mountbatten Report when, it was estimated, around 120 prisoners needed the highest level of security. Mountbatten recommended that these Category A prisoners should be held in a single fortress prison and that all other categories should be placed in other establishments, ranging from those with cells and high walls to those which were completely open. In the event, the top security prison was not built and Category A prisoners were dispersed in selected, closed training establishments.

5.3 Mountbatten was making recommendations for a Prison Service serving a very different society to that of today. He could scarcely have imagined the growth in violent crime, the lack of regard for authority or the increase in drug abuse which are now so much part of life and which influence the types of crime committed. In the years since his Report, the number of Category A prisoners has increased and is now around 750. The Prison Service found it necessary to create three sub-divisions within that category in order to identify those who represented the gravest danger to society. These sub-divisions were: Exceptional Risk, containing highly resourceful prisoners, valuable to criminal organisations outside and highly likely to escape; High Risk, containing prisoners who may be marginally less likely to obtain help to escape; and Standard Risk, for those who have fewer resources. The effect of the sub-division was twofold. First, certain security arrangements were left to local discretion and, second, some staff, as they told the Inquiry, found it extremely difficult to differentiate, in particular, between High Risk and Standard Risk Category A prisoners located in the same prison. Prisoners were able to manipulate and exploit the system, undermining the safe custody of some very dangerous offenders who continued to present a serious threat to the community.

5.4 There is, therefore, a need to develop rapidly an improved categorisation system. Procedures must be introduced which are better attuned to the security profiles of individual prisoners. The interim solution must be applicable to all sentenced prisoners, as well as making proper provision for those on remand. Objective information, such as personal and criminal history, should continue to be taken into account and the Prison Service should designate which categories each establishment may hold and review the procedures associated with each category. Rules must be clear so that Governors and their staffs are in no doubt about the mandatory security requirements for each type of prisoner.

5.5 The chart at Figure 11 suggests new categories, compares these with the existing categories and shows what type of accommodation is suitable for each. Remand prisoners would be treated as Category 4 but given higher designations when the need arose.

Fig. 11 **Possible New Categorisation Chart**

NEW CATEGORY	EXISTING CATEGORY	TYPE OF PRISON
1	A (EXCEPTIONAL RISK)	DISPERSAL
2	A (HIGH RISK)	DISPERSAL
3	A (STANDARD RISK) B	DISPERSAL DISPERSAL
4	B C	TRAINERS CELLULAR
5	C	NON-CELLULAR
6	D	OPEN

5.6 It is proposed that, until other options are available, prisoners in Categories 1, 2 and 3 should be accommodated in Dispersal Prisons. Those in Category 4 could be held in closed, cellular, training prisons; those in Category 5, in the closed, non-cellular estate; and those in Category 6, in open prisons. The numbers in each category, and the criteria for distinguishing between them, would approximate to the current position but it is anticipated that, with the fencing of some Category D prisons, fewer would be held in open conditions.

5.7 The Parkhurst Inquiry has shown that two of the escapees had a history of determined escape planning and, as such, qualified for a higher categorisation than Standard Risk. Furthermore, their background and prison histories, examined at Appendix G, indicate that neither would sit comfortably in either the High or Standard Risk definitions. What is needed, in the longer term, is a fundamental review of the whole categorisation process and a system which provides better protection for the public, has the confidence of staff and can be seen as fair to prisoners. During the course of the Inquiry, attention has been drawn to the work of Professor David Canter, a leading advocate and practitioner of a research method which may enable the Prison Service to develop a more reliable and flexible system of categorisation. This method is explained in Appendix N and, if accepted, should result in a much more responsive system which matches prisoners to security categories with greater objectivity. It is recommended that the Prison Service follows up this initiative as a matter of some urgency.

5.8 Categorisation is fundamental to security. It is the key to ensuring the safe custody of prisoners and work on its improvement must be given proper priority. The system outlined at Figure 11, supported by revised procedures, could remove the present confusion. The research work recommended would refine the system.

THE HIGH SECURITY ESTATE

5.9 The high security estate houses those prisoners who pose the greatest threat to the public, should they escape. The events at Whitemoor and Parkhurst have revealed, in the starkest possible terms, major inadequacies in the current accommodation. It is self-evident that effective arrangements, covering buildings, security measures and regimes, must be put in place, as a matter of urgency.

5.10 Redefining the security categories and clarifying procedures would be useful first steps, but what is really required is an examination of the levels of security afforded by every establishment and the will to bring each one up to the requisite standard.

Categories 1 and 2

5.11 At present, prisoners who would fall into the new Categories 1 and 2 are housed in Dispersal Prisons, which provide the best security defences in the prison estate. However, the recent escapes have cast doubts on the ability of these establishments to contain inmates who have the resources and the determination to escape. The continuous development of explosives and weapons and their availability to criminals and their associates, pose a much greater threat to the security of our maximum security prisons than the Service has previously encountered. For this reason, it is necessary to re-examine the policy of dispersing high risk prisoners amongst lower security, albeit still dangerous, prisoners and housing them within the same establishment.

5.12 There are two options. Use could be made of the current Dispersal estate by building even more secure SSUs in our existing prisons. This option presents a number of disadvantages. First, the responsibility for the command and control of our most high risk prisoners is at present split between six Dispersal Prison Governors, five Area Managers and two Operational Directors, with no single person responsible for this highly important group of inmates. Second, the management of SSUs within prisons distracts Governors and staff from dealing with the majority of inmates. Third, practices and procedures are likely to vary between Units and open the system to exploitation by inmates. In addition, there must be some doubt as to whether the upgrading of existing facilities in the Dispersal Prisons will meet the requirements of the next century.

5.13 The other option is to look again at Mountbatten's recommendation to place all high risk prisoners in a single high security prison. The arguments for and against putting maximum security prisoners under one roof have been extensively aired on a number of occasions since his Report was published. Appendix A looks at these in more detail. Suffice it to say, the escapes from Whitemoor and Parkhurst, together with the evidence of poor physical security throughout the estate, indicate that it is now time to re-examine the Mountbatten proposal. Accordingly, an experienced and widely respected architect, who has specialised in prison design, was asked by the Inquiry to develop proposals for the construction of a 21st century high security prison.

5.14 The aim was to design an establishment for around 200 Category 1 and 2 prisoners, with differing types of Units for each category. Every Unit would be as self-contained as practicable, with workshop, recreational facilities, exercise area and catering arrangements. Movement to any shared facilities, such as a health care centre, would be via secure corridors and there would be a similar corridor to provide a safe route for rapid staff response. Having studied similar establishments in other countries, the Inquiry placed great emphasis on designing the living Units to provide more light and a greater sense of space than traditional cell blocks. This led to a design for an establishment in which there are three Units, each containing six cells, for Category 1 prisoners, and ten Units, with up to 24 cells each, for Category 2 prisoners. The Inquiry recommends this approach.

High Security Prison

5.15 The design for the High Security Prison includes the following features:

- External security would be provided by a wall protected by cameras and other electronic detection devices. The prison would stand in open ground, which would be monitored by additional cameras and floodlighting in order to provide early warning of any external attack on the wall. There is no requirement for an on-site firearms capability. Two observation towers would give additional surveillance of the external ground and central recreational area and would provide warning of any approach by helicopter.

- Entrance buildings would be designed to include proper searching arrangements for visitors, with pedestrian access to the prison through a tunnel. A vehicle off-loading facility has been included in the design for use whenever practicable. Those vehicles which must enter the prison, such as those delivering food, would be channelled through a secure vehicle access point into the prison.

- Internal security would be provided by a perimeter fence and further concrete walls, which would encase the staff corridor and general access corridor. These corridors would be gated at each Unit; entrance to the Unit would be through another set of double gates. The corridor dedicated to the use of staff would provide ease of access to all living Units in emergencies, avoiding the need to enter other accommodation areas.

- Access to the central recreational area would be through a limited number of gates. Anti-helicopter wires would provide overhead protection in this area.

- CCTV cover would be provided for the sterile open area, between the perimeter wall and the external wall of the corridors, with dogs patrolling this area.

- The ECR would be the nerve centre of the establishment, as in other high security prisons.

- Once secured in a 'lock down' state, any potential escapee would have to negotiate three concrete walls and a fence. The prisoner would have to proceed over a wide sterile area guarded by dogs, CCTV cover, alarms and a sensor system. Any intruders would have the same obstacles to surmount if they succeeded in crossing the outside area.

- A staff training centre would provide facilities for training, particularly for control and restraint (C and R), searching and inter-personal skills.

- The pressures on staff would be recognised, with ample rest and recreational facilities.

- The spaciousness and light which are features of the design would reduce claustrophobia, to the benefit of both inmates and staff. The design would also assist staff by providing good sight lines, making observation easier.

- The design would provide for activities in the living Units, leaving little need for external movement of prisoners.

Figures 12-15 show: the layout of the proposed High Security Prison (Figure 12), the plan of the ground level (Figure 13), the plan of the first floor level (Figure 14) and a cross-section of one living Unit (Figure 15).

Fig. 12 **Layout - High Security Prison - 200 Places**

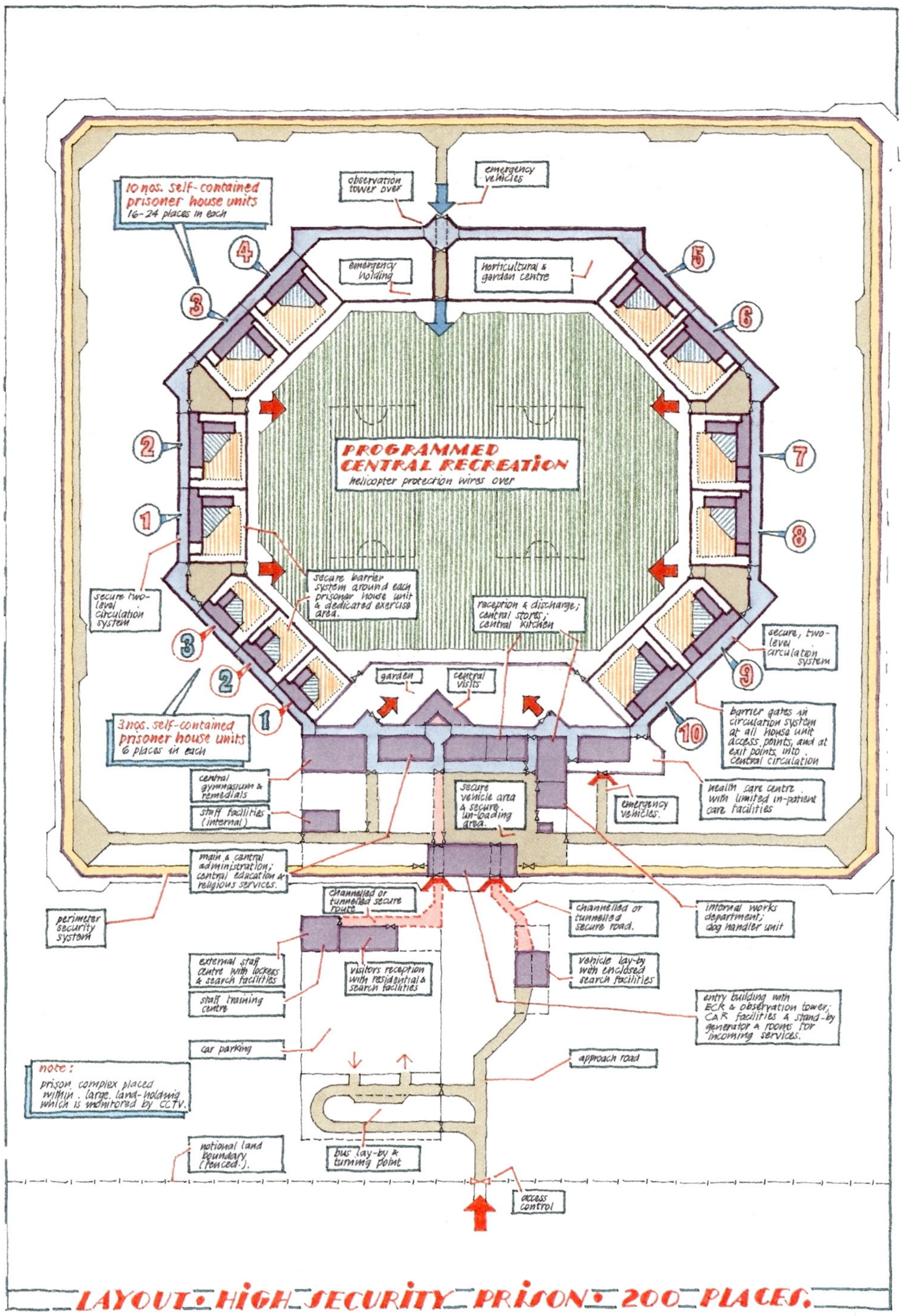

Fig. 13 **High Security Prison - 16 to 24 Place Living Unit - Ground Floor Plan**

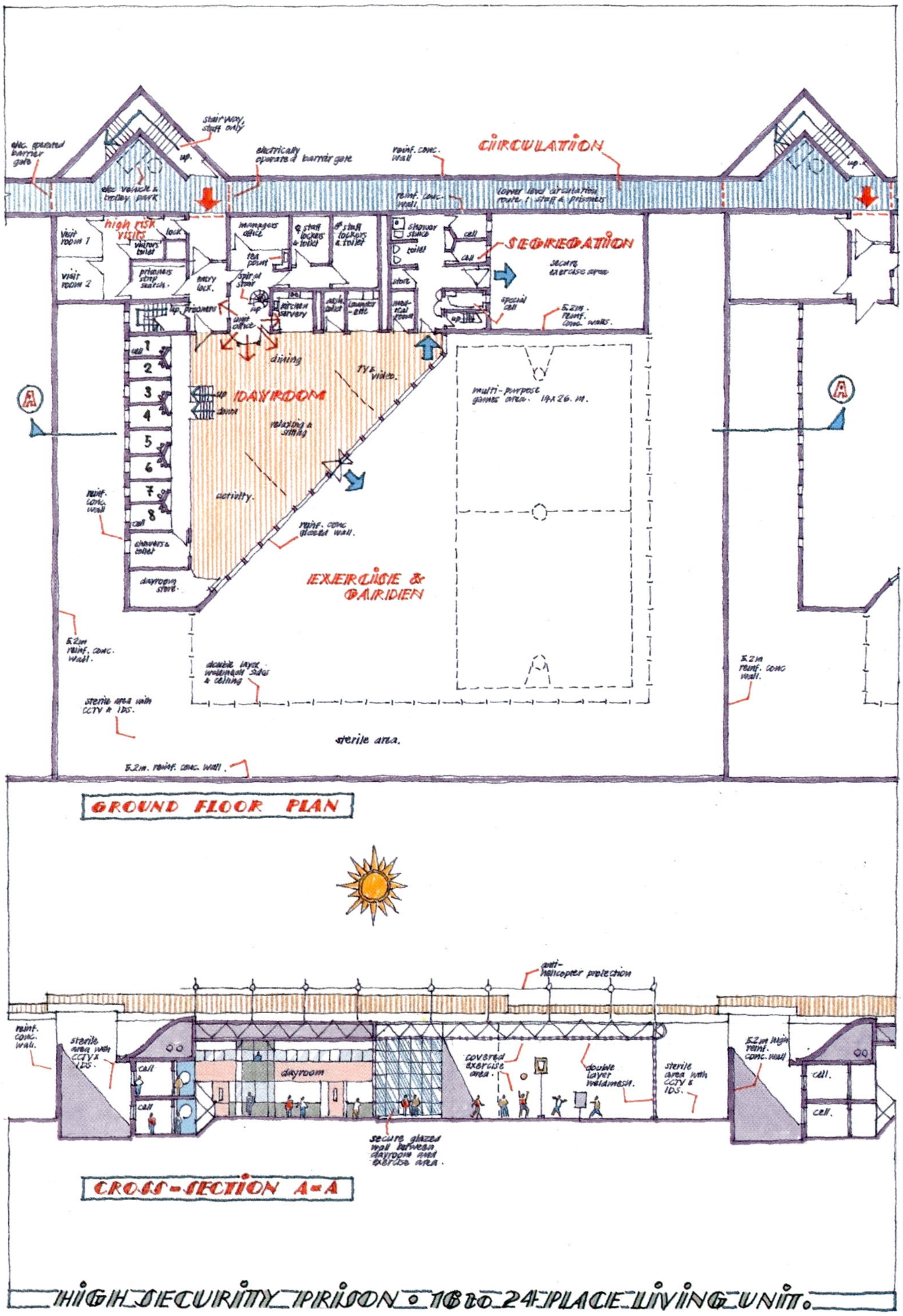

Fig. 14 **High Security Prison - 16 to 24 Place Living Unit - Upper Floor Plan**

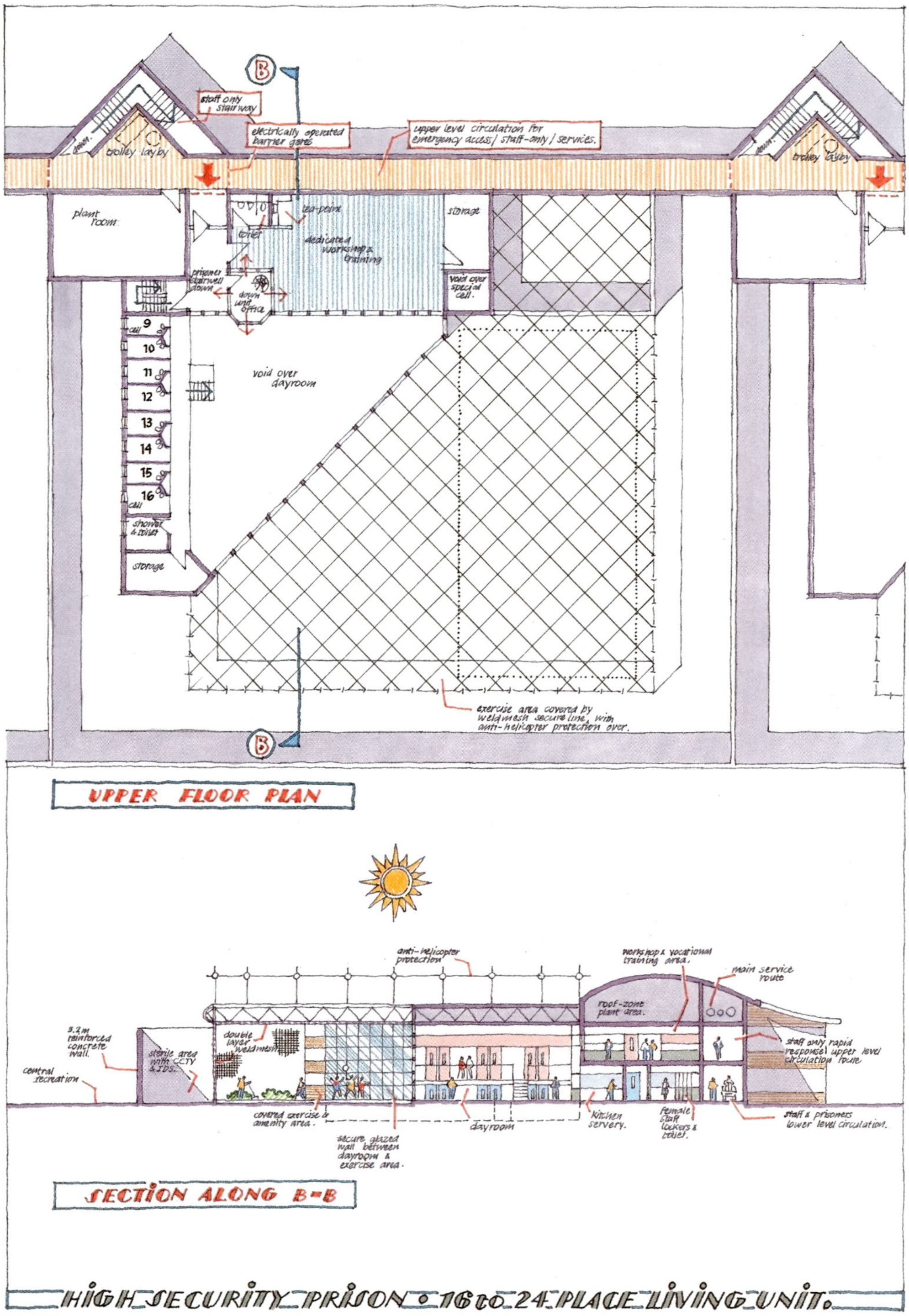

Fig. 15 **High Security Prison - 16 to 24 Place Living Unit - cross-section**

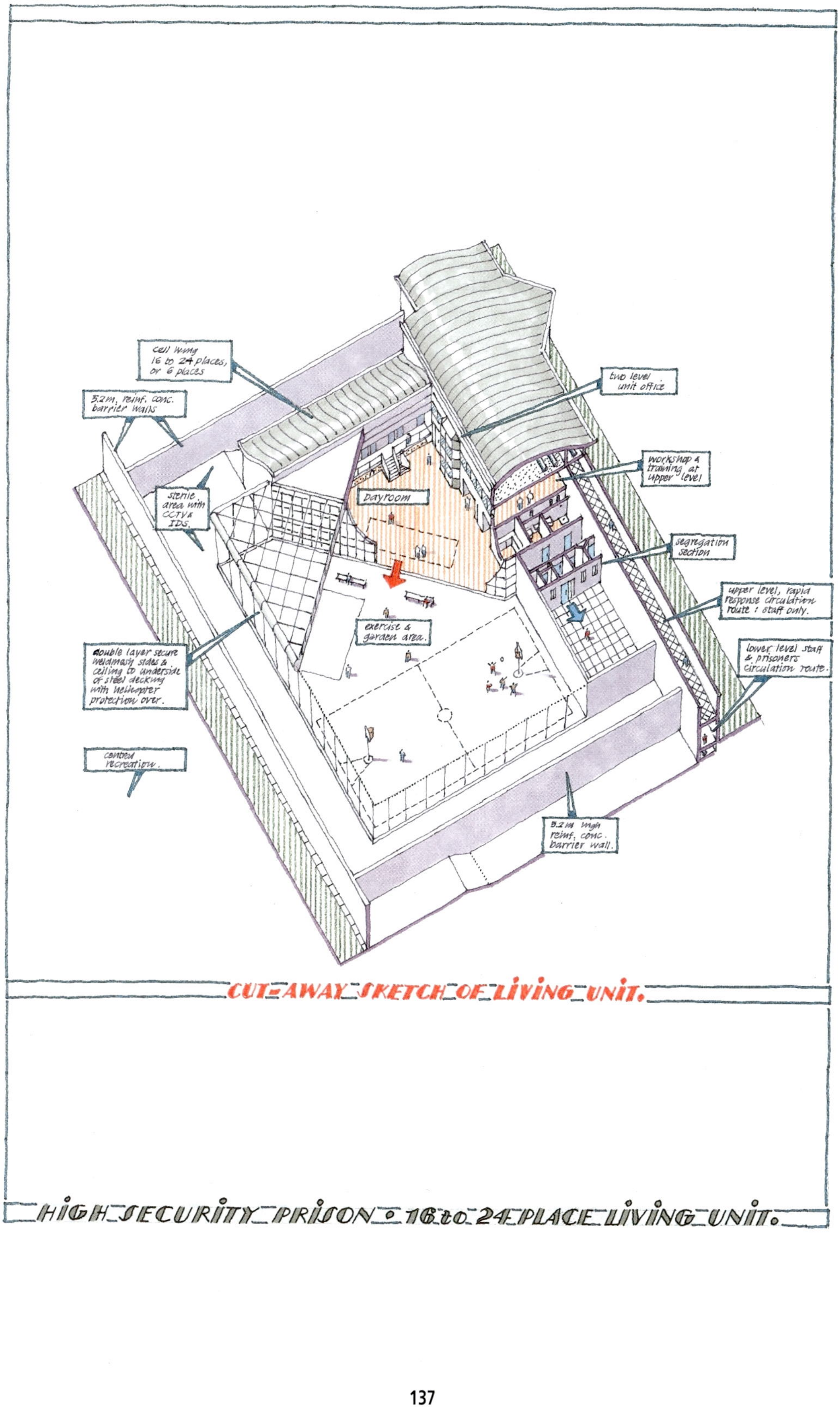

5.16 One of the persistent arguments against housing high risk prisoners in one High Security Prison has been doubt over the ability to produce a design that would provide both high security and humane living conditions for prisoners. As the illustrations show, modern building and design techniques can overcome these objections. The new design offers a sensitive and technologically advanced solution appropriate to British circumstances. It would facilitate maintenance of a purposeful training regime, similar to Dispersal Prisons, and prisoners would be encouraged to take part in a wide range of activities, to prevent the worst excesses of institutionalisation. Of major importance is the fact that the living Units would contain relatively small numbers of inmates, to assist the staff to manage prisoners effectively and help them to gain a sense of self-worth. There has been media speculation that this Inquiry would recommend a British "Alcatraz", which would provide a repressive environment where prisoners were subjected to a boring and bruising regime. The Inquiry's proposal represents exactly the opposite point of view.

Category 3

5.17 Currently, the Dispersal estate houses Category A Exceptional, High and Standard Risk prisoners, together with selected Category B inmates. This poses two main problems. First, the Exceptional and High Risk inmates require specific treatment; and the Inquiry has addressed this with the recommendation of the High Security Prison. Second, over the years, there has been a blurring of the distinction between Category A Standard Risk and those Category B prisoners held in the Dispersal estate, and this requires resolution.

5.18 It is proposed that the present Category A Standard Risk and those Category B prisoners held in the Dispersal estate should be amalgamated into the new Category 3. These prisoners should be housed in six Dispersal Prisons, which are in the process of being brought up to the standard required. Even when this work is complete, Parkhurst, for reasons outlined earlier in the Report, will remain unsuitable for the containment of Category 3 prisoners. In addition to concerns over its design, the location of Parkhurst, on the Isle of Wight, makes visiting extremely difficult for inmates' families, particularly as many have to travel from the London area. More importantly, it is difficult to provide Police Service support during serious incidents. It is recommended, therefore, that Parkhurst should become an establishment for Category 4 prisoners as soon as possible and should be replaced in the Category 3 estate by a more suitable establishment, perhaps Belmarsh Prison.

High risk male remand prisoners

5.19 The current practice of holding potential Category A remand prisoners in a large number of local prisons is unsatisfactory. Security conditions generally fall below the necessary standards and the potential for escape is high. The cost of bringing about 25 local prisons up to the required standards would be prohibitive and some of them would remain unsatisfactory, whatever sums were spent. However, the need to utilise a significant number of establishments will remain unless the recommendation on TV links (see paras. 4.37-38) is implemented. If it is implemented, Category 1 and 2 remand prisoners could be held in the High Security Prison when awaiting trial. During trial, they could be held in the High Security Prison, if it were geographically convenient, in an SSU within the Dispersal system or in one of a small number of suitable establishments across the country. These secure remand facilities could be provided in local prisons and some of the Dispersal Prisons. A judgement would need to be made as to whether an individual who is potentially Category 3 requires this level of security during remand.

High risk women prisoners and high risk young offenders

5.20 Whilst there are few high risk women prisoners, a number are extremely dangerous. The Prison Service has no suitable facilities and needs to address this matter urgently. Similarly, arrangements must be made for high risk young offenders.

THE REMAINDER OF THE ESTATE

5.21 Prisoners in the new Categories 1 - 3 would form only a small proportion of the prison population. Of a total of around 51,000, approximately 95 per cent would be in Categories 4, 5 and 6. These prisoners are accommodated in a variety of establishments.

5.22 Most prisoners enter the prison system through local prisons. The main purpose of these is to hold remand prisoners and transfer them, when sentenced, to training establishments. Most local prisons are situated in cities or towns but the prisoners may appear at Courts spread over a large geographical area. The local prison estate is generally old and is scarcely suited to the modern purpose. In recent years, particularly since the publication of the Woolf Report, accommodation has been improved and integral sanitation installed. The high levels of overcrowding, once a feature of these prisons, has been dramatically reduced. However, physical conditions often remain far from satisfactory. A 'model regimes' initiative has provided more positive activity for prisoners but many local prisons are still unable to provide the comprehensive programmes found in training establishments. Security and good order are extremely difficult to maintain.

Categories 4 and 5

5.23 Category 4 prisoners would be those now found in Category B Training Prisons and cellular Category C Prisons. These prisoners tend to have long sentences and are likely to be dangerous and keen to escape. For these reasons, they should be housed in closed, cellular prisons, with secure perimeters and buildings similar to those of a current Category B Training Prison.

5.24 Category 5 prisoners would represent one of the most difficult groups in the prison estate. They would tend to be young and serving short sentences, having committed less serious offences. Discussions with Governors indicated that the greatest threat lies in disturbances and riots. It was pointed out that inmates of this Category have not been susceptible to any form of discipline in their lives. Most have never had the opportunity to work and have been brought up to question authority as a matter of course. The problem has been exacerbated by the proliferation of drugs, causing considerable misery inside prisons and to prisoners' families. Gangs are formed which specialise in selling drugs and which practise intimidation, bullying and physical assaults. Prisoners in the new Category 5 are presently housed in campus style prisons on the basis of an assessment system developed 20 to 30 years ago. It is clear that, in the light of the current risk, enhanced security arrangements are needed for them.

5.25 Category 5 prisoner should, therefore, be held in establishments which are more secure than the current Category C, non-cellular prison. In particular, perimeter fences should be adequate and CCTV should be in place, to cover all vulnerable areas where bullying, intimidation and drug trading are likely to take place.

5.26 The Category 4 and 5 prisoners would cover a very wide spectrum. Some would be serving long sentences, others short; some would be mature and some volatile; but all would need to be occupied during their time in prison. It follows that Category 4 and 5 prisons must have a strong training element in their regimes. They must offer those prisoners who are willing to work, who want to earn a reasonable wage and who are not a control problem, the opportunity to enhance their rehabilitation prospects by working in a more normal environment.

Industrial Prisons

5.27 HM Chief Inspector of Prisons has supported the introduction of Industrial Prisons, which would clearly meet these requirements. An Industrial Prison is defined as an establishment where work comes first and leisure or educational activities are only available at the end of the working day. Where Industrial Prisons exist in European countries, the private sector, on occasion, has provided the capital, wages, materials and machinery: there is minimum cost to the public. Prisoners have the opportunity to help their families with savings, useful skills and the habit of work.

5.28 The Prison Service has attempted to run Industrial Prisons in the past. It has failed because of derisory wages; a feeling amongst prisoners that they were merely being used as cheap labour; and a sense of apathy in the workplace. Prisoners should be paid an acceptable wage, to encourage involvement in work. Out of higher wages, they should pay tax, National Insurance contributions, accommodation and food charges, victim support, family support and compulsory savings for release. If these were correctly balanced, there would be no question of lavish rewards. The right to work in an Industrial Prison should be regarded as a privilege to be earned by good behaviour and a co-operative attitude.

5.29 There may be resistance, from either an organised labour or political point of view, if it is seen that Industrial Prisons are putting at risk jobs outside the Service. For that reason, it may be wise to concentrate on import substitution. Goods now imported into the country from places where labour is cheap could be produced in Industrial Prisons without damaging home industries. Other grounds for concern, such as profiteering by private sector companies at prisoners' or public expense, would need to be carefully examined and handled.

5.30 Industrial Prisons are a sound proposition. They would not only contribute to security but would establish the habit of work and help to secure jobs for inmates after release. Advocates within the Service report frustration over the lack of progress in this field. Negative views are depressingly prevalent but it is self-evident that private sector executives will not wish to become involved with reluctant partners. Once faith and confidence are in place, an energetic public relations and marketing drive will be required, possibly using prominent and sympathetic businessmen as ambassadors. The concept of Industrial Prisons should be evaluated by the Prison Service as a matter of urgency, drawing on the recent work by private consultants.

5.31 Prisoners from any part of the Category 4 and 5 estate should be eligible to work in an Industrial Prison. They would earn this right by virtue of good behaviour and the recommendation of staff and Governors.

Category 6

5.32 Category 6 prisoners would be those who can be trusted in open conditions. The main purpose of the training regime in any prison is to prepare prisoners for release into the outside world. Some establishments have developed the role of preparing, for discharge, long-term prisoners near the end of their sentences. At present, there are several prisons and Units in prisons dedicated to this work, which focuses on the community and has close links with the caring agencies. Whilst they all aim to help with resettlement, they vary in the selection criteria applied and in the ways they operate.

5.33 One difficulty prevalent in open prisons is that some prisoners, who go into the community to work or see their families, come under considerable pressure from other prisoners to smuggle illicit items back to the prison. These pressures are often applied by prisoners who deal in drugs and are capable of extreme violence.

5.34 Open establishments have made an important contribution to the Service over the years. The experience of custody, without walls or bars at the windows, has assisted the rehabilitation of many offenders. The structured training programme inside these establishments, and the important part many have played in community life, have given them a special place in penal history.

5.35 Time, however, moves on and evidence has been given to the Inquiry that it is increasingly difficult to find suitable prisoners to fill the vacancies in open establishments. One likely reason for this is that Courts now have a wider range of options and the types of offender for whom open establishments were intended now receive non-custodial sentences. Another explanation is the deterioration in the general behaviour and quality of prisoners. Whilst hard to prove, this argument has sufficient force to make the Prison Service increasingly cautious about the use of open facilities.

5.36 Until recently, the general public has shown a tolerant attitude towards open prisons. However, recent escapes and the attendant publicity have created a less tolerant mood. Levels of absconding, which once attracted scant comment, are now regarded as unacceptable even though they have been reduced recently. Problems of drugs and alcohol are portrayed as little short of a public scandal.

5.37 Despite these problems, open establishments continue to have an important, albeit smaller, part to play in the Prison Service. Some should be retained in their present form but it does seem appropriate to regrade others to at least the current Category C standard. The very important resettlement work being done with long-term prisoners must be preserved and spread more widely through the prison system. Either some or all present open establishments could be used for this purpose. For these reasons, a review is recommended to assess the present open estate and to decide what is required for resettlement Units, what should be retained as open accommodation and what should be upgraded to new security standards.

Women prisoners

5.38 Opinion amongst informed pressure groups and many experienced Prison Service staff is that female prisoners should be treated differently to males. In general, women are imprisoned for less serious offences than men, their behaviour pattern in prison is different and they rarely riot. They frequently come from difficult circumstances and are given to bouts of depression and their form of protest is usually self-mutilation. A survey at one prison found 60 per cent of the women had been subject to sexual abuse and 80 per cent were victims of violence. Around one fifth of women in prison are foreign nationals, many of them imprisoned for drug smuggling and subject to deportation at the end of their sentences. This is the main group of women prisoners which needs an enhanced level of security. In addition, women inmates have expressed concern for their own security whilst housed in a predominantly male establishment.

5.39 The current prison estate does not provide an even geographical spread of places for women and many women are imprisoned far from home. For example, there is no female establishment in Wales. The problem is acute when the mothers of young families are imprisoned and it causes a great deal of distress. Provision for women who present an escape risk is poor and the regimes offered them are relatively limited. Many observers regard female prisoners as being worse off than their male counterparts, which cannot be right in a Service espousing equality of opportunity. Some women are being held in accommodation not appropriate to their security category and this must be rectified.

5.40 There is a clear requirement to provide focus to the particular problems posed by women in custody and ensure these problems receive proper recognition within the chain of command. The Inquiry believes that the women's Wings within male prisons should be closed as soon as is practicable and that all women prisoners should be housed in female prisons. In the longer term, there must be a thorough review of the estate, with the object of matching accommodation more closely to the needs of women prisoners. In principle, women should be held in small, self-contained Units in urban areas throughout England and Wales. The Units should provide the necessary levels of security and have incentive-based regimes. Former local authority hostels or other buildings, capable of being run as self-contained houses, are likely to provide the best model. All women's prisons should be placed under a single Area Manager, who would take responsibility for the totality of the female estate.

MANAGEMENT OF DISRUPTIVE PRISONERS

Uncontrollable prisoners

5.41 The prison population includes a number of prisoners who do not respond to the existing control mechanisms and become so disruptive that they make life unbearable for others. Whilst there are not many of them, their continuing presence in the prison estate is a constant threat to others and their disruptive influence is out of all proportion to their numbers.

5.42 Many of the recommendations in this Report are aimed at securing good behaviour from prisoners through incentives (see paras 5.60-85). The thrust of the recommendations is to make disruptive behaviour unattractive because it results in fewer privileges and facilities. Encouraging prisoners to do their best, rather than simply preventing them doing their worst, has to be the right way forward for a prison system in any civilised society. Unfortunately, there will always be those who fail to respond and who kick over the traces, despite the best efforts of staff to make prison life a tolerable training experience. Those in this hard core of persistent troublemakers create problems for themselves but, more significantly, for other prisoners and for staff. They form a disruptive element which seriously threatens the safety of others and the good order of the prisons.

5.43 Disruptive prisoners are not confined to any one security category, although the high security, long sentence group, in particular, contains some difficult inmates. Many have learned to be extremely manipulative and have long histories of violence, which intimidates others. Some have criminal associates who can be used to threaten the families of staff or other prisoners, undermining the efforts of the Service to control them. Currently, the Prison Service handles these disruptive prisoners in one of four ways. First, there are those who are allocated to two Control Review Committee (CRC) Units at Hull and Woodhill. Both Units are under-utilised and a number of prisoners who ought to be in them are not. The arrangements therefore represent an ineffective use of current resources and poor value for money.

5.44 Despite this under-utilisation of the CRC Units, a second group of disruptive prisoners, in excess of 100, is housed in Segregation Units across the prison estate. At the high risk end of the scale, these prisoners are so disruptive that they are put on a Continuous Assessment Scheme, which means that they take part in what has become known as the "merry-go-round". Those on the "merry-go-round" tend to move at frequent intervals, from prison to prison; in one well publicised case, a prisoner was moved 21 times in two years.

5.45 A third group of disruptive prisoners are those with a psychiatric condition who are presently housed in the CRC Unit at Parkhurst, which is a national resource. The disadvantages of this Unit are that it is on an island, with the attendant difficulties of moving prisoners across water; it is remote from the main population centres of England and Wales; and the current conditions are far from satisfactory, not least because the Unit cannot handle more than 18 inmates.

5.46 The fourth element consists of young, highly volatile prisoners with poor disciplinary records, many of whom are serving relatively short sentences and are found in the current Category C estate. These prisoners pose a control problem disproportionate to the crimes they have committed. Currently, they are controlled through transfers to local prisons or re-categorisation to Category B. Significant numbers of them end up in Segregation Units of Category C Training Prisons. This is wholly unsatisfactory. The Inquiry was pleased to note that the Prison Service now intends to examine the issue, under the 1995/96 Business Plan.

5.47 It is clear that the present arrangements do not adequately address the Service's control problems. The difficulties are not likely to go away, especially with society becoming more violent and with drug-related crime expanding. The portents point to the need for an imaginative solution that will take the Service forward into the 21st century. Put another way, the Inquiry believes that failure to produce a realistic resolution of the problems raised by these difficult prisoners will result in the Service having immense problems in carrying out its responsibilities.

5.48 The Prison Service requires an establishment or establishments to deal with:

- Those who are not mentally ill but whose behaviour has been thoroughly and maliciously disruptive.
- Disruptive inmates in need of psychiatric attention, including the small number of inmates who are so disturbed that it is necessary for several staff to be present whenever they are out of their cells.

5.49 For similar reasons to those outlined in the argument for a High Security Prison, it is highly desirable that the command and control of all these inmates should be concentrated rather than dispersed. This points to the establishment of a single Control Prison, preferably built on a green field site, to deal with prisoners with control problems.

5.50 The regime for prisoners without a psychiatric condition would be based upon a policy of 'bad behaviour gets you in; good behaviour gets you out'. The regime would be constructed on progressive lines. Prisoners would move between several regimes (three or more), starting with minimal privileges, restricted movement and little or no association with other inmates. Progress to other levels would be earned until, finally, the prisoners would have privileges more akin to a standard prison. A decision would be made at this stage about whether they should rejoin the mainstream. Behaviour would be continually assessed during a prisoner's stay.

5.51 The regime for disruptive inmates in need of psychiatric attention would be similar to that of Parkhurst C Wing.

Control Prison

5.52 The Control Prison would house around 200 inmates and its design would have the following main features:

- The Control Prison would have the same level of physical security as the High Security Prison and would contain similar security features. Thus prisoners in any security category could be accommodated.
- The construction of the living Units would vary in order to reflect the variety of regimes needed for a wide range of prisoner behaviour. For those receiving psychiatric treatment, there would be two Units, each housing ten patients, located near the hospital. For those who are very dangerously disturbed, there would be five suites for single occupation. These would be equipped with all the necessary medical facilities. In addition, there would be one Assessment Unit, containing 15 places.
- For those inmates who are not mentally ill, there would be seven Units. The buildings would reflect the different regimes, ranging from austere to near normality. These Units would provide 22 places

maximum per Unit and their configuration would aid movement between the regimes. To ensure continuity, each Unit would be managed by one group of staff.

- Whilst the size of Units throughout the prison would vary, all would be small and designed to help staff to acquaint themselves with inmates and provide good supervision. As in the High Security Prison, staff would be able to move between Units, using a corridor dedicated to their use.

- Staff facilities would be provided both inside and outside the perimeter.

- Multi-disciplinary staff resources would be available to support Unit staff and to provide a wide range of skills in dealing with difficult prisoners.

Figures 16-19 show: the proposed layout (Figure 16), plans of the ground and first floor levels of living Units (Figures 17 and 18) and a cross-section of a Psychiatric Living Unit (Figure 19).

Fig. 16 **Layout Principles - Control Prison - 200 Places**

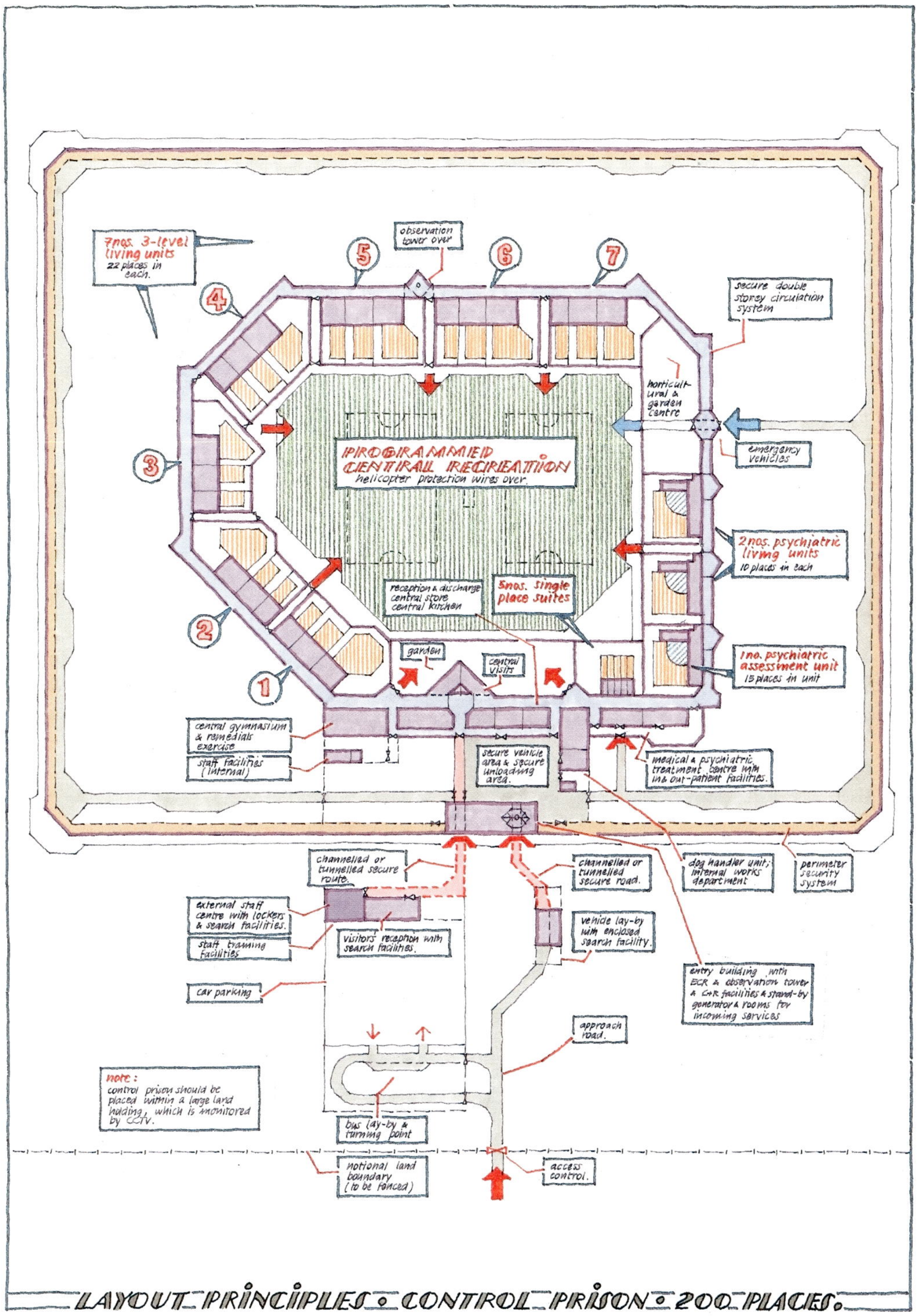

Fig. 17 **Control Prison - 3-Level Living Unit - Lower Level Plan**

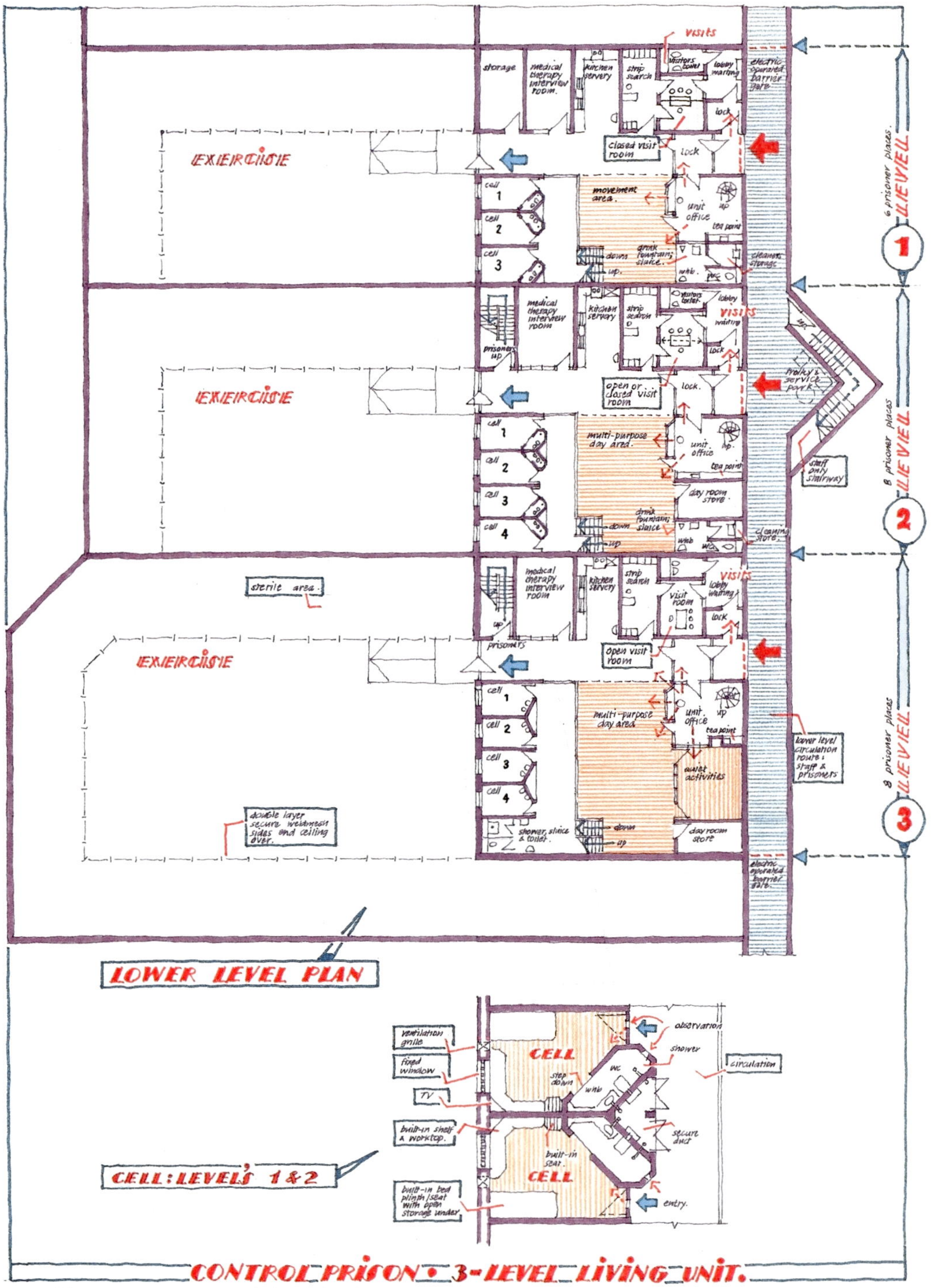

Fig. 18 **Control Prison - 3-Level Living Unit - Upper Level Plan**

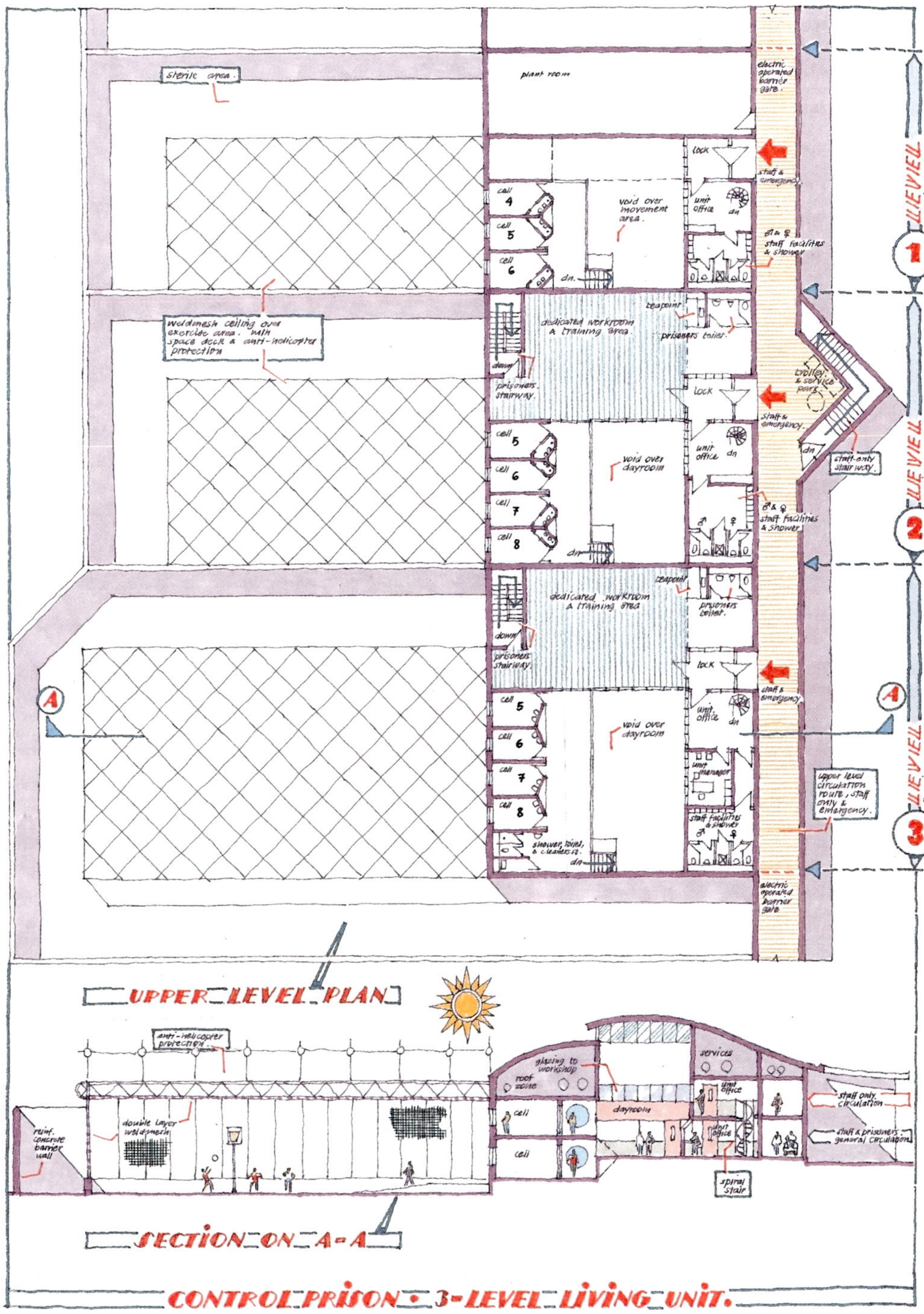

Fig. 19 **Control Prison - Psychiatric Living Unit**

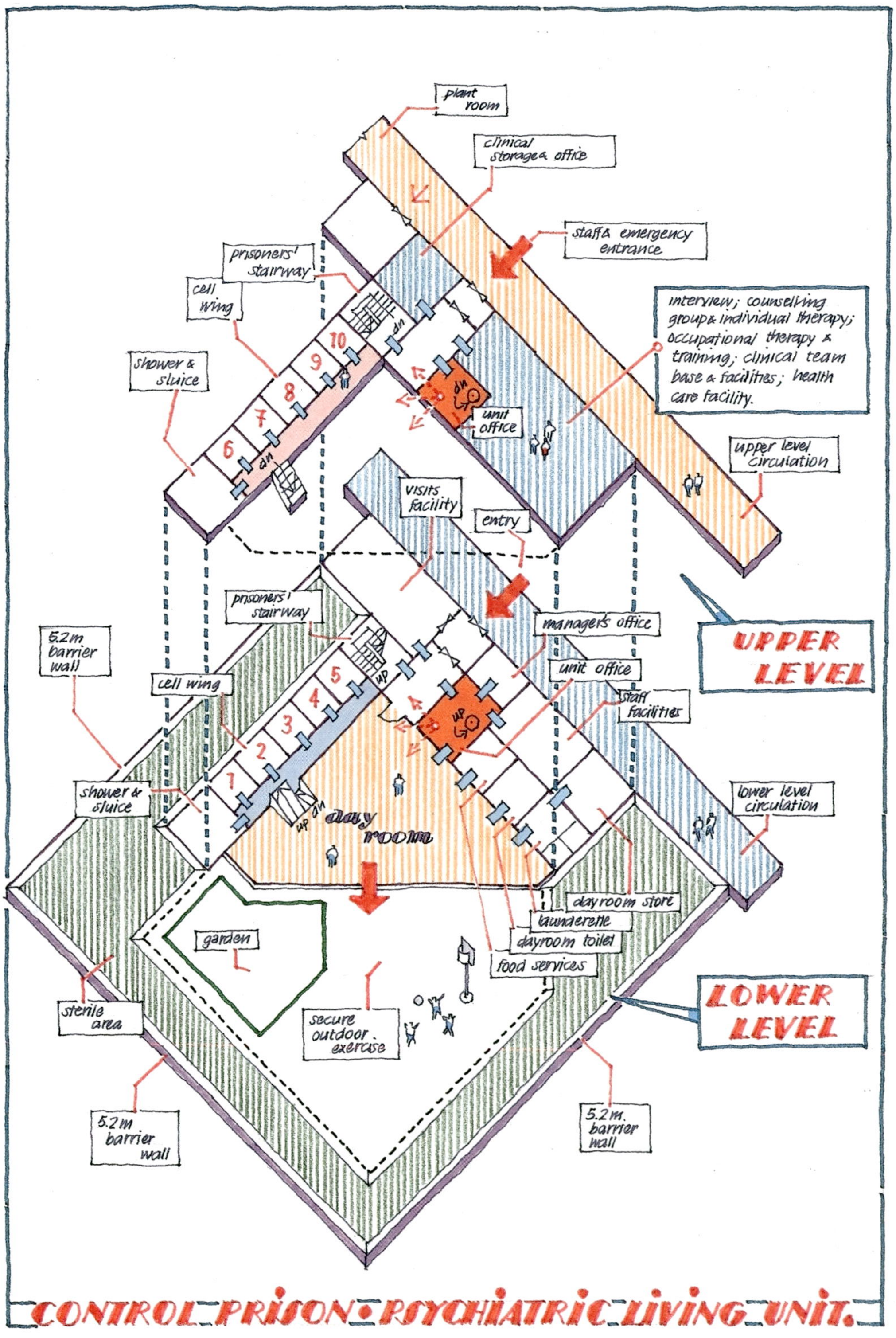

5.53 A site for the prison should be sought in the vicinity of other establishments in order to provide an opportunity for staff interchangeability.

5.54 The procedures associated with the Control Prison must be clear and published for the information of staff and prisoners. The criteria on which prisoners would be moved to the prison and the behaviour required to earn transfer out must be easily understood and seen as fair. Duty in the prison would be demanding and staff would need to be carefully selected and properly prepared for it. As with the High Security Prison, there must be a properly equipped centre for training in Control and Restraint (C&R), searching and interpersonal skills. It would be necessary to conduct a needs analysis to ensure the correct training is made available.

DYNAMIC SECURITY

5.55 In his much respected Home Office report, "A Sense of Direction", Ian Dunbar, a former Operational Director, explained the ways in which physical security is enhanced by activity and relationships in prisons:

> *"Individualism, relationship and activity come together in the widely shared concept of dynamic security. This approach to safety for the public (preventing prison escapes) and safety for the prison (internal control) recognises that both are only really possible through the relationship between staff and inmates. Dynamic security is knowing what is going on in a prison establishment, in addition to providing a safe and secure background against which the whole range of activity making up the life of a prison takes place."*

5.56 The Inquiry recognises the importance of dynamic security and acknowledges the work already undertaken with prisoner programmes. In the following paragraphs, a system of incentives is proposed which would considerably strengthen control by rewarding responsible behaviour.

Prisoner programmes

5.57 An essential element of security and control within prisons is the establishment of effective programmes for sentenced prisoners. Through these programmes, each inmate has his or her progress professionally administered by prison staff of all ranks and disciplines. There are two pillars to these programmes, the Personal Officer scheme and sentence planning. Prisoner programmes, well set up and properly administered, cover the whole inmate population of an establishment and involve all Prison Officers, in Wings or Units, as well as specialist staff, including psychologists, psychiatrists, probation officers, and education, workshop and PE instructors. Programmes embrace all aspects of daily life in an institution. They bring together, in a constructive way, staff and inmates and make the best use of the professional skills of Prison Service staff.

5.58 The appointment of Personal Officers, to deal with social, domestic and personal problems, is a vital element in building good working relationships between prisoners and staff. It helps inmates to feel valued, maintains stability and often provides good security intelligence. Sentence planning also has an important part to play because it provides a vehicle for target-setting and monitoring a prisoner's performance, thus encouraging positive attitudes.

5.59 Some excellent programmes exist and these models should be followed elsewhere. Every sentenced prisoner serving more than 12 months should be given a sentence plan and allocated a Personal Officer but the Inquiry found instances where this was not done. The value of this approach has been recognised by other Prison Services, which have also highlighted its potential effect on security. A report on the management of Canadian prisons stated:

> *"We feel strongly that good programmes contribute to good security and to the protection of society, both while the inmate is incarcerated and after release. At the same time we accept that good programmes can only be operated in a safe and secure environment."*

Incentives

5.60 The concept of incentives is one with which Prison Services throughout the world have been wrestling for many years. The idea of encouraging good behaviour and discouraging bad is a philosophy which runs through every strata of society and is the basis of parenting and education of the young. In the UK, Lord Woolf recognised the value of incentive schemes in his Report (para. 14.42):

> *"It seems to us incontrovertible that prisoners are likely to behave more responsibly, and to make the best use of their time in prison, if they feel that their responsibility and effort will be in some way rewarded."*

5.61 Regimes based on incentives are a sound foundation on which to balance custody and care, to establish positive co-existence between prisoners and staff and, more importantly, to rehabilitate or 'socialise' offenders for re-entry into normal life. This approach is widely used in other countries, although the level of sophistication varies. The common message from the countries visited by the Inquiry was that well thought out incentives are a spur to good, positive behaviour. They reduce the rate of relapse and give some hope for those facing long sentences, who otherwise feel that, however badly they behave, they have nothing to lose.

5.62 Life in prison was discussed with hundreds of inmates during visits by the Inquiry. The conclusion was drawn that there are six incentives and one disincentive (the removal of private cash) which might form the key elements in a positive, controlled regime. Each of these is discussed below.

(a) Earned early release (EER)

5.63 The discussions with prisoners indicated that the greatest incentive would be the chance to leave prison early. Arrangements currently in force in England and Wales are contained in Part II of the Criminal Justice Act, 1991, and came into force on 1st October 1992. Prisoners serving a sentence of under four years are released automatically at the half-way point but they remain 'at risk' until the end of their sentence. 'At risk' means that a Court dealing with a new offence could add all or part of the outstanding sentence to the new sentence. Prisoners serving over four years are eligible for parole (Discretionary Conditional Release) at the half-way point but release is automatic at the two-thirds point. They are similarly 'at risk' until the end of their sentence.

5.64 The key word is automatic. Early release is a right which can only be lost through 'Additional Days Awarded' (ADAs) for misconduct. This represents a very negative approach.

5.65 In some other countries, the minimum amount of sentence spent in prison is comparable with the 50 per cent which is normal in the UK. The difference is that the inmates have to earn every day of remission through good behaviour.

5.66 In England and Wales, prisoners have grounds for believing that ADAs will be cancelled as their release or parole date draws near. They are therefore frequently difficult and disruptive in the early part of their sentence and only begin to improve once they come near to the half-way mark. A prisoner serving 20 years has no inducement to behave well for the first eight years or so. The change can then often be so dramatic that the Service congratulates itself, believing that the treatment and help provided is reaping rewards.

5.67 A more positive approach is needed, under which early release is a privilege, earned a day at a time, through regular good conduct. Visits to prisons in the United States of America disclosed that prisoners, by a combination of good behaviour and good work attendance, were able to earn remission from their sentences of as much as 15 days per month. The Inquiry found an advanced penal system in Catalonia which had been granted virtual independence from the rest of Spain in this respect. In Catalonia, two full days of work earned one day's remission. A refinement here was that inmates were not allowed to work at first. They had, by good conduct, to earn the right, initially to half a day's work and then to a full day's work. Work was thus seen as a privilege and a work ethic is established at the outset of the sentence. The Inquiry was told by a prison psychologist that, after a period of time, this behavioural change can lead to a cognitive change of attitude. The Catalan system produces a very high degree of work attendance, with prisoners behaving exceptionally well. Any remission not earned day by day is lost for good, with the result that inmates are always anxious to maintain a good record. Life in prison is constructive from the outset and work for Prison Officers more rewarding.

5.68 Two and a half months after the Inquiry began, a Prison Service discussion paper formed a draft submission suggesting two options for EER. One would entail retaining automatic release at the half-way point but allowing inmates to earn even earlier release through good behaviour. The alternative would oblige the prisoner to 'earn' the period normally spent 'in the community' (ie the remainder of sentence from the half-way or two-thirds point).

5.69 The paper points out the legislative barriers to the first option and the potential accommodation problems arising from the second. The recommendation which emerges is that neither option should be adopted immediately but that further work should be carried out. The principle of EER appears to be accepted but only as a long-term objective. The paper admits a major difficulty, in that work and training facilities are still not available in all establishments so it is impossible, at this stage, to produce fair and uniform opportunities for inmates. That is a sad commentary on Prison Service management so many years after purposeful activity was acknowledged as a primary goal. The Inquiry does not accept that a workable scheme of purposeful activity cannot be readily devised, a view confirmed by discussions with operationally experienced staff.

5.70 The Prison Service paper is moving in the right direction with the second option but it could go further. If every day by which release was brought forward had to be earned, as in some other countries, a cornerstone of good behaviour throughout the period of the sentence would be laid. This is fundamental to the security of our prisons and the idea should therefore be taken forward as a matter of urgency. A simple scheme, whereby each day on which a prisoner is judged to have participated fully and willingly, with good behaviour, in a mandatory activity, would earn one day's early release, is highly attractive. As at present, the offender would remain 'at risk' after release, until the end of sentence.

(b) Work and wages

5.71 Sentenced prisoners are required to work. During visits to prisons by the Inquiry, it became clear that the work available is seen by inmates as boring and irrelevant because it seldom benefits the prisoners and does not relate to the work to which they aspire after release. In one workshop, prisoners were sewing underpants for a few pounds a week, work which they found especially unrewarding. The Inquiry sees the need for an internal Prison Service economy, in which prisoners make goods for consumption in establishments, but believes more could be done to attract a greater variety of profitable work.

5.72 The concept of Industrial Prisons has already been discussed. Other prisons should also offer meaningful work with realistic wages. This would enable prisoners to pay their way in prison, save a little in preparation for release and avoid being a financial burden on their families. It would also assist security and control by giving prison staff the opportunity of employing financial sanctions against those who do not conform.

5.73 In some establishments, Governors have explored the practicalities of bringing in quality work for prisoners. A few have been successful but, generally, it is felt there is no real point in pursuing these initiatives because profits made go to the Treasury, under normal Government accounting rules, and are lost to the establishment. This policy should be reversed so that prisons gain financial benefit from their commercial enterprises. Accountability for financial management should be devolved to Governors in order that product ranges can be developed and wages increased. Although realistic wage schemes can be notoriously difficult to introduce, because of tax and state benefit implications, ways can be found to overcome these problems. Commercial advice should be available in Headquarters to assist Governors in making prisons more self-financing.

5.74 The payment of higher wages to prisoners raises difficult political, moral and social questions. The public might not wish to see prisoners in employment and earning reasonable wages at a time of high unemployment. The policy could, however, help to create a more settled prison population and improve security and control.

(c) Removal of private cash

5.75 The present opportunities for prisoners to receive and use private cash starkly highlight the difference between the 'haves' and the 'have nots' within the prison population. It cannot be right for some prisoners to have available to them sums of money (sometimes many thousands of pounds) which can be used to buy a wide range of goods, including drugs, whilst others have nothing. "Money equals power" is an alarming truism on the prison landings. Drugs are the root cause of many problems in prisons. Staff and prisoners described to the Inquiry the intimidation, bullying and assaults which are associated with drug abuse and the lengths to which addicts and dealers will go in order to obtain supplies. Prisoners temporarily released into the community, and visitors to prisons, frequently come under pressure to smuggle drugs; and some families feel obliged to provide money to sustain the habits of relatives inside. Addicts build up debts with their suppliers, which are repaid through favours, such as administering beatings to other debtors, or by families, who have to commit crimes to obtain the money. This cycle of criminal activity poses serious problems of control and security.

5.76 The recommendations contained in the Working Party Report on Incentives and Privileges included a plan to phase out the availability of private cash which has, until recently, been unlimited in Special Security Units within Dispersal Prisons. In the longer term, the Prison Service proposes to phase out completely the use of unearned private cash by convicted prisoners. This step will be welcomed by Prison Officers and will prevent many prisoners having large sums of money, possibly the product of criminal activity and used to finance the drug habit. The proposal will help to eliminate the difference between the 'haves' and the 'have nots' and should eventually lead to a system where the only cash available to inmates will be earned money. It is of interest that all prisoners with whom this matter was discussed agreed with the proposal, provided that they could earn a meaningful wage themselves.

(d) Visits

5.77 The prisoners placed enormous value on visits as the prime source of contact with family and the outside world. The importance of visits, for both humanitarian and security reasons, must not be underestimated, especially as a prisoner who is worried about family matters is more likely to contemplate escape than one who can discuss concerns with relatives.

5.78 The starting point should be a mandatory minimum entitlement to visits which takes account of the effect on family members. The Prison Service fully supports this view. Additional visits, with frequency, duration and quality (eg contact allowed) as variables, would be an excellent incentive to good behaviour. The problems presently experienced, of clashes with work sessions and other disruptions of establishment routine, need to be consciously avoided in any incentive scheme.

(e) Telephone calls

5.79 Prisoners consider telephone calls to friends and relatives as an important form of contact and prize them highly. As with visits, a mandatory entitlement to minimum standards is necessary. Telephone calls, however, also provide a suitable element for an incentive scheme, with the variables being frequency and duration. Currently, prisoners can buy phonecards, subject to fixed limits. This system gives rise to a market in phonecards, which encourages disorder. In an effort to overcome the problem, the Prison Service plans to install new technology in all prisons which will allow inmates to use a PIN number. Prisoners will be able to call only approved numbers.

(f) Television in cells

5.80 Discussions with prisoners indicated a degree of intimidation and bullying in prisons far in excess of that indicated by other sources. The drive for time out of cell and free association has accentuated this problem, producing the ingredients for boredom and confrontation between inmates. The greater the confrontation, the more likely the riot or serious disturbance; hence the need to find ways and means of reducing potentially explosive situations.

5.81 One solution would be the introduction of TV in cells. To the general public, TV in cells might appear a luxury or, at least, an undue recreational privilege. If introduced in a planned and controlled manner, however, it would be possible to limit the programmes, as well as the total amount of TV time, available to each prisoner. The extent of access to TV would then become another variable in the incentive and sanction package.

5.82 The first stage of earning the right to TV in cells might be to earn the right to electricity, with the authorities controlling the power supply to each cell. This would allow the individual use of radios, shavers and other minor electrical appliances. In Scotland, prisoners have electricity in cells and are allowed to have such items as their own electric kettle. The fact that a prisoner can make himself a hot drink during the night is much valued and has a calming influence.

5.83 The next stage would be to earn limited access to TV. The control over programmes allowed would permit a high proportion of viewing time to be devoted to information, news or educational subject matter. It would also allow the authorities to communicate (directly or through pre-recorded video) with inmates on issues affecting the Service. This could include an induction video, which explained clearly the incentive and sanction system and the alternative regimes available. Similarly, videos could be produced on combatting drugs and AIDS or to advertise the availability of counselling. The Inquiry commends this approach.

(g) Home leave

5.84 Another important incentive for a prisoner is the opportunity to earn the right to a home visit. Such a privilege can sustain hope within an inmate for a long time and can be a positive inducement to good behaviour. When such visits are successful, they help to reunite families and assist in preparing prisoners for re-entry into society. Failures bring condemnation of the Service and adversely distort the escape statistics, causing considerable embarrassment.

5.85 Despite the many problems, the positive aspects of home leave are worth further investment, for it is a powerful incentive. The Service should explore ways of increasing the availability of home leave to inmates. The Prison Service should not be discouraged from pursuing this general policy because of failures to return to establishments; but when they do occur, firm sanctions should be applied to those who have abused the privilege.

MANAGING THE PRISON ESTATE

High risk prisoners and uncontrollable prisoners

5.86 At present, sentenced prisoners in the three sub-divisions of Category A are held, with some of the more dangerous Category B prisoners, in six Dispersal Prisons. The Dispersal Prisons are currently managed by two Operational Directors and five Area Managers, all based at Prison Service Headquarters (see Appendix K). For prisoners posing the greatest security threat, these organisational arrangements appear fragmented and ineffectual.

5.87 It is crucial that the high security estate is managed as a whole rather than piecemeal. The interpretation of policy and the implementation of procedures must be carefully orchestrated to ensure consistently high standards. The special nature of the work of these prisons, and the likely political and public sensitivity to any operational problems, make it necessary for them to have direct and dedicated representation at Prisons Board level. Individual Area Managers, with their wide variety of establishments, cannot be expected to give this important part of the estate the attention it needs. It follows that an Operational Director should be appointed with the sole task of managing the High Security Prison, the Control Prison and the six Dispersal Prisons. This Director should be a full member of the Board, have operational experience as the Governor of a Dispersal Prison and have no substantial work other than the management of these prisons. It is important that these prisons are staffed by Governor Grades and Prison Officers with Dispersal Prison experience. They will have to be rotated regularly and not left for protracted periods to deal with the most dangerous and difficult prisoners in the prison estate. The skills, experience and flexibility required can only be provided by HM Prison Service. There should be no question of contracting out the High Security Prison, the Control Prison or the Dispersal Prisons for the foreseeable future.

The remainder of the estate

5.88 Category B, C and D prisoners are the responsibility of the two Operational Directors and of 15 Area Managers, also based at Prison Service Headquarters (as shown in Appendix K). There are two major problems with these organisational arrangements. First, the span of control of Operational Directors is too great, a view shared by the Operational Directors themselves. Second, it is difficult to see how Area Managers can effectively control their areas while based in London.

5.89 Note has been taken by the Inquiry of work currently being undertaken by the Prison Service relating to the size and number of areas in England and Wales. In particular, the concept of community prisons, as recently introduced into Kent, is supported by the Inquiry. This involves the allocation of inmates to prisons within range of their homes, as recommended in the Woolf Report in 1990, which stated that:

> *"Where this is practical, prisons should be community prisons sited within reasonable proximity to, and having close connections with, the community with which the prisoners they hold have their closest links."*

5.90 A 1993 paper by HM Chief Inspector of Prisons, "Doing Time or Using Time", saw a conflict between this desirable goal and the need to prepare inmates better for release to normal life:

> *"The narrow definition of a community prison is that prisoners should be confined as closely as possible to their home environments; but if imprisonment is to be about preparing prisoners for release, then a wider definition and strategy is needed. This must be based on the realisation that the prison population consists of many groups with widely differing needs. A*

regime driven Prison Service has to respond to the needs of the groups in different ways. To do this prison establishments need to design regimes which are integrated across the system."

5.91 From this paper, the White Paper entitled "Custody, Care and Justice" and Lord Woolf's Report, emerged the concept of a community prison cluster. The rationale, as explained in the Corporate Plan, 1994-97, is to:

> *"... develop the prison estate as far as we can, on the basis of community clusters. Within each geographical area, there should be a sufficient 'mix' of establishments to allow most prisoners to be held within reasonable distance of their homes at an establishment which provides appropriate security and regimes."*

5.92 The Service has proposed that there should be 13 regional 'clusters', each one of which should form a management entity. Within each group, there would be a sufficient range of regimes to accommodate most types of background and need. Inmates would progress through establishments and regimes according to attitudes, behaviour and work records. This would ultimately give Area Managers and Governors the tools with which to deliver sentence planning and inmate management, in response to a clear policy laid down by top management and endorsed by Ministers.

5.93 This initiative is supported by the Inquiry with two modifications. First, high security establishments, covering new Categories 1 - 3, should be removed from the cluster concept, because of their extreme sensitivity, and managed directly by an Operational Director, as discussed earlier. Second, women's prisons, because of the specific and unique considerations also referred to earlier, should be managed by one Area Manager covering the whole country.

5.94 Leaving aside the high security establishments, under the command of one Director, there would be 12 groups of prisons, including the women's group. It is proposed that these should be organised into three Directorates, each headed by a Board member. Each Directorate would consist of four groups or 'Areas' and the Area Managers should have sufficient staff to manage the group. Each Area (with the exception of women's prisons) would form a cluster, containing a range of establishments including:

- Training Prisons of Categories 4 and 5 (including Industrial Prisons).
- Young Offender Institutions.
- Prisons with remand facilities.
- Resettlement Units of Category 6.

This structure is shown in Figure 20.

Fig. 20 **Proposed Board Structure**

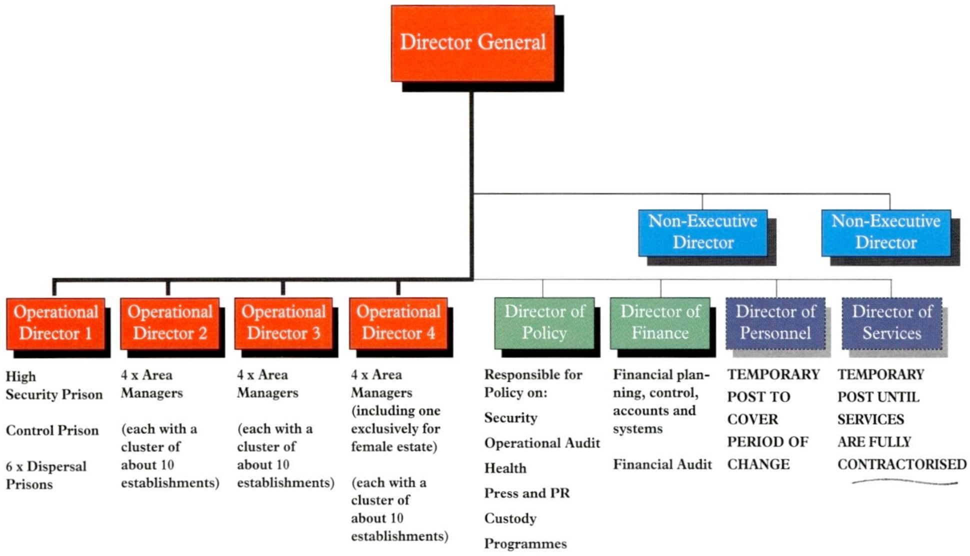

5.95 As outlined in paragraph 3.105, this structure would increase the number of Operational Directors from two to four, reducing their spans of command and putting substantial extra operational weight onto the Board and therefore enhancing security across the Prison Service. It would end the predominance of functional interests and ensure that functional Directors do not have undue influence in Board deliberations. Above all, it would ensure that the Director General could not be isolated from vital operational matters.

ACCREDITATION

5.96 In recent years, the Prison Service has considered the accreditation of establishments but, as yet, taken no firm steps towards it. Accreditation would require each establishment to hold a certificate, awarded following the objective measurement of performance against approved national standards. Where a prison failed to meet the required standard, the certificate would be withdrawn and a notice of improvement served. If the improvements were not then delivered within the required timescale, sanctions would follow.

5.97 Accreditation is a way of improving standards. The Prison Service already has security audit systems capable of measuring performance against objective criteria. It would be a simple step to move to security accreditation. The necessary information, including comment from the Area Manager, might be provided to the relevant Operational Director, who would grant the certificate or issue an improvement order. Later, the system could be extended to include accreditation of the standards in the manual "Operating Standards." With the introduction of a national coding of operational standards in April 1994 and an Audit Team operating independently of the operational line, the Prison Service has taken the first steps towards accreditation of establishments and should continue this work as a matter of urgency.

ROLE OF THE INSPECTORATE

5.98 The current role of HM Chief Inspector of Prisons, in England and Wales, is to report to the Secretary of State on prisons inspected, placing particular emphasis on the treatment of prisoners and conditions in prisons. Whilst the Secretary of State may refer other matters to the Chief Inspector, for consideration during an inspection, the Chief Inspector at present has no security role.

5.99 To reinforce the central importance of security, and to complement the internal security audits and proposed prison accreditation system, the Inquiry recommends that the role of the Chief Inspector be extended to include security issues and that he be provided with staff for this purpose.

CONCLUSIONS

5.100 This Section proposes a new Board structure with four Operational Directors, all of whom should be Prison Service professionals. It proposes a new categorisation system for prisoners and highlights the need to put the command and control of the most dangerous categories under a single Operational Director. Two new prisons are recommended, one to house the current Exceptional and High Risk prisoners and the second to house those prisoners who are deemed uncontrollable within the normal prison system. Standard Risk prisoners would be held in the current Dispersal estate. The remaining prisons would be grouped into 11 clusters, each under an Area Manager, with an additional Area Manager taking responsibility for the totality of the women's prison estate. Three Operational Directors at Board level would control four Area Managers each. The roles of the Functional Directors are outlined in Section 3.

5.101 The Section also proposes the development of incentives schemes and of the Industrial Prison concept. Incentives and privileges should be earned by good behaviour and the Service needs to give further thought to earned early release and meaningful work and wages. Visits and telephone calls are other incentives to good behaviour, as would be the introduction of electricity and subsequently television into cells. The removal of private cash should follow the introduction of meaningful work. The need for self-respect and contact with the outside world are two very important aspects of the prisoner psyche. If these needs can be satisfied, within the basic security requirements, improved prisoner behaviour, greater control and less likelihood of disturbances should follow.

5.102 The Prison Service has no accreditation system in force and therefore has no means of measuring the security effectiveness of individual establishments. The recent introduction of an audit team, under the Director of Security, is a step in the right direction but this initiative must now be pursued vigorously throughout the Service.

RECOMMENDATIONS (SECURITY - THE WAY FORWARD)

102 The Prison Service should introduce a new interim categorisation system as soon as possible.
(Paras. 5.4-5)
[See recommendations 38 and 103]

103 The Prison Service should further refine the system, drawing on the work of Professor David Canter.
(Para. 5.7)
[See recommendations 38 and 102]

104 Prisoners in new Categories 1 and 2 should be housed in a new purpose-built High Security Prison.
(Paras. 5.14-16)

105 Prisoners in the new Category 3 should be housed in the existing Dispersal system.
(Paras. 5.17-18)

106 Parkhurst should be downgraded to become an establishment for prisoners in the new Category 4 as soon as possible and should be replaced in the present Dispersal (Category 3) estate by a more suitable establishment, perhaps Belmarsh Prison.
(Para. 5.18)
[See recommendation 40]

107 In the long term, subject to revised arrangements for remand hearings (see recommendation 98), remand prisoners in the new Categories 1 and 2 should be held in the proposed High Security Prison when awaiting trial. During trial, they should be held in the High Security Prison, if it is geographically convenient, in an SSU within the Dispersal system or in in a small number of suitable establishments across the country.
(Para. 5.19)

108 The Prison Service should provide suitable accommodation for high risk women prisoners and young offenders.
(Para. 5.20)

109 Prisoners in the new Category 4 should be housed in closed, cellular prisons with secure perimeters.
(Para. 5.23)

110 Prisoners in the new Category 5 should be housed in the present Category C, non-cellular establishments with adequate perimeter security and CCTV coverage of vulnerable areas.
(Para. 5.25)

111 The Prison Service should evaluate the concept of Industrial Prisons as a matter of urgency. Prisoners from any part of the new Category 4 and 5 estate should be eligible to work in them. They would earn this right by virtue of good behaviour and the recommendation of staff and Governors.
(Paras. 5.27-31)

112 The Prison Service should undertake a review to assess the present open estate and to decide what is required for resettlement Units, what should be retained as open accommodation and what should be upgraded to new security standards.
(Paras. 5.32-37)

113 Women's prisons should be the responsibility of one Area Manager. All women prisoners should be housed in women's prisons. In the longer term, there should be a thorough review of the female prisoners' estate.
(Paras. 5.38-40)

114 A Control Prison should be established for particularly disruptive prisoners including disruptive prisoners who are mentally ill.
(Paras. 5.48-54)

115 Prisoner programmes should be adopted nationally. Every sentenced prisoner serving more than 12 months should have a sentence plan and should be allocated a Personal Officer.
(Para 5.59)

116 Early release should be a privilege earned through good behaviour and the Prison Service initiative on this matter should be taken forward urgently.
(Paras. 5.67-70)

117 All prisons should offer meaningful work and wages. Prisons should be allowed to keep the profits from their commercial activities and commercial advice should be available to Governors.
(Paras. 5.71-74)
[See recommendation 45]

118 Private cash should be phased out.
(Paras. 5.75-76)

119 There must be a mandatory minimum entitlement to visits which takes account of the need to retain family links. Additional visits can be used as incentives to good behaviour.
(Paras. 5.77-78)

120 Telephone privileges should feature in an incentive scheme.
(Para. 5.79)

121 Television in cells could provide a calming influence and a powerful incentive to good conduct. It could also be used for educational and communication purposes. The right to this privilege should be earned by good behaviour, once the prisoner has earned the right to electricity in the cell.
(Paras. 5.80-83)

122 The Prison Service should explore ways of increasing the availability of home leave and apply firm sanctions to those who abuse the privilege.
(Paras. 5.84-85)

123 The high security estate should be managed as a whole rather than piecemeal. An Operational Director should be appointed with the sole task of managing the High Security Prison, the Control Prison and the six Dispersal Prisons. This Director should be a full member of the Prisons Board, have operational experience as the Governor of a Dispersal Prison and have no substantial work other than the management of these prisons. The High Security, Control and Dispersal Prisons should remain in the public sector.
(Paras. 5.86-87)

124 The remainder of the prison estate should be organised into 11 clusters, each cluster working to an Area Manager, supported by sufficient staff to run the Area. The 12th Area Manager would control the women's estate.
(Paras. 5.89-94)

125 An Operational Director at Board level should control no more than four Area Managers. The number of Operational Directors should be increased from the current two to four, reducing their span of control, putting substantial extra operational weight onto the Board and enhancing security across the Prison Service.
(Paras. 5.94-95)

126 The Prison Service must introduce, as a matter of urgency, an accreditation system which would require each establishment to hold a certificate, awarded following the objective measurement of performance against approved national standards. Where an establishment's performance failed to meet the required standard, the certificate would be withdrawn and sanctions would follow.
(Paras. 5.96-97)

127 The role of HM Chief Inspector of Prisons should be extended to include security issues and he should be provided with staff for this purpose.
(Para. 5.99)

SECTION 6 : CONCLUDING REMARKS

6.1 As 1994 drew to a close, the Prison Service should have been reeling in the aftermath of a devastating period, with the uproar over the Whitemoor escape still ringing in the ears of staff. It would not have been unreasonable to expect the whole Service to have entered 1995 with an absolute determination to apply the lessons of Whitemoor across the prison estate. The Service might also have been expected to put in place, once and for all, the proper practices already promulgated in the Manual on Security but which the Woodcock Report had shown to be honoured in the breach. Any such aspirations were to be short-lived for on 3rd January the Parkhurst escape occurred.

6.2 Despite every effort to prevent them, escapes from prison establishments will occur from time to time. The status of Parkhurst as a high security prison, however, made this escape unacceptable. The fact that all the basic weaknesses of Whitemoor, which had been so clearly identified by the Woodcock Enquiry, reappeared at Parkhurst, with other failings, makes the escape inexcusable.

6.3 Section 2 graphically illustrates the failures and omissions at Parkhurst which allowed the escape to occur and which brought condemnation on and despair to the Service. At the same time, Frederick West who was in custody at Winson Green, Birmingham, on charges of multiple murders, committed suicide; and there were riots at Everthorpe Prison on Humberside over drugs problems. The combined effect of these incidents was a deluge of damaging publicity. The chain of disasters has produced a Service in which morale is low, with ordinary Prison Officers feeling devastated and unfairly treated. They want to do well and are willing to work hard but need direction and visible leadership to take them forward.

6.4 The many shortcomings at Parkhurst poignantly illustrate how far short the Service has fallen of reasonable public expectations in security matters. The poor practices revealed have led to the recommendations in this Report and there is a desperate need for the Service to look critically and objectively at all its procedures. It became very evident to the Inquiry that there was a vast difference in the perception of the Prisons Board and the reality at establishment level. The Board rarely discussed operational matters and, in consequence, the fundamental and extremely dangerous security weaknesses found by the Inquiry were obscured by the plethora of management initiatives outlined in Appendix L. A change of ethos at Board level is therefore essential and an increase to four in the number of Operational Directors with Prison Governor experience is imperative, because the current span of their commands is far too great. The operational chain of command should be the core of the business, with Area Managers playing a much enhanced role.

6.5 In its Salmon response, the Prison Service has submitted its own assessment of its achievements since it became an Agency on 1st April 1993 (see Appendix I). Much progress has been made over care for prisoners and the performance of the Board in bringing about better sanitary conditions and reducing over-crowding is most commendable. The quality of life in prisons, for both inmates and staff, has been improved and, in many cases, establishments visited by the Inquiry were under control and running well, despite the deficiencies outlined in this Report. Reference has been made in the Report to the need for prison establishments to maintain a balance of custody and care, with control playing a key role in keeping these elements in equilibrium. If the emphasis is placed too heavily either way or if there is neglect of any one element, including control, the result is tension within the prison. The embarrassing escapes from Whitemoor and Parkhurst show that the balance had been lost.

6.6 Throughout the Inquiry, there were complaints about the amount of paperwork arising in every corner of the Service. The proliferation of paper has reached epidemic proportions and there is a crying need for a simplification strategy. Any organisation which boasts one Statement of Purpose, one Vision, five Values, six Goals, seven Strategic Priorities, and eight KPIs, without any clear correlation between them, is producing a recipe for total confusion and exasperation amongst those undertaking a most difficult and dangerous task on behalf of the general public. People and their actions are far more important than paper. This philosophy should never be forgotten.

6.7 The fact that so much is wrong with the Prison Service appears to be finally dawning. Since the start of the Inquiry, a series of audits has confirmed that Whitemoor and Parkhurst were not aberrations of the norm but symptomatic of the practices in place in similar establishments throughout the country. The pity is that it has taken recent catastrophes to produce such obvious supervisory and audit procedures.

6.8 The Report is littered with recommendations for a more humanitarian approach to prisoners. These touch upon community clusters, Industrial Prisons and the management of women prisoners. A large number of the recommendations arise directly from discussions with both Officers and inmates and, if implemented, should assist to take the Service forward, with rehabilitation the ultimate goal. It is the humanitarian argument which has led the Inquiry to recommend that all visits should be open, with two exceptions. These are visits to Exceptional Risk prisoners (Category 1) and to those whose behaviour justifies the temporary withdrawal of the open visit privilege.

6.9 It is recognised that some of the recommendations will cause political difficulties. The need for both the Control and the High Security Prisons has been carefully thought out and the Control Prison is essential if the "merry-go-round", constantly shifting the most disruptive prisoners from pillar to post, is to end. Whilst the present practices are understandable they are positively dangerous and few will lament their discontinuance. It is anticipated that the media may well see such security prisons as the reincarnation of a prison on an island in the south west of the United States of America or the modern equivalent of such a fortress. Nothing could be further from the truth for it is a British solution to a long-standing problem and deserves deeper consideration. The management and control of the most dangerous and disruptive prisoners in the system must have the top priority. They must remain in the public sector and must be the responsibility of a single Operational Director at Board level.

6.10 Television in cells will be seen by many as an unwarranted luxury. It is essential equipment for all the reasons explained in the Report and is strongly supported by everyone who knows the business of maintaining control. The fact that so many other countries have already gone down this road is proof positive of its advantages.

6.11 The recommendation on re-categorisation of prisoners, using a less subjective and more scientifically-based formula than at present, is considered essential. Throughout the Inquiry, there were suggestions that categorisations were decided according to the vacancies in particular prisons. No evidence was found to substantiate this assertion but it would be of benefit to the Service if both Officers and prisoners could understand how such decisions are reached.

6.12 The rewards for good behaviour, outlined throughout the Report, should be attractive to prisoners. Many incentives to earn privileges and even reductions in sentences are suggested. However, the privilege must be dependent on good behaviour and not granted automatically on entering prison. It is recognised that some prisoners will still misbehave and attempt to disrupt the lives of the majority. For such prisoners, there are special sanctions, including the Control Prison, aimed at producing a change in behaviour but intended, above all, to protect those who simply want to serve their sentence in the most constructive way possible.

6.13 The costs of implementing the recommendations contained in the Report are set out at Appendix Q. What must be recognised is that a window of opportunity is open at this time. Additional prisons are already in the planning pipeline and the cost of these can be partly offset against additional expenditure. The cost of Prison Service failure to other Services within the Criminal Justice System, must be taken into account, particularly police, probation and Court costs. The proposals in the Report are worthy of serious debate.

6.14 The Inquiry has studied reports on previous escapes and similar problems. The words, *"if only they had implemented it"*, echoed constantly. The Inquiry hopes that this Report does not become yet another such document to be regurgitated in the future by others with similar terms of reference.

what about Radzinowicz?

6.15 It must be appreciated that, unless security measures are in place which can be managed with confidence, then any hope of progress towards humanitarian objectives is pious. The Prison Service must fulfil its primary function of keeping in custody those committed to its care by the Courts. The escapes from Parkhurst and Whitemoor have revealed considerable lapses in security which violate the excellent set of rules provided in the Manual on Security. The Service must now get the basics right, including staff training, for it can ill afford another episode which erodes the very foundation of a long established and respected Service. The rules are in place. What is now needed is the resolve to abide by them. There is an abundance of excellent people within the Prison Service whose most fervent wish is to do a good and worthwhile job. They are yearning to be led to better things. Although much has been done to improve the corporate planning within the Service, this Inquiry has starkly illustrated the need to address urgently shortcomings in leadership, operations and security.

SECTION 7: CONSOLIDATED RECOMMENDATIONS

STRUCTURE

7.1 The operational chain of command should be the core of the business. Functional activities should play a supporting role. The number of layers in the structure should be minimised. (Para. 3.75) [**Recommendation 68**]

7.2 Service structure should deliver the right messages to the organisation. The Board should be re-structured to strengthen operations:

(a) An Operational Director at Board level should control no more than four Area Managers. Operational Directors should have previous experience as a governing Governor. The number of Operational Directors should be increased from two to four, reducing their span of control, putting substantial extra operational weight onto the Board and enhancing security across the Prison Service. They should be in the chain of command in emergency situations.

(b) Responsibility for policy at Board level should be vested in one Policy Director, with operational experience gained, ideally, from within the Prison Service.

(c) The Head of Health Care should report to the Policy Director and need attend Board meetings only when medical matters are discussed.

(d) The Finance Director should be a professional, with financial experience gained in an operational environment.

(e) The Director of Personnel appointment should be reviewed within the next three years, after devolution of personnel matters to operational directorates, areas and establishments, when responsibility for personnel policy at Board level could pass to the Policy Director, supported by a professional personnel manager.

(f) Services should be contractorised by competitive tendering, with contracts renewable only if standards are met. The Director post might then be reviewed.

(g) The number of non-Executive Directors should be reviewed.

(Paras. 3.92, 3.100-114 and 5.94-95) [**Recommendations 72 and 125**]

SERVICE MANAGEMENT

7.3 The Service Statement of Purpose should be clarified, to make custody the primary purpose. (Paras. 3.35-40) [**Recommendation 62**]

7.4 The Board should review its approach to Key Performance Indicators, to reinforce the main objectives of the Service and to ensure meaningful and valid interpretation:

(a) "Escapes" is too negative an indicator on its own and should be supplemented by indicators that show progress towards preventing escapes.

(b) Figures for assaults should show percentage changes separately for assaults on staff, inmates and others.

(c) Greater care should be taken to monitor the way "purposeful activity" data is captured, to prevent exaggeration and ensure credibility.

(d) The Service should develop new KPIs to indicate:

(i) the extent to which staff training fulfils a clear staff development policy (the Service having first introduced a clear development policy).

(ii) staff morale. Three obvious indicators are turnover, sickness and absence. Complaints by staff are also an indicator, if a sufficiently well-developed complaints scheme is in place.

(iii) recidivism rates. Examples might be the percentage of new inmates who have a previous conviction, the percentage of inmates released during the past two, five and ten years who have been re-convicted and the average number of years before released inmates re-offend. There are difficulties in expressing these figures meaningfully but there are ways of handling them.

(iv) the degree of success in dealing with the drug problem in prisons.

(v) inmate behaviour, eg disciplinary cases and suicides.

(vi) standards of physical security.

(vii) reduction in Headquarters personnel.

(viii) reduction in the percentage of the total Prison Service budget absorbed by Headquarters and support (ie non-operational) activities.

(Paras. 3.54-56 and Appendix J) [**Recommendation 65**]

7.5 An "owner" should be nominated for the Service, to fulfil the role of line manager for the Director General. A small, professional unit should be formed to support the "owner". (Para. 3.82) [**Recommendation 69**]

7.6 The Home Office should undertake an in-depth study of the relationship between itself and the Prison Service. (Para. 3.87) [**Recommendation 71**]

7.7 Area Managers should be an integral part of the corporate planning process, monitor service delivery and manage the area's resources. They should be located in their areas and hold their own budgets. They must concentrate on operational management of establishments and make their voices heard at Board level through the Operational Directors.
(Paras. 3.133-136) [**Recommendation 75**]

7.8 Boards of Visitors should be properly resourced and the Liaison Section should be moved out of Headquarters.
(Paras. 3.142-143) [**Recommendation 78**]

7.9 The role of HM Chief Inspector of Prisons should be extended to include security issues and he should be provided with staff for this purpose. (Para. 5.99) [**Recommendation 127**]

PRISON MANAGEMENT

7.10 Prison managers should set aside a minimum number of hours to walk around their establishments. (Para. 2.228) [**Recommendation 53**]

7.11 The applications system should be urgently reviewed so that minor matters are resolved at the appropriate level and only serious issues are referred to Governor Grades. (Para. 2.229) [**Recommendation 54**]

7.12 Wings and Units should each have a single Manager, empowered through direct access to a Senior Management Team oriented towards operational needs. The management structure should be built from the bottom up and have only five levels.
(Paras. 2.231-238) [**Recommendation 56**]

7.13 Officers should work in regular teams under a Senior Officer responsible to one Manager. Wing and Unit Managers should report directly to the Head of Operations and Security. The Head of Operations and Security and the governing Governor should both be supported by a Secretariat, including a Staff Officer for the Governor. (Paras. 2.235-237) [**Recommendation 57**]

7.14 All staff, including Governors, should normally wear uniform, with name badges. Civilian members of staff should be clearly identifiable from inmates. (Paras. 3.46 and 3.48) [**Recommendation 63**]

7.15 The Service must look for better ways of dealing with the proliferation of paperwork and take urgent action to reduce it.
(Paras. 3.129-132 and Appendix M) [**Recommendation 74**]

7.16 The Prison Service must introduce, as a matter of urgency, an accreditation system which would require each establishment to hold a certificate, awarded following the objective measurement of performance against approved national standards. Where an establishment's performance failed to meet the required standard, the certificate would be withdrawn and sanctions would follow. (Paras. 5.96-97) [**Recommendation 126**]

LEADERSHIP

7.17 Visible leadership must be demonstrated by Wing Managers, who should work from an office located on their Wing.
(Paras. 2.194-196 and 2.228) [**Recommendation 42**]

7.18 Positive and visible leadership must be shown at all levels.
(Para. 3.27) [**Recommendation 61**]

7.19 The problems of intimidation, manipulation and boredom must be thoroughly addressed during recruitment and training, continuously monitored by line managers and carefully studied by the Service with a view to appropriate action. More important still is visible leadership which recognises the human dimension, shows enthusiasm for peoples' efforts and promotes feelings of self-respect and self-confidence.
(Paras. 4.39-48) [**Recommendation 99**]

THE DIRECTOR GENERAL

7.20 The Director General and Board should have regular contact with those who have operational responsibilities so that security weaknesses do not go unnoticed. (Para. 3.16) [**Recommendation 58**]

7.21 The problem of the Director General's pre-occupation with parliamentary matters must be overcome. He must redress the balance between keeping Ministers informed and running the Service.
(Paras. 3.83-86) [**Recommendation 70**]

PRISON SERVICE HEADQUARTERS

7.22 The momentum to downsize Headquarters and Central Services, by at least 500 posts by 1998, must be maintained. Activities not essential to operational management, such as the Lifer Group (excluding the operational management of Lifers through the Allocation Unit), Parole Unit and Superannuation Section, should be moved out of Headquarters.
(Paras. 3.123-124) [**Recommendation 73**]

STAFF ASSOCIATIONS

7.23 The procedures for handling disputes with the Prison Officers Association need to be reviewed. (Para. 2.230) [**Recommendation 55**]

7.24 The Board should build on the willingness of staff associations to co-operate in taking the Service forward. (Para. 3.50) [**Recommendation 64**]

PERSONNEL POLICY

7.25 A coherent personnel policy needs to be established and reflected in the Establishment Plan. (Para. 2.220) [**Recommendation 49**]

7.26 Procedures need to be put in place to select, for Dispersal Prisons, staff with the necessary skills and experience for the work, with additional incentives to enhance the status of those selected.
(Paras. 2.225-227) [**Recommendation 52**]

7.27 Headquarters and other senior appointments should be filled largely by Prison Service professionals. (Para. 3.18) [**Recommendation 59**]

7.28 The Service must rapidly become a more caring and people-oriented organisation. Gallantry and good service should be recognised.
(Paras. 3.22-23 and 3.25) [**Recommendation 60**]

7.29 Personnel management systems should be introduced to ensure equal opportunities and common standards, to identify talent for fast-streaming and to develop top managers. (Paras. 3.71-72) [**Recommendation 67**]

7.30 The Prison Service should ensure that the contribution of civilian staff is properly recognised. (Paras. 4.49-50) [**Recommendation 100**]

TRAINING

7.31 Training should not be regarded as a dispensable task.
(Paras. 2.220-222) [**Recommendation 50**]

7.32 Additional training should be given to Dispersal Prison staff, to counter the extra problems inherent in dealing with the Dispersal population.
(Para. 2.227) [**Recommendation 51**]

7.33 Deficiencies in training must be rectified without delay. The identification of core competencies, for training purposes, should be extended to all grades. Before line managers take up new posts, they should receive leadership and management training. Over the next five years, annual training for all staff should rise to 14 days. (Paras. 3.66-69) [**Recommendation 66**]

SECURITY MANUAL

7.34 The Manual on Security should be mandatory and used as the basic document for training purposes. Copies should be widely distributed in all establishments and concise versions should be available to operational staff. (Paras. 4.14-15) [**Recommendation 83**]

SEARCHING AND PATROLLING

7.35 A clear written policy on searching procedures should be available to all staff, inmates and visitors and should be monitored and supervised to ensure implementation. (Para. 2.41) [**Recommendation 12**]

7.36 'Rub-down' searches should be carried out consistently and to a standard specified in the annual security audit, agreed by the Area Manager. (Para. 2.56) [**Recommendation 20**]

7.37 Cell searches should be undertaken in accordance with the Manual on Security. (Paras. 2.57-65) [**Recommendation 21**]

7.38 There must be a coherent strategy for searching of communal areas and appropriate records must be maintained. (Para. 2.73) [**Recommendation 24**]

7.39 All curtains, blinds and obstructions should be removed from the association areas. (Para. 2.217) [**Recommendation 47**]

7.40 Officers should patrol all areas of each Wing unannounced and at frequent but irregular intervals. (Para. 2.217) [**Recommendation 48**]

7.41 All prison establishments must implement a searching programme in accordance with the Manual on Security. (Paras. 4.29 and 4.31) [**Recommendation 92**]

7.42 The Prison Service should establish dedicated search teams at all Dispersal Prisons and at the two new prisons recommended in Section 5. Such teams should have available to them, on a regular basis, dogs trained to identify firearms, explosives and drugs. (Paras. 2.59 and 4.31) [**Recommendations 22 and 93**]

7.43 Across the rest of the estate, better use must be made of search teams, supported by appropriate equipment and the wider deployment of trained dogs. (Para. 4.31) [**Recommendation 94**]

SEARCHING OF VISITORS

7.44 Sufficient accommodation and equipment should be provided, at the main gate of all prisons holding Category A inmates, to enable searching of all staff and visitors to take place at all times. This should be subject to CCTV observation. The main reception area should have direct communication with the visits reception area. (Para. 2.31) [**Recommendation** 4]

7.45 Procedures for searching visitors are laid down in the Manual on Security and must be obeyed, to minimise the risk of smuggling. Staff must have the latest equipment and be properly trained and proficient in the use of X-ray and metal detecting machinery, in sufficient numbers to ensure that, at each establishment, all such equipment, in particular at the gatehouse, is operated by qualified staff, who should be fully aware of searching procedures and relevant rules/legislation. Searching procedures should be regularly supervised. (Paras. 2.31, 2.41, 4.19 and 4.25) [**Recommendations 5 and 86**]

7.46 Visitors to prisons holding Category A inmates must be subject to a 'rub-down' search and X-ray check, in accordance with existing instructions. All hand baggage and loose items (eg coats) should be X-rayed. All baggage and property, except cash for canteens and vending machines, should be left in secure containers at the gatehouse or in a Visitors Centre situated outside the prison perimeter. (Para. 2.32) [**Recommendation 6**]

7.47 The Prison Service must develop visitor searching standards for each type of prison and maintain a system for auditing performance. (Para. 4.21) [**Recommendation 87**]

CONDUCT OF VISITS

7.48 Any prisoner or visitor needing to use the toilet facilities during a visit should be searched before and after visits to the toilet. In addition, all toilets should be searched before the end of a visits session and before inmates and visitors are allowed to leave. (Para. 2.41) [**Recommendation 13**]

7.49 The Prison Service must develop standard designs for visits rooms, commensurate with the levels of security and facilities required for differing establishments or circumstances. Existing rooms should be surveyed and, where practicable, brought up to these standards. There should be full 360° fixed CCTV cover in visits rooms in secure establishments, with video recording facilities. (Paras. 2.34 and 4.23) [**Recommendations** 7 **and 88**]

7.50 Visits rooms should have fixed furniture with a formal and observable layout. (Para. 2.35) [**Recommendation 8**]

7.51 Inmates on visits should wear some form of distinguishable clothing. (Para. 2.35) [**Recommendation 9**]

7.52 A visitor recognition system should be introduced.
(Paras. 2.36-37) [**Recommendation 10**]

7.53 Visitors should not make cash transactions in visits rooms except at canteens or vending machines. (Para. 2.42) [**Recommendation 14**]

CLOSED VISITS

7.54 The closed visits room at Parkhurst should be reconstructed to an appropriate design and brought back into use for all prisoners suspected of receiving illegal items from visitors and for inmates on the escape list.
(Para. 2.40) [**Recommendation 11**]

7.55 In most cases, some physical contact should be allowed between inmates and family. Mandatory closed visits are recommended only for Exceptional Risk Category A prisoners. For other than Exceptional Risk Category A prisoners, the option of imposing closed visits should be available in all secure establishments, to be used at the Governor's discretion. Governors should make more use of the option, when they have reasonable grounds for suspicion, and Headquarters should support them.
(Paras. 4.26-28) [**Recommendations 90 and 91**]

FAMILY VISITS

7.56 Family visits are not appropriate for Dispersal Prisons and should cease.
(Para. 2.47) [**Recommendation 15**]

7.57 In high security prisons, visiting children should be restricted to toys provided in the children's area. In other prisons, imitation weapons should be banned and other toys brought in by children should be checked.
(Para. 2.50) [**Recommendation 16**]

SEARCHING OF STAFF

7.58 All staff entering Dispersal Prisons, and the two new establishments, should be searched and there should be random searches of staff leaving these prisons. Elsewhere, programmes for searching staff should be agreed between Governors and Area Managers.
(Paras. 2.52 and 4.32) [**Recommendations 17 and 95**]

7.59 Facilities should be provided for all staff at Dispersal Prisons to leave civilian clothes and personal possessions outside the prison perimeter.
(Para. 2.52) [**Recommendation 18**]

PRISONERS' PROPERTY

7.60 Other than in exceptional circumstances, a prisoner's property should accompany its owner on transfer and should be checked against the inventory, searched and X-rayed by fully trained staff at each prison establishment. (Paras. 2.54 and 2.68) [**Recommendation 19**]

7.61 A volumetric control of all prisoners' possessions should be introduced forthwith, to reduce dramatically the amount of property in possession/storage and facilitate effective searching. The volume allowed should be standard to all inmates, whatever their category. Prisoners should be allowed only that amount of property which fits into a maximum of two transit boxes. Prisoners should not be allowed to add to their property, if it would then exceed the allowance, until arrangements are made for excess property to be collected by relatives/friends or stored centrally. (Para. 2.68) [**Recommendation 23**]

PRISONER MOVEMENTS

7.62 Supervisors must ensure that high standards of control on the movement of dangerous inmates are enforced and that movement books always accompany Exceptional and High Risk prisoners.
(Paras. 2.111-114) [**Recommendation 30**]

7.63 Inmates should not be allowed access to the Wing Office.
(Para. 2.116) [**Recommendation 31**]

7.64 In Dispersal Prisons, a prisoner movement system must be introduced in a form which provides a permanent record and is not accessible to inmates. Inmates must be required to give advance notification of discretionary movements off the Wing. Such movements should be co-ordinated, monitored and properly controlled. (Para. 2.117) [**Recommendation 32**]

WORKSHOPS

7.65 Throughout the prison estate, establishments with workshops should set up daily audits of tools and materials. Workshops should be designed to ensure that prisoners can be observed at all times and, subject to health and safety regulations, safety screens should be made of transparent material.
(Paras. 2.21 and 2.29) [**Recommendation 1**]

7.66 Such establishments should also ensure that Officers supervising workshops have basic knowledge and understanding of the work they are supervising, to ensure that they can identify security breaches and risks.
(Para. 2.23) [**Recommendation 2**]

7.67 The Prison Service should review the type of work and training available to inmates in Dispersal Prisons, with emphasis on the central importance of security in all aspects of activity. (Para. 2.29) [**Recommendation** 3]

PHYSICAL SECURITY

7.68 Appropriate facilities, including CCTV, must be provided at the entrances to Dispersal Prisons. The prison estate must conform to up-to-date security standards and minimum physical security standards need to be set for all establishments and applied. Remedial work identified by security audits should be a high priority.
(Paras. 2.74-101, 4.4 and 4.9) [**Recommendations 25, 80 and 81**]

7.69 Locking schedules for secure establishments need to be reviewed with modern electronic or magnetic systems in mind. Current policy in respect of locks for non-residential buildings should be urgently reviewed.
(Paras. 2.75-76) [**Recommendation 26**]

7.70 Designs for all prisons must be agreed nationally.
(Para. 4.3) [**Recommendation** 79]

ELECTRONIC SECURITY

7.71 Home Office recommended standards for CCTV systems should be applied throughout the Prison Service. (Para. 2.100) [**Recommendation** 27]

7.72 The Prison Service Headquarters Security Survey, on electronic security defences, should be actioned without delay. The Service must provide national solutions to technical problems.
(Paras. 4.7-9) [**Recommendation 81**]

7.73 CCTV cameras should be covered for protection against tampering and to disguise movement. Full video recording facilities must be available.
(Para. 4.25) [**Recommendation 89**]

EMERGENCY CONTROL ROOMS (ECRs)

7.74 Before Officers are deployed to an ECR, they must be fully trained to nationally agreed standards and familiar with the establishment.
(Paras. 2.108-109 and 4.10-12) [**Recommendations 28 and 82**]

7.75 The ECR at Parkhurst must be upgraded in accordance with the findings of the Director of Works. (Para. 2.110) [**Recommendation 29**]

7.76 Each Dispersal Prison must have a properly equipped ECR and every Governor of a Dispersal Prison must have a Command Suite for use in emergencies. (Paras. 4.10-12) [**Recommendation 82**]

EMERGENCIES

7.77 Contingency plans must be regularly tested and practiced, with all staff trained in realistic situations, in line with the instructions in the Manual on Security. Emergency packs must be subject to regular testing. Paras. 2.118-122) [**Recommendation 33**]

7.78 Contingency plans must be reviewed annually, as part of the security audit. (Para. 2.122) [**Recommendation 34**]

7.79 Directions in the Manual on Security, in respect of Duty Governors, must be strictly followed. (Paras. 2.123-126) [**Recommendation 35**]

7.80 Clear instructions must be issued throughout the Service directing that staff must co-operate fully with any police investigation and, if requested, make a verbal and/or written statement without delay. (Paras. 2.127-129) [**Recommendation 36**]

7.81 The Service must keep abreast of work on chemical incapacitants and consider the use of CS gas to quell riotous behaviour. There is a need also for the Service to re-examine the argument for an armed response capability. (Paras. 4.53-55) [**Recommendation 101**]

INTELLIGENCE

7.82 A working party should be set up to review intelligence and management information needs throughout the Prison Service, building on best practice, available IT systems and experience of other Agencies. (Paras. 2.131-145) [**Recommendation 37**]

CATEGORISATION

7.83 Security categorisation should be reviewed and researched to remove dangerous anomalies produced by the current system. (Paras. 2.146-149) [**Recommendation 38**]

7.84 The Prison Service should introduce a new interim categorisation system as soon as possible. (Paras. 5.4-5) [**Recommendation 102**]

7.85 The Prison Service should further refine the system, drawing on the work of Professor David Canter. (Para. 5.7) [**Recommendation 103**]

CONSTRUCTION

7.86 Prison establishments must properly supervise on-site contractors and their vehicles particularly when entering and leaving establishments. (Para. 4.33) [**Recommendation 96**]

PARKHURST

7.87 The decision to retain a hospital at Parkhurst, as a Service-wide resource, should be reviewed. (Para. 2.178) [**Recommendation 39**]

7.88 Parkhurst should be downgraded as soon as possible to become an establishment for prisoners in new Category 4 and should be replaced in the present Dispersal (Category 3) estate by a more suitable establishment, perhaps Belmarsh Prison. (Paras. 2.179 and 5.18) [**Recommendations 40 and 106**]

7.89 The relevance of current building work should be examined so that unnecessary work can be stopped. (Para. 2.179) [**Recommendation 40**]

7.90 The SSU at Parkhurst should not be re-opened in that capacity. The accommodation should be put to other use.
(Para. 2.179) [**Recommendation 41**]

PURPOSEFUL ACTIVITY

7.91 Prisoners should be offered sufficient, regular and meaningful work and wages or education facilities. Those not taking up work places should be locked in their cells during the day.
(Paras. 2.210-213 and 5.71-74) [**Recommendations 45 and 117**]

7.92 The Prison Service should evaluate the concept of Industrial Prisons as a matter of urgency. Prisoners from any part of the new Category 4 and 5 estate should be eligible to work in them. They would earn this right by virtue of good behaviour and the recommendation of staff and Governors.
(Paras. 5.27-31) [**Recommendation 111**]

7.93 Prisons should be allowed to keep the profits from their commercial activities and commercial advice should be available to Governors.
(Paras. 5.71-74) [**Recommendation 117**]

PRIVILEGES AND INCENTIVES

7.94 Cooking facilities on Wings should be treated as a privilege and not a right. Access to stores of food must be supervised and regulated.
(Paras. 2.214-216) [**Recommendation 46**]

7.95 Prisoner programmes should be adopteded nationally. Every sentenced prisoner serving more than 12 months should have a sentence plan and should be allocated a Personal Officer. (Para. 5.59) [**Recommendation 115**]

7.96 Early release should be a privilege earned through good behaviour and the Prison Service initiative on this matter should be taken forward urgently.
(Paras. 5.67-70) [**Recommendation 116**]

7.97 Private cash should be phased out.
(Paras. 5.75-76) **[Recommendation 118]**

7.98 There must be a mandatory minimum entitlement to visits which takes account of the need to retain family links. Additional visits can be used as incentives to good behaviour. (Paras. 5.77-78) **[Recommendation 119]**

7.99 Telephone privileges should feature in an incentive scheme.
(Para. 5.79) **[Recommendation 120]**

7.100 Television in cells could provide a calming influence and a powerful incentive to good conduct. It could also be used for educational and communication purposes. The right to this privilege should be earned by good behaviour, once the prisoner has earned the right to electricity in the cell. (Paras. 5.80-83) **[Recommendation 121]**

7.101 The Prison Service should explore ways of increasing the availability of home leave and apply firm sanctions to those who abuse the privilege.
(Paras. 5.84-85) **[Recommendation 122]**

TELEPHONES

7.102 Telephone monitoring should be intelligence driven. Improved facilities need to be in place to monitor foreign language conversations.
(Paras. 2.201-205) **[Recommendation 43]**

7.103 In the short term, the current £40 limit per week for phonecards at Parkhurst must be reviewed and set at a lower level. In the long term, the issue of phonecards needs to be reassessed throughout the Service, to remove abuses of the system. (Paras. 2.201-209) **[Recommendation 44]**

DRUGS

7.104 The concepts of drugs-free Wings and of drugs testing should be implemented where appropriate. (Para. 4.16) **[Recommendation 84]**

7.105 To deal with drug abuse, all prisons must have programmes which inform, educate and help prisoners combat the drug habit. Success on such programmes should be rewarded through the incentive scheme.
(Para. 4.18) **[Recommendation 85]**

THE HIGH SECURITY ESTATE

7.106 Prisoners in new Categories 1 and 2 should be housed in a new purpose-built High Security Prison. (Paras. 5.14-16) **[Recommendation 104]**

7.107 A Control Prison should be established for particularly disruptive prisoners including disruptive prisoners who are mentally ill. (Paras. 5.48-54) [**Recommendation 114**]

7.108 The high security estate should be managed as a whole rather than piecemeal. An Operational Director should be appointed with the sole task of managing the High Security Prison, the Control Prison and the six Dispersal Prisons. This Director should be a full member of the Prisons Board, have operational experience as the Governor of a Dispersal Prison and have no substantial work other than the management of these prisons. The High Security, Control and Dispersal Prisons should remain in the public sector. (Paras. 5.86-87) [**Recommendation 123**]

OTHER ESTABLISHMENTS

7.109 Prisoners in the new Category 3 should be housed in the existing Dispersal system. (Paras. 5.17-18) [**Recommendation 105**]

7.110 The Prison Service should provide suitable accommodation for high risk women prisoners and young offenders. (Para. 5.20) [**Recommendation 108**]

7.111 Prisoners in the new Category 4 should be housed in closed, cellular prisons with secure perimeters. (Para. 5.23) [**Recommendation 109**]

7.112 Prisoners in the new Category 5 should be housed in the present Category C, non-cellular establishments with adequate perimeter security and CCTV coverage of vulnerable areas. (Para. 5.25) [**Recommendation 110**]

7.113 The Prison Service should undertake a review to assess the present open estate and to decide what is required for resettlement Units, what should be retained as open accommodation and what should be upgraded to new security standards. (Paras. 5.32-37) [**Recommendation 112**]

7.114 Women's prisons should be the responsibility of one Area Manager. All women prisoners should be housed in women's prisons. In the longer term, there should be a thorough review of the female prisoners' estate. (Paras. 5.38-40) [**Recommendation 113**]

7.115 The prison estate, apart from the High Security, Control and Dispersal Prisons, should be organised into 11 clusters, each cluster working to an Area Manager supported by sufficient staff to run the area. The 12th Area Manager would control the women's estate. (Paras. 5.89-94) [**Recommendation 124**]

REMAND PRISONERS

7.116 In the short term, whenever possible, remand Category A prisoners should be held in Dispersal Prisons but it will be necessary for many of them to be held in other strategically placed prisons with accommodation to Category A standard. (Para. 4.35) [**Recommendation** 97]

7.117 The practicality of installing TV links between prisons holding remand prisoners and Magistrates' Courts should be explored. (Paras. 4.36-38) [**Recommendation 98**]

7.118 In the long term, subject to revised arrangements for remand hearings (see para. 7.117), remand prisoners in the new Categories 1 and 2 should be held in the proposed High Security Prison when awaiting trial. During trial, they should be held in the High Security Prison, if it is geographically convenient, in an SSU within the Dispersal system or in one of a small number of suitable establishments across the country. (Para. 5.19) [**Recommendation 107**]

PRIVATE PRISONS

7.119 The Service should ensure that, when contracts are drawn up for private prisons, staffing levels are set on the basis of staff and prisoner safety and the protection of the public. (Paras. 3.137-138) [**Recommendation** 76]

7.120 A substantial public Prison Service should be retained but the advantages arising from competition and private sector involvement should be applied across the Service. (Paras. 3.140-141) [**Recommendation** 77]

APPENDIX A
BACKGROUND AND HISTORICAL INFORMATION

Background and Historical Information

1. The Inquiry covered a number of areas of Prison Service policy and practice and some of the terminology used will be unfamiliar to the lay reader. In addition, a number of historical facts are relevant to the discussions held and recommendations made. This Appendix sets out the historical background and explains a number of terms.

THE DISPERSAL PRISON SYSTEM

2. In the early 1960s, there were no specially secure prisons in England and Wales. This lack of provision was clearly brought into focus by the escapes of two of the Great Train Robbers, Charles Wilson and Ronald Biggs (respectively, from Birmingham in 1964 and Wandsworth in 1965) and the spy George Blake (from Wormwood Scrubs in 1966).

3. The first attempt to deal with this problem was the establishment, in 1965, of small Special Security Wings at Durham and Leicester but these could not provide a complete or permanent solution. They were expensive to build and the lack of a suitable design produced oppressive conditions. In 1966, Lord Mountbatten carried out an enquiry into Prison Service security and made a number of recommendations, including the following:

   - Prisoners should be divided into four categories, according to the degree of security necessary for their containment (A, B, C and D, with A the highest).
   - Category A prisoners should be concentrated in a purpose-built, fortress prison on the Isle of Wight.
   - Standards of security in other prisons should receive attention.
   - In parallel, physical conditions should be improved and a liberal and constructive regime adopted in order to reduce tensions and the desire to escape.

4. Whilst the thrust of the recommendations was accepted by the then Home Secretary, he asked the Advisory Council on the Penal System to consider the nature of the regime under which the high security, long-term prisoners might be held. The Council appointed a sub-committee, under Professor Radzinowicz, which, in 1968, produced a Report entitled "The Regime for Long-term Prisoners in conditions of Maximum Security".

5. This Report came out against the "concentration" philosophy recommended by Mountbatten and, instead, recommended a system of "dispersal", under which Category A prisoners would be distributed among the larger prison population of three or four specially selected establishments, with appropriately upgraded perimeter security. The main arguments against concentration were: the risk that the regime of a fortress prison would become repressive; the possible effects of labelling the entire population of a prison as the most difficult; anxieties about dealing with a concentrated group of prisoners who might feel they had nothing to lose; and the difficulty of providing varied regimes within a single prison.

6. Despite these reservations, and its final recommendation, the sub-committee recognised the validity of both alternatives. It recognised the danger posed by a few. It stated:

> *"The choice between concentration and dispersal is obviously one that is central to the future of any penal system: it is a difficult choice, and we would emphasise that there are strong arguments on both sides, and that neither solution is a panacea."*

7. In 1968, seven prisons were selected as Dispersal Prisons and plans were put in hand for an additional, new establishment. These prisons contained a mixture of Category A and the higher risk Category B inmates.

8. The Dispersal system was reviewed in 1983, following serious disturbances at Albany and Gartree Prisons, on the Isle of Wight and in Leicestershire respectively. This review gave qualified support to the Dispersal system but recommended substantial strengthening of and modifications to existing facilities and the addition of two 'Control Units', for those inmates identified as persistent trouble makers.

9. Both Radzinowicz and the subsequent review recognised the potential conflicts between high security and care of the most disruptive. Both questioned how best to impose control on the highest security inmates. The first of the Control Units was opened in 1974 but closed a year later as it had not been used to the extent expected and was considered wasteful of resources.

10. Following riots at Hull Prison in 1976, the Chief Inspector of Prisons touched on the concentration -v- dispersal debate:

> *"The Dispersal system does offer flexibility, despite the obvious difficulties of operating in establishments that were not purpose-built ...We may not have the Dispersal system right but we have not got it all wrong."*

11. This subject was considered in 1979 by the May Committee, which concluded that the Dispersal system should continue but accepted that two major problems were inherent. First, the mixing of Category A and B inmates was unsatisfactory from the security point of view. Second, the classification of inmates on security grounds alone could not solve all control problems, as not all the most disruptive inmates were in the very highest security categories.

12. In September 1983, the system was examined by the Control Review Committee (CRC), set up with the following terms of reference:

> *"To review the maintenance of control in the prison system, including the implications for physical security, with particular reference to the Dispersal system, and to make recommendations."*

13. This Committee identified five main problems with the Dispersal system:

- Entry into the Dispersal Prisons was too automatic and came too soon after sentencing.
- It was unrealistic to assume that the Dispersal Prison regime was suitable for all long-term prisoners.
- The existing facilities to deal with persistently disruptive inmates were inadequate and not all the necessary services were available within the system.
- The system lacked sufficient disincentives to bad behaviour or incentives to good.
- Responsibility for allocation of inmates was divided between different authorities for lifers, Category A and other inmates.

14. The CRC Report recognised the need for high standards of physical security but concentrated mainly on internal control issues. The Committee acknowledged that the Dispersal system was in need of substantial support and confirmed the widely held belief that:

> *"There will inevitably be control problems if long-term prisoners are held in a system that gives inconsistent messages about the course of their sentences or the consequences of their actions, and if prison managers' only recourse in the face of disruption is to switch prisoners between normal location and the Segregation Unit, and between one prison and another."*

15. It proposed a strategy based on two complementary initiatives. First, it recommended an improvement of inmate allocation and sentence planning, to provide individual programmes and regular reviews. Second, it recommended a small number of specialised Control Units for those

inmates who did not respond to incentives. It explained why it saw no alternative to these Units in the following terms:

> *"For other kinds of inmate who constantly threaten control we shall have to develop a few small Units of a new kind, and we strongly recommend that this should be done as a positive, developmental initiative, with outside academics participating in the planning and evaluation, and with as much openness as possible about the whole project."*

16. The Dispersal system presently consists of six prisons, located at Frankland, Full Sutton, Long Lartin, Parkhurst, Wakefield and Whitemoor. Following a helicopter-assisted escape from Gartree prison, in 1987, the Dispersal system was again reviewed and prisoner classifications were refined to reflect potential for escape. The review introduced three escape risk sub-classifications of Category A, namely Exceptional Risk, High Risk and Standard Risk, those in the two lower categories to be housed in Dispersal Prisons and the Exceptional Risk prisoners in the Special Security Units.

SPECIAL SECURITY UNITS (SSUs)

17. SSUs were a response to the same events that eventually produced the Dispersal system, namely the escapes of 1964/65. It was quickly recognised, after Wilson's escape, that especially secure Units were needed to house the very small number of prisoners who posed the greatest threat to the public. By August 1965, two Special Security Wings, at Durham and Leicester, had been established and had started receiving prisoners, including the remaining four Great Train Robbers. Plans were put in place to open a third such Wing at Parkhurst, on the Isle of Wight.

18. Following the Reports of Mountbatten and Radzinowicz, Special Security Wings were regarded as a temporary measure, pending the full introduction of the Dispersal system with its increased security.

19. By 1978, with the emergence of terrorist prisoners and a number of others who would previously have been subject to the death penalty, a continuing demand for these small maximum security Units was recognised. It was also seen that the capacity of the system needed to be increased and that each Unit should be purpose-built, rather than adapted from existing premises.

20. In 1988, the first purpose-built SSU was opened at Full Sutton near York. By that time, Leicester SSU had been recognised as unsuitable, because of its cramped conditions and location within a non-Dispersal ("local") prison; and the SSU at Parkhurst was in desperate need of upgrading and refurbishment.

21. In mid-1989, in view of the increasing demand for secure accommodation and the escape from Gartree Prison, the decision was taken to construct a second purpose-built SSU within the next new Dispersal Prison. That was to be HMP Whitemoor. Following the re-classification of Category A inmates, SSUs were used to house those deemed to pose an exceptional risk.

22. There are presently three SSUs, at Full Sutton, Parkhurst and Whitemoor.

PARKHURST PRISON

23. Parkhurst is located next to Camp Hill and Albany Prisons, close to Newport on the Isle of Wight. It has traditionally housed some of the most disruptive prisoners within the prison system.

24. Parkhurst was originally the site of a military hospital (from 1798) and was first used as a prison in 1838, when it was converted to hold young male offenders. It was designed to house 102 boys, originally those awaiting deportation to Australia. After 1853, when the transportation of boys was discontinued, it was allocated to short-term prisoners, then some female inmates and, finally, in 1869, solely to male convicts serving long-term sentences.

25. Most of the buildings originate from the period after 1838 and the last Wings were built in 1886. Construction of the SSU started in 1963 and, between 1970 and 1979, the prison was upgraded to a high security establishment. During the same period, C Wing was designated as a Special Unit to house disruptive and disturbed inmates. In 1987, the hospital theatre was reopened after refurbishment. It has become a national Prison Service resource, reaching NHS standard for operations.

26. The Prison has four accommodation blocks and two hospitals. The present gate lodge, visiting rooms and administrative buildings were added in 1988. A and D Wings were damaged during a prison riot in 1979 and were left empty until refurbished in July 1993. A programme of reconstruction work is planned to continue until the end of the century.

27. At the time of the escape, Parkhurst could accommodate up to 227 prisoners. On 3rd January 1995, it contained 223 prisoners, 53 in Category A, of which 18 were considered to be highly dangerous with the ability to effect an escape.

APPENDIX B
THE LEARMONT INQUIRY TEAM

The Learmont Inquiry Team

ASSESSORS

General Sir John Learmont KCB CBE

Sir John Woodcock CBE QPM

Mr G Dadds

ADVISERS

Mr M S Heath CB CBE

Mr P Leonard - seconded from Prison Service

Sir Peter Wallis KCVO CMG

PARKHURST TEAM

Deputy Assistant Commissioner	A G Fry QPM	-	Metropolitan
Detective Chief Inspector	B Morris	-	Metropolitan
Detective Inspectors	M Barley	-	Metropolitan
	A Rennison	-	Metropolitan
	A Sellers	-	Metropolitan
Detective Sergeants	N Benwell QPM	-	Metropolitan
	D Buck	-	Metropolitan
	N Harris	-	Dorset
	T O'Neill	-	Sussex
Detective Constables	S Clark	-	Sussex
	M Curran	-	Metropolitan
	C Munro	-	Metropolitan
	R Mutch	-	Dorset
Typist	Mrs A Sturmey	-	Hampshire

SECRETARIAT

Mr A T Williams

Mrs D Ruddell

Mrs R C Hembury

Mrs J Purssell

Miss M Kingswood

Mr B Bell (Driver) - seconded from Metropolitan Police

REPORT COMPILATION

Superintendent P A Todd - Bedfordshire Police

Detective Inspector P MacKay - Bedfordshire Police

COSTINGS TEAM

Mr R Kettle

Mr B Mehta ACMA

APPENDIX C
REFERENCE DOCUMENTS

Reference Documents

Report by Earl Mountbatten into Prison Escapes and Security - December 1966

Managing the Long-Term Prison System: The Report of the Control Review Committee - 1984

Prison Disturbances - Report by Rt Hon Lord Justice Woolf and His Honour Judge Stephen Tumim - April 1990

Custody, Care and Justice: The Way Ahead for the Prison Service in England and Wales - 1991

Report of an Audit of Custody Arrangements for Category A Prisoners and of an Inquiry into DOC1 Division by Hadfield and Lakes - December 1991

Prison Service Management Review by Admiral Sir Raymond Lygo - December 1991

Review of Prison Service Headquarters: Taskforce Report - January 1994

The Woodcock Enquiry on "The Escape from Whitemoor Prison on Friday 9 September 1994" - December 1994

Final Report of the Enquiry into the Escape of 3 Prisoners from HMP Parkhurst on 3 January 1995 by Richard Tilt, Director of Security - January 1995

HM Prison Service Framework Document (April 1993), Corporate Plan (1994-97) and Business Plans (1994-95 and 1995-96)

Prison Service Annual Report and Accounts (April 1993 - March 1994)

HM Chief Inspector of Prisons Reports (on prisons visited)

APPENDIX D
LIST OF PRISON ESTABLISHMENTS VISITED

List of Prison Establishments Visited

ENGLAND AND WALES

HMYOI Aylesbury

HMP Albany

HMP Bedford

HMP Belmarsh

HMP Birmingham

HMP Brixton

HMP Camp Hill

HMP Cardiff

HMP Channings Wood

HMP Dartmoor

HMP Downview

HMP Everthorpe

HMP Exeter

HMP Featherstone

HMPYOI Feltham

HMP Frankland

HMP Full Sutton

HMP Gartree

HMYOI Glen Parva

HMP Grendon

HMP Holloway

HMP Leicester

HMP Leyhill

HMP Lincoln

HMP Long Lartin

HMP Morton Hall

HMYOI Onley

HMP Parkhurst

HMP/YOI Prescoed

HMP Risley

HMP Stocken

HMP Usk

HMP Wakefield

HMP Whitemoor

HMP Woodhill

HMP Wormwood Scrubs

PRIVATE PRISONS

Blakenhurst

Doncaster

Wolds Remand Centre

MILITARY PRISONS

Military Correctional Training Centre, Colchester

COLLEGES

PSC Newbold

PSC Wakefield

NORTHERN IRELAND

HMP Maghaberry

HMP The Maze

SCOTLAND

HMP Corton Vale

HMP Shotts

THE NETHERLANDS

Penitentiary Institutions 'De Schie', Rotterdam

Penitentiair Complex Scheveningen, The Hague

Nieuw Vosseveld, Vught

SPAIN

Centre Penitenciari, Barcelona (Male)

Centre Penitenciari, Barcelona (Female)

UNITED STATES OF AMERICA

Federal Bureau of Prisons, Washington

Maryland Correctional Adjustment Centre, Baltimore

Maryland Correctional Adjustment Annex, Jessup

Northern Correctional Institution (Ultramax), Connecticut

Federal Administrative Maximum United States Penetentiary, Colorado

United States Penetentiary, Florence

Cybuishi Correctional Institute, Florence, Californian Department of Corrections, Sacramento

APPENDIX E
LIST OF INTERVIEWS HELD AND SUBMISSIONS RECEIVED DURING THE COURSE OF THE LEARMONT INQUIRY

List of Interviews Held and Submissions Received During the Course of the Learmont Inquiry

INDIVIDUALS

Mr David Abelson	-	Chairman, Board of Visitors (BOV) Co-ordinating Committee
Mrs Millie Banerjee	-	Non-executive member of Prison Board
Mr Tony Batchelor	-	HM Treasury
Mr Bill Bentley	-	Non-executive member of Prison Board
Mr Bill Brister	-	Ex-Deputy Director General of Prison Service
Ms Frances Crook	-	Howard League for Penal Reform
Mr Nick Flynn	-	Prison Reform Trust
The Rt Hon Michael Forsyth MP	-	Minister for Prisons
Ms Lucy Gampell	-	Prisoners' Families Support Groups (submission)
Mr Richard Gully	-	Vice-Chairman, BOV Co-ordinating Committee
Mr John Halliday	-	Home Office, Criminal Department
Sir Robin Ibbs	-	Chairman, Lloyds Bank
Mr John Ingman	-	Home Office, Prison Service Monitoring Unit
Mr David Jenkins	-	Independent Researcher working with the Inspectorate of Prisons
Mr Gordon Lakes	-	Ex-Deputy Director General and joint author of Hadfield/Lakes Report
Mr John Lynch	-	Architect

Mr Robin Masefield	-	Home Office, Efficiency Scrutiny of Police
Ms Ann McTaggart	-	Co-ordinator, Save The Children Scheme, HMP Holloway
Professor Rod Morgan	-	London Prisons Community Links
Mr Chris Nuttall	-	Home Office, Research and Statistics Department
Ms Una Padel	-	London Prisons Community Links
Mr Joe Pilling	-	Ex-Director General of the Prison Service
Mr Paul Pugh	-	Home Office, Prison Service Monitoring Unit
Mrs J S M Roberts	-	Association of Chief Officers of Probation (submission)
Mr Andrew Rutherford	-	Howard League for Penal Reform
Mr Peter Salisbury	-	Marks and Spencer
Mr John Sandy	-	Ex-Regional Director of the Prison Service
Mr Michael Saunders	-	Home Office, Legal Advisers Branch
Mr David Seymour	-	Home Office, Legal Advisers Branch
Mr Stephen Shaw	-	Prison Reform Trust
Ms Vivien Stern	-	National Association for the Care and Resettlement of Offenders (NACRO)
Ms Beverley Thompson	-	NACRO
His Hon Judge Stephen Tumim	-	Her Majesty's Chief Inspector of Prisons
Sir Peter Woodhead	-	Prison Ombudsman
The Rt Hon. Lord Justice Woolf	-	Author, Report into Prison Disturbances, April 1990

STAFF ASSOCIATIONS AND TRADE UNIONS

Association of First Division Civil Servants

Civil and Public Services Association

Institution of Professionals, Managers and Specialists

National Union of Civil and Public Servants

Prison Governors Association

Prison Officers Association

Prison Service Trade Union Side Secretariat

Prison Service Union (submission)

OTHERS

The Learmont Inquiry Team also interviewed a wide range of people from within the Prison Service and three independent consultants.

APPENDIX F
SCHEDULE OF CORRESPONDENCE REGARDING GEOPHONES

Schedule of Correspondence Regarding Geophones

Date	Comments
30.3.84	*Memo: Governor Parkhurst to P5 (Security) Division* "The need for geophones was identified by the Parkhurst Project Control Team as long ago as February 1974." "In November 1975 it was agreed to geophone the perimeter."
25.11.85	*Internal Headquarters memo* "... the remainder has no CCTV cover or geophones ... The clear need is to improve the Prison's perimeter security before the SSB [Special Security Block] equipment is withdrawn."
1.9.86	*Parkhurst SSB - Security upgrading meeting* "... need to clarify the position in regard to the provision of full perimeter CCTV, the geophoning of the inner security fence and the installation of Method 5 on the gander device."
30.6.87	*Memo: Deputy Governor Parkhurst to P5 Division* Re: weaknesses of perimeter security - "There are no geophones fitted around the inner fence or the outer wall (excluding the SSB), so the ECR is utterly dependent upon the vigilance of the perimeter patrols and the dog handlers on duty."
20.8.87	*Internal memo: P5 to P1 re CCTV at Parkhurst* "... we should be seeking to install the CCTV system as soon as possible with a full [*sic*] back date for completion (operational) of 1991/92. Perimeter security at Parkhurst falls far short of the standards laid down for a Dispersal Prison and in the absence of other improvements, P5 would urge that the scheme to provide CCTV coverage is given a high priority." "Long term, P5 look to installation of a geophonic alarm system to the inner fence ... However, it is accepted that realistically this is unlikely to be a viable proposition until the end of the redevelopment building programme."

Date	Comments
13.10.87	*Parkhurst perimeter security meeting* "It was thought infeasible (*sic*) to install geophones before the work on A and D Wings was completed, as the vibrations of contractors' traffic would constantly set them off. However, it was pointed out that geophones would be valuable at those times when the contractors were not working in the prison."
17.12.87	*Parkhurst perimeter security meeting* "Mr **** proposed that due to the rebuilding of A, B and D Wings and kitchen, it would be preferable for the geophones and Method 5 security system to be delayed until the building project has been completed. The committee [including technical and scientific advisers] concurred ... In the light of the geophones and Method 5 being postponed, Mr **** asked if the CCTV and lighting could be brought forward ..."
5.1.88	*Internal memo in Directorate of Works (DOW)* "... geophones and Method 5 perimeter security be delayed until after completion of new Wings ... ie early 1992" ... suggestion by P5.
21.1.88	*Minutes of No 1 Design Team meeting regarding upgrading of perimeter security in Parkhurst* "It was confirmed that geophones and Method 5 be delayed until after A, B, D Blocks and new kitchen project had been completed."
26.2.88	*DOW/Architects Branch rough preliminary estimate* Supply and installation of a geophone system - £150,000.
August 1988	*Report of the Working Group on Category A Security. Appendix 9 Parkhurst* 1. Incomplete perimeter wall and part detection device. 2. Inner fence - no detection device, no CCTV. 3. External and internal perimeter - no complete floodlighting system.
12.8.88	*Memo from P5* "... work on an alarm system is programmed for 1991/92 on completion of the refurbishment of A, B and D Wings."

Date	Comments
24.11.88	*Internal P5 memo* "Perimeter security at Parkhurst falls short of the standards laid down for a Dispersal Prison .... For years, proposals to upgrade perimeter security have been linked to the redevelopment plans ... Arrangements are now in hand to provide CCTV surveillance of both the external and internal perimeter barriers within the next 12 months."
24.11.88	*Letter from MP to Home Office Minister* "Why does Parkhurst still not have a geophone fence?"
13.1.89	*Letter from Home Office Minister to MP* "The security fence surrounding the SSU is geographically (*sic*) alarmed. It is intended to install an alarm system on the inner perimeter security fence as soon as the upgrading and refurbishment of A, B and D Wings is completed."
17.1.89	*Letter from MP to Home Office Minister* "... However I am concerned that the inner perimeter security fence is still not protected by a geophone alarm and my understanding of that is that that does not conform with the security specifications for the type of prisoner being held in that prison."
27.1.89	*Observations on MP's letter provided by P5 to Private Office* "There is little point in alarming the fence until the refurbishment and upgrading of A, B and D Wings is complete."
10.2.89	*Memo from P5 to Governor Parkhurst* States that Method 5 system will be removed from Parkhurst for use by Northern Ireland Office.
9.3.89	*Reply from Home Office Minister to MP* Letter cannot be traced.
25.6.90	*Memo from Prison Building (PB2) Division to Governor Parkhurst and others* "Perimeter lighting is being upgraded and design work is proceeding on geophone for implementation when major redevelopment completed."

Date	Comments
21.8.90	*Memo from PB2 Division to DOW* £800K is for geophones, Method 5, ECR consoles etc.
11.10.90	*London South Area progress meeting* "Upgrade Perim Security Cat B ... Geophone, control room, Method 5 etc scheduled for when main part of redev. complete 1994/95." Action DOW.
1991	*Hadfield/Lakes Report* "Only the fences around the SSU have geophones: no other internal perimeter fence has any form of audible warning device fitted."
10.1.91	*London South Area progress meeting* "Upgrade Perim Security Cat B ... Geophone, control room, Method 5 etc scheduled for when main part of redev. complete 1994/95." Action DOW.
11.4.91	*London South Area progress meeting* "Upgrade Perim Security Cat B ... Geophone, control room, Method 5 etc scheduled for when main part of redev. complete 1994/95. DOW to update BE [Budget Estimate]." Action DOW.
9.5.91	*Meeting on the redevelopment of HMP Parkhurst* "... need to introduce some additional measures, such as geophones and CCTV to improve the perimeter security. DBS1 [Department of Building Services] said that the intention was to implement these measures once the Wing refurbishment programme had been completed and the breach in the wall had been secured."
11.7.91	*London South Area progress meeting* "Upgrade Perim Security Cat B ... Geophone, control room, scheduled for when main part of redev. complete 1994/95. DOW to update BE." Action DOW.
17.7.91	*Memo from DBS1 to Directorate of Custody (DOC1)* "A bid to upgrade perimeter security at Parkhurst was made in 1987. ... The second phase included geophones, ECR consoles and Method 5. This phase was postponed until the wings refurbishment was completed ..."

Date	Comments
25.7.91	*Memo from DOC1 to DBS1* Geophones identified as the greatest priority for perimeter security. "The absence of geophones in a prison which takes high risk Category A prisoners in its normal accommodation and in its hospital must be seen as a serious reduction of the level of perimeter security that should be provided in such a Dispersal Prison."
12.8.91	*Memo from DBS1 to Governor Parkhurst in response to memo from DOC1 dated 25.7.91* "... whether there is any way the geophones can be installed early ... In the present climate on security he is worried that Parkhurst does not reach the security standard expected at a Category B Dispersal."
20.8.91	*Memo from Head of Custody Parkhurst to DBS1* "Geophones and cameras go hand in glove and one without the other seriously compromises the security of the establishment."
6.9.91	*Memo from DOC1 to DBS1* "In view of the Governor's view that it is possible to fit geophones down the majority of perimeter fence lines around a prison, I would recommend that this be brought into the programme of work at the earliest possible point."
18.9.91	*Memo from DBS1 to DOW* "At the moment there were no funds ... to meet the remaining elements of the ... project to upgrade perimeter security at Parkhurst..."
19.9.91	*Meeting on redevelopment of Parkhurst* "Following correspondence from DOC1, the Governor would submit a major capital works bid to Area Manager for geophones."
10.10.91	*London South Area progress meeting* "Upgrade Perim Security Cat B ... DBS1 have asked DOW to provide costings on geophones and wall re-alignment." Action DOW.

Date	Comments
25.10.91	*Letter from MP to Home Secretary* "... you may imagine my dismay that the geophones, about which I wrote to [the Minister of State], and his reply is dated the 9th March 1989, are still waiting to be fitted!"
undated	*Memo to Private Office from Gov II DOC1* "There is no early plan to install geophones at Parkhurst ... DSP1 [Directorate of Services and Personnel] have taken the view up to now that major rebuilding work needs to be completed before geophones can be installed. The earliest date quoted had been 1994-5 but there is no current planned date for their installation. I take the contrary view that geophones should be installed as early as possible to as much of the perimeter fence as practicable. If short gaps need to be left because of major redevelopment work that is a smaller price to pay than delaying the whole project for several more years. I believe the Governor takes a similar view."
undated	*Reply to MP from Home Secretary* "Geophones are highly sensitive and their effectiveness depends upon the existence of a relatively stable physical environment. The difficulty with installing geophones while building work is being undertaken is that they might not provide substantial extra security, and the consequent danger exists that the building work itself would damage, or regularly immobilise the equipment."
14.1.92	*Memo Governor Parkhurst to Area Manager* "As I understand it geophones for Parkhurst are not included in any programmed building work approved for this establishment ... in my professional view geophones should be put in place rather earlier than is envisaged [1997/98]. ... I acknowledge that there are technical difficulties in introducing geophones while the redevelopment programme is under way, but it would certainly be of benefit during nights and weekends."
--.1.92	*Memo to Area Manager from DOC1* "I support the Governor's view that geophones should be added to the perimeter defences at Parkhurst. They act as a complementary defence to CCTV and have been for many years part of the standard hardware for our perimeter defence system. Historically Parkhurst has always been poorly provided, as it is only of recent years that perimeter CCTV was installed."

Date	Comments
21.1.92	*Memo to Governor from Area Manager* "It may well be that there are parts of the inner fence which will rarely be affected by the building work and these sections could be installed at an early stage."
22.1.92	*London South Area progress meeting* "Upgrade Perim Security Cat B ... DSP1 have asked DOW to provide costings on geophones and wall re-alignment. AM [Area Manager] exploring options for funding provision and installation of geophones." Action DOW/AM.
23.1.92	*Memo to Directorate of Works from Area Manager* "I came to the conclusion that I wanted to immediately alert you and other colleagues in DOW that I wish for the installation of geophones to proceed earlier than 1997/8 if this was practical, both technically and as far as funds are concerned. It seems to me difficult to justify asking Parkhurst to continue their massive building programme without the aid of geophones when they now have the new ECR and CCTV coverage in operation."
14.2.92	*Memo from Governor to Area Manager* Expresses his concerns about the way the redevelopment is being taken forward. "... I believe that returning to the original proposals will reduce the possibilities of escape, enable us to introduce geophones more easily and also help us to run this prison more sensibly."
19.2.92	*Parkhurst Redevelopment meeting* "Area Managers raised the question of the geophones which had been earmarked for installation after the completion of the Wing programme. Directorate of Services & Personnel [DSP1] said it was extremely difficult to see how this could be funded within the next three years. DOW could cost a scheme if DOC1 provided them with a brief showing how this work could be taken forward bearing in mind the extensive work which was already ongoing or planned at the establishment. Once a costed scheme was available, DSP1 would consider this again."

Date	Comments
24.2.92	*Internal memo on costings* "A rough order of cost for the above work has been estimated at £250K."
24.2.92	*Memo to DSP1* "... as agreed DT1 have produced a rough order of costs."
25.2.92	*Memo to DSP1 from DOC1* "There are a number of matters which have been raised in connection with Parkhurst by Mr ****. They include the omission of any specific reference to the installation of geophones at Parkhurst ..."
28.2.92	*Memo to DOC1 from DSP1* "We accept the need for geophones to be installed at Parkhurst but it is difficult to see how this could be funded within the period in question (DOW have recently provided us with a rough order of costs £250,000). Even if funds could be secured, careful consideration would have to be given as to how the installation could be fitted in with the extensive building programme already planned, particularly bearing in mind that, at various times in the next few years there will be one or more breaches in the wall and building work will be carried out close to the perimeter ... You may be assured that if the opportunity arises to introduce the installation of geophones into that programme we shall look at the position again."
2.3.92	*Note of meeting at Parkhurst prepared by DSP1* "Parkhurst remains the only Dispersal Prison without geophones. The building work should not be a sufficient reason not to install these devices, since the geophones could still be used outside the hours that the contractors are on site. The costs are estimated at £250K - but it is not clear where the funds will come from."
4.3.92	*Internal memo to Head of DOC1* "I have to express doubt that in spending large amounts of capital on refurbishing living accommodation sight has been lost of the need to provide a secure perimeter. If geophones cannot for funding reasons be provided within the programme until 1995/6 at the earliest, the threat of escape from within the prison should be reconsidered."

Date	Comments
13.3.92	*Internal memo to Head of DOC1* "The argument that Parkhurst has avoided a perimeter breach for many years without geophones will not really be sustainable for very long, but I think a further delay in installation can be justified if: (i) as seems to be the case, it makes NO PRACTICAL SENSE to install geophones other than as a coherent part of the large scale building work now in progress and planned. Adjacent building work and necessary gaps in the fence may materially reduce the effectiveness of geophones and/or result in disproportionate installation/disinstallation expenditure; and (ii) relevant OTHER MEASURES be taken in the interim. I am thinking here of enhanced patrolling."
17.3.92	*Internal memo to Head of DOC1* "The recent loss of high risk places at Frankland placed considerable strain on the rest of the Dispersal estate. If Parkhurst were to be similarly restricted, at a time when Gartree and Albany have withdrawn and when Frankland was not yet up to complement, then I think it would be very difficult indeed to manage the high risk population ... If availability of funds or other factors get in the way of early installation of geophones at Parkhurst, then we need to look for alternative security measures which will enable the establishment to continue to hold high escape risk prisoners."
20.3.92	*Memo from Governor to DOC1* "I agree that if we went down such a road it might expose weaknesses elsewhere in the system, and we should not be railroaded into making hasty decisions. There is no doubt that the building programme currently underway is a major security nightmare, and I would welcome any opportunity to discuss how we might best enhance our security arrangements so that all of us can be reasonably confident that adequate safeguards are in place."
26.3.92	*Internal memo DSP1* Reviews the contents of the previous memos and states that the Governor and Area Manager have asked for a feasibility study to be carried out to look at ways of phasing in geophones in the most effective way.

Date	Comments
27.3.92	*Memo to DOC1 from DSP1* Agrees that it would be useful to have an early meeting re Parkhurst geophones and asks that DSP1 and DOW should attend.
6.4.92	*Memo to Director of Custody from Area Manager* "Have made a bid for additional dog handlers and installation of geophones wherever possible."
6.4.92	*Internal memo to Head of DOC1* "I understand from Mr **** that DSP1, following a recent planning meeting with Area Manager, is exploring further just how geophones might be installed, perhaps on a piecemeal basis to fit in with the building programme as a whole."
7.4.92	*Letter from Area Manager to Governors London South* "Once the programme of work for the construction of the new kitchen and the refurbishment of B, C and M Wings had been settled, DSP1 would look at the possibility of installing geophones in phases in a way which fitted in with that programme. It was possible, therefore, that some of this work would be done before 1995/6."
9.4.92	*London South Area progress meeting* "Geophones & Stores In Transit" due to start 1995/96. Current position "DSP1 to look at possible piecemeal installation of geophones." Action DOW/AM.
19/20.5.92	*Attempted escape by five prisoners at Parkhurst* In the report of his investigation, Head of Custody recommended "All internal perimeter fences to be fitted with geophones as a matter of urgency."
28.5.92	*Minutes of Redevelopment Commission Team Meeting No.8* "Head of Custody has had a meeting with DOC1 who can see no reason why we should not have geophones. Governor to submit to Area Manager."
24.6.92	*Memo from DOC1 to DOW* "There is particular concern because the perimeter of Parkhurst is substandard having no geophone alarms except around the SSU."

Date	Comments
29.6.92	*Memo Area Manager to Operational Director* "... the installation of geophones would be taken forward ... as and when the programme of buildings allowed for the geophones to have any practical benefit."
17.8.92	*London South Area progress meeting* "Geophones & Stores In Transit" due to start 1995/96. Current position "DSP1 to look at possible piecemeal installation of geophones." Action DOW/AM.
14.10.92	*London South Area progress meeting* "Geophones & Stores In Transit" due to start 1995/96. Current position "DSP1 to look at possible piecemeal installation of geophones." Action DOW/AM.
10.11.92	*Letter from local MP to Home Secretary* "... my ongoing concerns about the lack of geophones at HMP Parkhurst."
8.12.92	*Memo to Area Manager's Office from Governor Parkhurst re: MP's letter* "... I have requested that geophones be provided on a number of occasions but I understand that money is not available."
14.12.92	*Memo from DSP1 to Private Office* "I offer a contribution along the following lines: As Kenneth Baker explained in his letter of 3 February, the installation of geophones will need to be carefully planned in conjunction with the other building work at the establishment. As you know, this year's public spending round was a particularly difficult one and it was not possible to make firm plans until we had a clearer idea of the resources which would be available. We are now in the process of finalising our plans for major building work in the light of the recent public expenditure settlement and we shall be examining how the installation of geophones might be phased in with this work."

Date	Comments
21.12.92	*DOC1 to Operational Director re prison building programme 1993/96* "... it is important that the money spent will bring us the greatest gains in terms of enhanced security and control ... arguable that much more significant improvements could be achieved by up-rating Category 'C' fences and/or fitting alarm systems to prison fences and possibly walls [than spending money on improved roof security]."
1993	*HMP Parkhurst Directorate of Works Building Strategy Study 1993* "A complete geophone system protecting the inner security fence would cost in the order of £200,000. It may be technically possible to integrate the CCTV cameras with the geophone system but some additional research needs to be done in this area. For preliminary costing purposes an additional £10,000 should be allowed for this."
18.1.93	*Letter from Home Office to local MP* "... the installation of geophones will need to be carefully planned in conjunction with other building work at the establishment. As you know, this year's public spending round was a particularly difficult one and it was not possible to make firm plans for building work at every establishment until we had a clearer idea of the resources which would be available. We are now in the process of finalising our plans for major building work in the light of the recent public expenditure settlement and we shall be examining how the installation of geophones might be phased in with this work."
20.1.93	*London South Area progress meeting* "Geophones & Stores In Transit." Current position "DSP1 to look at possible piecemeal installation of geophone." Action DOW/AM.
27.1.93	*Memo from Governor Parkhurst to Area Manager* Re attached correspondence "... I thought you should be aware of it in case it is appropriate to discuss with Headquarters colleagues. As you know, we are seeking the introduction of geophones to enhance our perimeter security."

Date	Comments
4.2.93	*Letter from Area Manager to DSP1* "..on 20 January I encouraged you to look for some way in which sections of the internal perimeter fence could be linked to the geophone system."
1.3.93	*Memo DSP1 to DOC1* "... seek view on whether installation of geophones should take precedence over other security schemes - must emphasise no additional funds can be made available."
9.3.93	*Meeting of a Working Party on the future of the Dispersal estate* "Again on a development issue the WP noted that the perimeter geophone installation needed to be accommodated in the programme budget. Its early installation, hampered by development access needs, would need to be piecemeal."
19.3.93	*Note of meeting at HMP Parkhurst* "The perimeter defences could be strengthened by the installation of geophones, and perhaps later by the addition of Diamond software (allowing "blank screen" technology) if trials elsewhere were successful."
25.3.93	*Memo DSP1 to DOC1* Invited DOC1 to allocate priorities amongst all security schemes then featuring in major capital building programme for 1993/94 and 1994/95. Asked how work arising from security audits in next three years is to be handled. "There is no scope in the current programme to admit new work (irrespective of the design/lead-in time necessary) unless it is to be at the expense of other security schemes." The attached table showed geophones not programmed to start until 1995/96 but suggested installation of geophones "may need to be done in 1994/95".
7.4.93	*London South Area progress meeting* "Geophones & Stores In Transit." Current position "DSP1 to look at possible piecemeal installation of geophones." Action DOW/AM.
7.7.93	*London South Area progress meeting* "Geophones & Stores In Transit". Current position "DSP1 to look at possible piecemeal installation of geophones." Action DOW/AM.

Date	Comments
6.10.93	*Memo to Area Manager from Governor Parkhurst* "I just wanted to make sure that in among all the other work, that we did not lose sight of the need for geophones to be installed at Parkhurst as soon as possible."
12.10.93	*Memo to Area Manager from DOC1* "The lack of any firm date for the installation of geophones or another perimeter alarm system must be of continuing concern. I need hardly set out the security arguments in favour of completing this investment."
15.10.93	*Memo to DOC1 from Area Manager* "I continue to press at every progress meeting that funding should be provided for the perimeter alarm system for the whole prison."
27.10.93	*Memo to DSP1 from DOW enclosing report on Building Programme* "HMP Parkhurst - Perimeter security. A final decision is awaited on the nature of these works - they are at present being designed."
10.11.93	*Memo to DOW from DSP1* "As you probably know, there is a long-standing requirement to improve the security of the inner perimeter fence at Parkhurst. DSP1 requested to carry out a feasibility study."
6.12.93	*Internal memo DSP1* "Area Manager saw me today and expressed concern that the Parkhurst perimeter security was not in the programme."
13.12.93	*DSP1 Executive Committee paper* For planning purposes the Executive Committee agree in principle to defer numerous security and other projects (including Parkhurst perimeter security) until 1995/96 or beyond to find money for houseblock programme (total of £110-120 million needed - Woolf). However they immediately put in hand measures to secure efficiency savings to enable these projects to be restored.

Date	Comments
20.12.93	*Review of Perimeter Security by DOC1* "... a lack of geophones on fences other than round the SSU..."
29.12.93	*Memo Area Manager to DOC1* "I shall continue to press for geophones and I understand that the latest list of major capital works programmes earmarks 1995/96 as the earliest this commitment can be undertaken."
21.1.94	*London South Area progress meeting* Perimeter security due to start 1996/97. Current position "Mr **** to provide feasibility study". Action DOW.
15.2.94	*Memo to DOW from DSP1* Requests information on options for improving the perimeter security at Parkhurst.
1.3.94	*Memo from Technical Services to DSP1* "Regarding options in Parkhurst Perimeter Security, there is only one system suitable for this type of prison and there are no staff savings." Enclosed is a report "1. Geophones £210K."
March 1994	*Memo to DOC1 from Area Manager* Expresses growing concern that the commitment to install geophones at Parkhurst has not yet been met.
23.3.94	*Memo to Area Manager from Governor Parkhurst* Re DOW co-ordinating meeting 1.2.94. "Items d and e refer to CCTV and geophones. It says that these have been withdrawn from the programme. Is this to be funded elsewhere."
5.4.94	*Memo to DOW from DSP1 re: Parkhurst perimeter security* "We are now hopeful that funds can be found in the financial year 1994/5 to allow work on the above project to go ahead."
6.4.94	*London South Area progress meeting* Perimeter security due to start 1996/97. Current position "Mr **** to provide feasibility study." Action WS [Works Services].

Date	Comments
14.4.94	*Report to Area Manager from Physical Security Adviser Works Services* "... there is a fundamental weakness in perimeter security at HMP Parkhurst ... the outer wall ... is actually in contact with the weld mesh fence which forms the inner perimeter ... problems exist with geophonically alarming the old wall section which runs parallel to the sides of the gate building. We recommend that this wall should be demolished and replaced by a security fence which can be effectively geophonically alarmed ... a programme of replacement of these panels is recommended but this is not vital to the installation of geophones. A good geophonic performance could be obtained by tensioning the existing panels."
4.5.94	*Internal memo DOW* "... BPS [Building Planning Services] request advice on as to whether the implementation of this during the course of other contracts on site will levy significant or disruptive effect on these contracts ..."
6.5.94	*Memo to DOW from Building Planning Services* Refers DOW to Physical Security Adviser's report of 14.4.94, describing a scheme to fit geophones at Parkhurst.
27.5.94	*Memo Area Manager to Financial Support Section re Capital Availability Planning* Area Manager prioritised bids showing Parkhurst perimeter security to be among the "essential" bids.
3.6.94	*Memo from Area Manager to Physical Security Adviser* Governor and he wish to take forward proposals about geophones.
7.7.94	*London South Area progress meeting* Current schemes show "Perimeter security - Geophones" due to start 1996/97. Current position "BPS to liaise with WS in preparation of a draft scheme for implementation when funding becomes available. Mr **** to provide feasibility study." Action BPS/WS.

Date	Comments
9.9.94	*Memo from Area Manager to Director of Works* "I am writing to confirm that with the assistance of Governors in London South I am able to provide £400,000 to pay for the upgrading of perimeter security at Parkhurst ..."
17.9.94	*Memo to Director of Custody from Area Manager* Asks for the removal of High Risk Category "A" inmates whilst building work, including upgrading of perimeter security, takes place.
20.9.94	*Internal memo DOW Copy Governor Parkhurst* Funding has been secured to upgrade perimeter security.
22.9.94	*Minutes of meeting between Governor and POA* Governor confirms that geophones will be fitted this year.
Nov 1994	Construction Services inform Area Manager that area funding would not actually be required - Directorate funding was available.
6.12.94	*Note of Area Co-ordinators Meeting at Parkhurst* Perimeter Security Upgrade - Work started 5 December.

APPENDIX G
BACKGROUND INFORMATION ON ESCAPEES

Background Information on Escapees

Schedule from prisoner's security file - Case A

27.4.89 Sentenced to Life Imprisonment for conspiracy to cause explosions, acting with intent to cause explosions, conspiracy to pervert the course of justice, administering poison, attempted arson, theft, arson, possessing an article with intent to endanger life, damaging property and possessing an explosive substance.

4.5.89 Confirmed Category A (Standard).

15.5.89 Suspected of packing match heads into pen top and causing explosion.

24.7.89 Senior Officer Category A report: considered him to have the ability and determination to plan and activate a serious escape attempt.

2.8.89 Found with alcohol.

16.8.89 Governor issued notice to all staff stating he is extremely dangerous.

27.8.89 Found with alcohol.

13.10.89 Found with fermenting liquid.

28.12.89 Found with broken clock face in cell.

23.1.90 Made suggestion to another Category A about building work going on in prison grounds - drive JCB up to the wall, extend the bucket arm and escape.

8.2.90 Unauthorised possession of oil.

2.3.90 Caused unrest in which another inmate was threatened with knifing.

6.3.90 Covered cell observation glass and found with quantity of oil.

15.3.90 Warned re stirring up other inmates.

7.9.90 Requested bio-chemistry books.

15.9.90 Requested bio-chemistry books.

18.9.90 Requested bio-chemistry books.

25.10.90 Seen taking an interest and notes on switch mechanism on cleaning machine.

30.11.90 Warned re going to work without an escort.

14.1.91	Tried to buy LEDs [light - emitting diode], solar cells, switches.
5.2.91	Produced three 2 litre bottles of liquid with stoppers. All the bottles under pressure and when undone gave off a foul smelling gas. Stated that the liquid had gone off but was for propagating seeds.
23.5.91	Cell search revealed radio equipment, home-made transmitting device, radio jamming device, electronic timing device, morse code machine.
2.9.91	**Cell in segregation searched and a map of Court of Appeal found, showing fire escapes etc.**
6.9.91	**Items found in his cell after transfer ie white crystals, container of white powder, washing bowls containing fine powder, film box containing brown crystals - the Chartered Chemist who examined the items stated they were bomb mixtures.**
6.11.91	Collected string and plant food.
24.11.91	Threatened to kill staff if moved.
10.12.91	Used IT in education to make forged documents.
31.12.91	Lead found running from his cell to VHF grid socket in TV room.
21.1.92	Banned from education centre. Used IT to make up dubious letter-headings.
4.2.92	Mixed with Irish terrorist.
7.5.92	Found to have an excessive amount of contact base solution in cell (irritant to body.).
7.5.92	Applied for full-time education or engineering VTC course.
27.5.92	Paid great attention to building work in B Wing.
29.6.92	Commenced 18 week VTC course in welding.
3.7.92	Applied for discretionary visits from brother's fiancee which was refused. Overheard making arrangements on the phone for her to visit on another inmate's VO [Visiting Order].
17.10.92	Cell door found to be locked 'out of frame' overnight.
13.2.93	**Paid particular attention to section of perimeter fence.**
20.2.93	Inmates stated he was responsible for spate of false alarms.
10.4.93	**Seen pacing out distance between cameras on perimeter.**
16.5.93	Believed responsible for series of false alarms.

20.5.93	Seen to pull up man-hole cover near to perimeter.
7.7.93	Climbed ladder into tank room. Asked questions about plumbing system.
15.7.93	Attempted to escape during an escort by threatening an Officer with a needle infected with HIV.
15.7.93	Transferred to Parkhurst.
21.7.93	Spent time near fence and remained in camera blind spot.
31.7.93	Seen on grass verges near perimeter fence, looking at roof of VTC and pacing out distances.
4.8.93	Seen regularly walking in grass area near perimeter fence.
6.8.93	Acting suspiciously near perimeter fence.
20.8.93	Charged with tampering with cell light switch.
29.9.93	May have been responsible for fracturing of a gas pipe.
4.10.93	Head of Custody issued instruction to the ECR: "Inmate to be followed by camera cover at all possible times whilst on compound."
13.10.93	Failed to return to cell - passive demonstration.
3.11.93	In wood store unaccompanied for 20 minutes and using power tools.
29.6.94	Intended to obtain an exercise bike to utilise it to set up an 'electrocution' arrangement.
18.8.94	Found on compound recess roof.
25.10.94	Cell search revealed electronic lighter, 2 wires attached, screwdriver and a drill bit.
25.10.94	Visitor brought in chemicals for him which could be used to make explosives.
1.11.94	Conditioned staff into allowing him into VTC class to finish a project started earlier in the year and which he had finished.
22.11.94	Found in an unauthorised place, in the VTC.

Schedule from prisoner's security file - Case B

1.2.90	Confirmed as a Category B prisoner.
5.2.90	Charged with murder and changed to Category A Standard Risk.
24.2.90	Found in possession of £10 in hospital Wing.
10.7.90	**Attempted to escape from Exeter Magistrates' Courts.**
14.9.90	Sentenced to 15 years imprisonment for kidnapping etc.
21.9.90	Placed on Escape ('E') list.
2.11.90	Information received that he intends to escape.
9.11.90	Review of 'E' list: remained 'ON'.
14.11.90	**Planning to escape. Confirmed by reliable police informant.**
15.11.90	Placed on High Risk visit instructions.
7.12.90	**Named with 3 other inmates as planning an escape.**
17.1.90	Review of 'E' list: remained 'ON'.
4.3.91	5 razor blades found in cell. 5 razor blades found hidden in heel of his shoe.
19.3.91	Sentenced to life imprisonment for murder.
22.3.91	Placed on 'E' list.
25.4.91	Removed from High Risk visits restrictions.
3.5.91	Removed from 'E' list.
4.7.91	**Believed involved in escape attempt.**
18.7.91	Computer discs found in cell, taken from education.
20.7.91	**Anxious to get to Court.**
6.1.92	**Information received re escape plan.**
24.9.92	Confirmed Category A.
5.1.94	**Information received re escape plan.**
10.1.94	Arrived at Parkhurst.
19.5.94	Wire and crocodile clips found in cell.
18.11.94	Category A reviews: remained Category A (Standard).

Schedule from prisoner's security file - Case C

22.8.86	Confirmed as a Category A prisoner.
6.11.87	Life imprisonment for murder.
16.2.88	Removed from Category A list. Recommendation to keep him in Dispersal system.
18.8.88	Assessment stated that he must be considered an escape risk.
4.1.89	Involved in assault on gym staff by throwing weights at them.
17.12.89	Smashed up a workshop.
5.4.90	Petitioned for a move to a prison with better gym facilities. Supported by Wing Governor.
21.5.90	Refused to work in workshop.
3.7.90	Confirmed Category B prisoner.
4.1.91	Arrived Parkhurst.
5.1.91	Profile described him as extremely violent, psychiatrically disturbed.
23.6.93	Violent outburst. Damaged cell in Segregation Unit.
7.9.93	Violent outburst.
14.9.93	Threatened staff with violence.
14.10.93	Recommended for a progressive transfer.
18.10.93	Psychologist agreed with progressive transfer. Supported by Probation Officer and Wing Personal Officer.
14.11.93	Violent outburst.
22.12.93	Probation Officer recommended progressive transfer.
25.4.94	Informed Home Secretary has declared a 17 year sentence. Judge had recommended 12.
15.11.94	Refused permission to attend weight-lifting championship. Security risk.

APPENDIX H
EXISTING PARKHURST MANAGEMENT STRUCTURE

EXISTING PARKHURST MANAGEMENT STRUCTURE

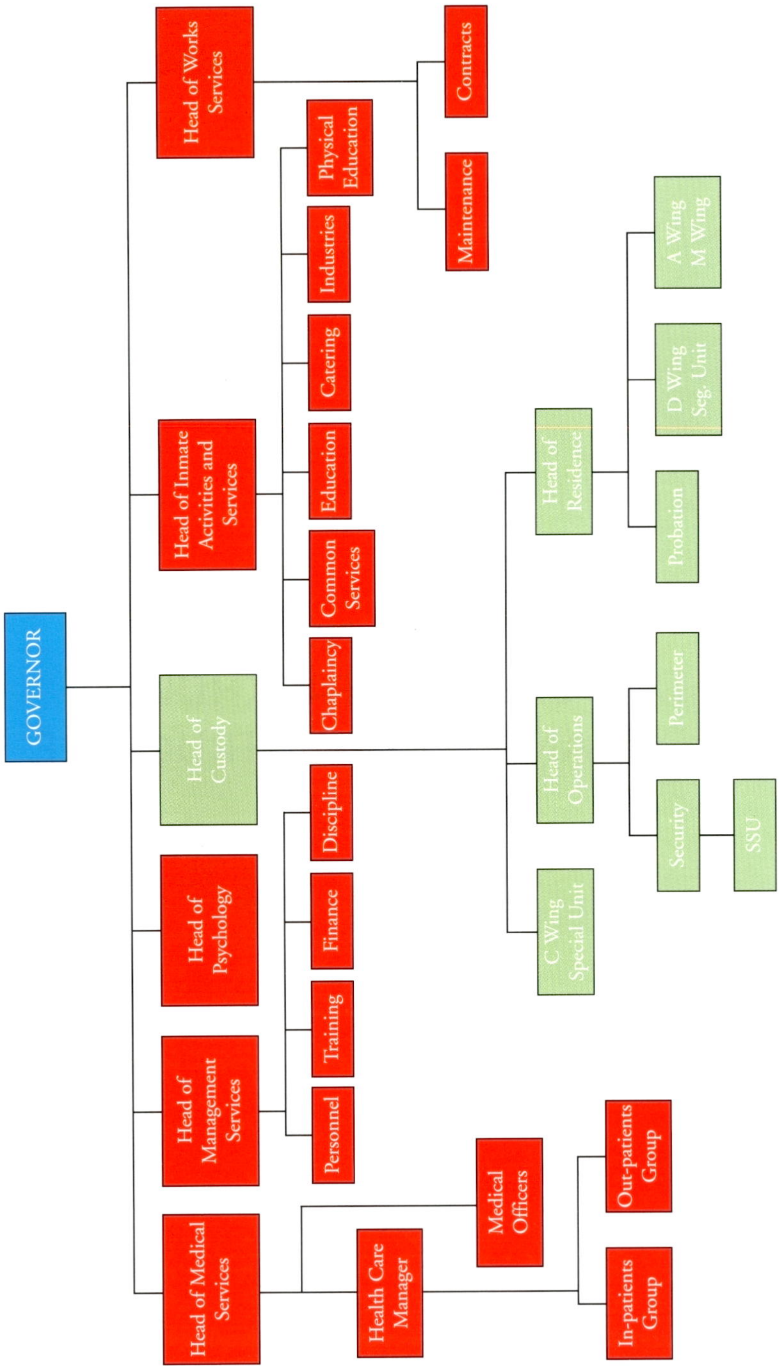

APPENDIX I
PART OF PRISONS BOARD'S SALMON RESPONSE – ACHIEVEMENTS OF THE PRISON SERVICE SINCE IT BECAME AN AGENCY ON 1ST APRIL 1993 – REPRODUCED WITHOUT COMMENT

Part of Prisons Board's Salmon Response – Achievements of the Prison Service since it became an Agency on 1st April 1993 – Reproduced without Comment

Key Performance Indicators

- The rate of escapes from prison and escorts has been reduced by 49% since the Service became an Agency in April 1993 (targets exceeded).
- Escapes in the period October 1994-March 1995 were 67% down on October 1992-March 1993.
- Absconds from open prisons have been reduced by 33% since April 1993.
- Assaults on staff and prisoners rose by 21% in 1993/94 (as a percentage of the prison population), continuing the historical trend. However so far this year, the trend has been reversed, one year ahead of the target set for the Agency, with a reduction of 6.5% (target achieved).
- Trebling was eliminated in 1993/94 (target achieved) and that has been maintained this year.
- Nearly 11,000 additional prison places have been provided with 24 hour access to sanitation since April 1994 (target exceeded). Over 95% of prisoners have access to sanitation, and we are on target to complete the sanitation programme by February 1996.
- The average hours of purposeful activity per prisoner per week have been increased by 11% since April 1993 (ahead of target).
- Prisoners with 12 hours or more out of cell have increased from 24% in April 1993 to 40% in March 1995.
- The proportion of prisoners with the opportunity for visits in excess of the legal minimum has increased from 84% to 100% since April 1993 (target achieved).
- Cost per baseline CNA place has been reduced by around 3% in real terms over the two years since the Service became an agency. Cost per in-use CNA place (a more meaningful short-term measure) has been reduced by 5% over the same two years.

Security

- Escorting procedures and hardware have been substantially improved, producing a 71% reduction in escapes from escorts in the period October

1994 – March 1995 compared to October 1992 – March 1993.

- Category C prison procedural and physical security has been improved, producing a 41% reduction in escapes. Action includes the cladding of all Category C fences.

- Security Group was created in January 1995. Early activities include:
  - issuing security handbooks of Dos and Don'ts to all staff
  - developing security awareness training with Training Services for all staff who come into contact with prisoners
  - organising a security poster campaign in establishments

- 30 of the Woodcock Report's 64 recommendations have been implemented. Work continues on the implementation of the remaining recommendations. Those already implemented include:
  - improved training in the use of X-ray and metal detection equipment
  - improved cell searching procedures
  - the security awareness training and security handbooks mentioned above.

- The re-opening of Whitemoor's SSU is imminent, with improved operating procedures that have entailed the implementation of a further 21 Woodcock recommendations within that Unit.

Home Leave/Temporary Release

- Home leave and temporary release failures have been reduced by 49% since the Prison Service became an Agency and a radical new home leave policy has been successfully introduced (so far without causing major disturbance).

Incentives and privileges

- A national framework of incentives for good behaviour and hard work has been developed and was published on 9 June. Implementation starts in July.

Prison Discipline

- Governors powers under the prison discipline and adjudication system have been strengthened by increasing penalties.

High Intensity Training Programme

- A pilot project for young offenders based on the successful elements of the high impact programmes in the United States has been developed.

Health Care

- Responsibility for health care in establishments has been devolved to Governors.

- Methods of providing health care in establishments have been developed to raise standards and provide better value for money:
  - prison establishments have entered into cluster arrangements for complementary health care provision to minimise unnecessary duplication of services; and
  - pilot contracts for mental health and genito-urinary medicine services have been placed with the NHS and are under evaluation for further development of contracting throughout the service. A model contract for the purchase of primary care services is in final stages of development.
- The first "Heath Care Standard" was published in 1994. Since then 8 further Standards have been produced.
- The "Audit for Nursing Standards" was produced in 1994 and provides a framework for assessing standards of nursing provision throughout the service.
- Major improvements in the care of the mentally ill have occurred over the last 3 years and are continuing including:
  - increased transfers of mentally ill to appropriate NHS care from 325 in 1990 to 760 in 1994; and
  - improved management of the mentally disordered within prison with an increase in professional skills (e.g. mental health nurses) and improved treatment approaches, including decrease in use of unfurnished rooms.
- Continuing development of approaches to treatment and care of those with addiction has been an important area of work.
- In line with the national strategy "Health of the Nation", the Prison Service instituted pilot health promotion programmes in 5 establishments in 1993/94. Smoking policies are now widespread in establishments.
- Prevention of HIV infection has been a particular health promotion focus and much has been achieved:
  - 93% of prisons have multi-disciplinary HIV teams;
  - 88% of prisons have trained HIV counsellors; and
  - 2 award-winning videos have been produced for use in prisoner induction programmes.
- Important advances have been made in staff health, including the provision of lifestyle screening to over 13,000 members of staff in establishments, since 1933.

- The 3-year registered nurse training for Prison Health Care Officers has to date accepted 24 Officers. Other Officers have been encouraged to undertake National Vocational Qualifications. To date, 287 applications for these courses have been approved.
- Recruitment and allocation of pharmacists has increased significantly.
- Major strides have been made in improving the training for prison medical officers.

Offending Behaviour and Training

- All adult male prisoners convicted of serious sex offences now have access to the intensive sex offender treatment programme. The number of prisoners completing the core programme increased from 284 in 1992/93 to 568 in 1994/95.
- Anger management programmes have been introduced at 45 prisons.
- A centrally co-ordinated cognitive skills programme was introduced in 1993/94 and 109 prisoners completed the programme that year. This figure increased to 213 in 1994/95, and is projected to be over 400 in 1995/96.
- Sentence planning, using standard documentation, is in place for all adult male prisoners serving 12 months or more.
- Separate life sentence plans, incorporating a comprehensive risk assessment, have been introduced for all lifers.
- 737 NVQ schemes are now being implemented in 1994/95.
- By the end of 1994:
  - 106 prisons were running prisoner development and pre-release courses
  - 115 prisons were offering an employment and housing advice service following training from NACRO's Prison Links Unit
  - 59 prisons were operating the Employment Focus scheme.

Prisoner Activities

- In 1994/95, 8 individual workshops achieved accreditation to ISO 9002/BS5750 for their quality assurance systems.
- As of April 1995, over 800 prisoners were employed in self-financing enhanced wages schemes, in which substantial increases in productivity more than covered the costs of the additional pay.
- During 1994/95, over 6m hours of organised physical education activity were delivered.

- Vocational Qualifications (NVQs) are now available to prisoners in 650 occupational areas. 13,470 NVQ Units were achieved in 1994/95, compared with 7,790 in the previous year.

Management

- The Board has been restructured and for the first time has taken operational command, supplemented by a new Executive Committee for detailed operating matters and the assignment of clear responsibility and accountability to the management line.
- Management information is now being provided regularly for the Board and at establishment level.
- Private sector financial management, including a private sector finance director, has been introduced.
- Governors have been given overall budgets with the responsibility and authority to manage those resources to the best effect and they have been made accountable for everything that happens within their prison.
- Targets have been set for each establishment and Governors are held accountable for their achievement.
- Communication systems have been changed and improved to ensure that Governors are clear what new instructions are mandatory and what are discretionary.
- A fundamental review of Headquarters has been completed. As a first stage, staff levels will be reduced from 2200 to 1600. Responsibilities have been clarified and service functions (which have been made accountable to their "customers" in establishments and elsewhere) split from Headquarters.
- The process for implementing change has been radically overhauled with the introduction of project teams operating to specific briefs, with firm milestones and deadlines and follow-up monitoring.

Personnel policy

- The Prison Service has successfully taken over from the Treasury responsibility for determining the pay of staff in the Prison Service and the first settlements (1994 pay round) were within the remit approved by Ministers.
- A new performance planning and review system which is tailored to the needs of the Service and to the delivery of its objectives has been introduced.
- A Code of Conduct and Discipline founded on ACAS principles has been introduced.

- A dedicated Prison Service Staff Care and Welfare Service has been established.
- Average training time for unified grades increased from 4.7 days per year in 1993/94 to 5.8 days per year in 1994/95.
- A National Training Plan was issued for the first time in 1995/96. It specifies the mandatory training requirements for all staff occupational groups.

Industrial Relations

- Industrial relations, which have been a major barrier to progress, have been transformed after decades of inaction.
- The POA has been confronted and legislation introduced and court rulings obtained that will create the basis for proper industrial relations.
- Local industrial relations have also been transformed and the POA successfully confronted at the prisons with notoriously obstructive local branches - such as Wandsworth, Gartree, Preston and Liverpool.
- The consistent and firm position taken by the Prison Service has brought about crucial changes in the composition of the National Executive Committee of the POA.

Private Sector Involvement

- Four out of ten court escort areas have been put under private management, producing:
  - cost reductions of about 15% (£13 million a year);
  - a 40% reduction in escapes; and
  - a better service to the courts.
- Contracts have been awarded to provide court escort services in another two areas and are out to tender on three of the remaining four.
- Four prisons are under private management, producing beneficial competition for the rest of the Service, as well as innovations in regimes and reductions in Unit costs of 15% to 25% (£5 million a year).
- The Prison Service has been breaking new ground for Private Finance with the DCMF (Design, Construct, Finance and Manage) contracts for new prison building.

Capital Expenditure

- Entirely new procedures have been introduced to ensure effective planning, prioritisation, line management, authorisation and control of capital expenditure. This was fully in place for the current PES allocations.

- Dramatically different construction techniques were introduced for the building of Buckley Hall which have resulting in:
  - construction of a complete prison in 10 months since the receipt of the planning permission (less than half of the conventional time of 2 years plus); and
  - construction at half the cost of previous construction (£50,000 per place compared with an average of £126,000 per place for other new gallery prisons).
- New designs of kitchen have been introduced which have reduced costs by up to two thirds. (Previously kitchens cost between £2 and £3 million each, compared with £0.7 to £1.0 million for the new design.)
- Costs of new houseblocks have been reduced by over a third.

Construction work

- A total of 2378 additional prison places have been provided. This includes the completion of new Category B prisons at Blakenhurst and Doncaster and a new Category C prison at Buckley Hall.
- Major refurbishment work has been completed involving the upgrading of a total of 1891 cells. This included the upgrading of security and installation of sanitation.
- A further 6750 existing cells had sanitation installed and the Prison Service is on schedule to end "slopping out" by the revised target date of February 1996.
- Major phases of redevelopment work have been completed at Wormwood Scrubs (the spinelink) and at Leeds (new accommodation and regime facilities).

Internal Audit

- The number of establishment audits has increased by a third (45 visits in 1993/94, 60 visits in 1994/95). In addition, 20 short visits and 6 follow up visits were carried out in 1994/95.
- The systems covered during the audit visits have been expanded to include: payroll, SPAR, LIDS, works etc.
- Audit testing of transactions has also been increased eg in the areas of procurement and travel and subsistence claims.
- The cost per audit day has been reduced by 35% (from £324 to £210) and the full economic cost of the service has been reduced by 10%.
- Governors and Area Managers have confirmed their satisfaction with the enhanced customer focus. Feedback from establishments (post-audit

questionnaires are issued after every audit) indicates that the vast majority are satisfied with the service provided.

- More frequent audit visits and presentations at Area Manager seminars (9 in 1994/95) and the HOMS conference have raised the profile of Internal Audit.

Standards Audit

- For the first time, a comprehensive code of operating standards, covering everything from security to hygiene and visiting arrangements, was introduced in April 1994.
- The Standards Audit team will now audit every prison at least once every two years to ensure that standards (including security) are being met.
- This audit work commenced in January 1995. A security audit will have been completed in the 33 establishments holding Category A prisoners by the end of June 1995.

IT Services/Systems Strategy

- A number of IT services have been contracted out:
  - IT Help Desk services
  - UNIX systems installation
  - application integration testing
  - PC installation
  - CAD system specification, design and implementation
- The development of Version 22 of LIDS was completed and it was installed in all establishments on time.
- PHASE I development of the personnel system has been completed and the system installed in 47 establishments in five months. PHASE II requirements have been defined and 81 management seminars held in three months.
- CCCJS: equipment was installed for a pilot project at Winchester. Equipment will be installed at Norwich in June.

Planning

- A Fully integrated planning system was designed and launched (May 1995).
- A Scoping study for an Information Strategy was completed. The study is now underway.

- A new strategic R&D programme was developed and is in the process of implementation.

Finance/Accounting

- A cost per place reduction strategy was established, using savings to help fund additional accommodation and improvements to existing establishments.
- The Prison Service budget was managed so as to finance £52 million additional capital expenditure through use of in-year savings.
- Objective efficiency comparisons into the internal budget setting process have been introduced.
- Responsibility for Prison Officers and other budgets totalling £690 million has been devolved to establishments (in April 1993, April 1994 and April 1995).
- Budget profiling arrangements for the Prisons Vote were introduced in April 1994.
- A financial regime for the Agency with considerably simplified Treasury delegations was introduced in April 1993.
- A revised process for prioritising capital expenditure and evaluating project cost benefits was in place by May 1995.
- A new Service-wide financial information system to provide Vote, accruals and functional costs data has been established and piloted.
- Arranged to produce trial accruals accounts with effect from 1994/95 (March 1995).
- A full assets register was completed in March 1995.
- Prison Service accounts and banking functions were established in Autumn 1994.
- A Service-wide financial training initiative was launched in Summer 1994.
- A programme to provide professional accountancy skills for all establishments has commenced.
- The Finance Manual has been revised and simplified and will be issued in June 1995.
- A scoping study for the general use of private finance in the Prison Service was established in Spring 1995.
- Shadow charging for 6 internal services commenced in April 1995.

Supply and Transport Services

- Substantial progress has been made in the introduction of a cash catering system to prisons, so that it is now operating in 116 establishments.
- There has been continued improvements in the supply of prisoners' socks and underpants so that by the end of June 1995 all prisoners will be able to have a daily change of these items.

Population

- The performance of the Prison Service must be assessed against a background of an unprecedented rise in the prison population. From a low of 40,600 in December 1992 the population has now reached 52,000 - an increase of nearly 30%.
- This has been accommodated with minimum recourse to police cells. There have been an average of about 170 prisoners in police cells this year (this will end this month) compared with nearly 2000 in 1992. Trebling has been eliminated and there was only one significant disturbance (Wymott).

APPENDIX J
KEY PERFORMANCE INDICATORS (KPIs)

Key Performance Indicators (KPIs)

KPIs and Other Standards

1. The Prison Service has a number of ways of describing standards which its staff should strive to meet. The Corporate Plan, 1994-97 includes, in addition to the **Statement of Purpose**, a **Vision**:

   "Our vision is to provide a service, through both directly managed and contracted prisons, of which the public can be proud and which will be regarded as a standard of excellence around the world."

2. There are five **Values**:

   " ■ *Integrity is fundamental to everything we do.*

   ■ *Commitment by our staff and to our staff.*

   ■ *Care for prisoners.*

   ■ *Equality of opportunity.*

   ■ *Innovation and Improvement."*

3. There are seven **Strategic Priorities:**

   " ■ *Providing sufficient accommodation for the projected prison population.*

   ■ *Reducing the level of violence and drug misuse in prisons.*

   ■ *Improving the quality, relevance and delivery of regime activities and introducing differential regimes based on prisoners' behaviour and willingness to co-operate.*

   ■ *Setting standards for establishments and developing a system of performance review and audit.*

   ■ *Improving cost efficiency and value for money.*

   ■ *Devolving responsibility to Governors and transforming the relationship between establishments and Headquarters.*

   ■ *Developing a well trained, well motivated staff with a shared commitment to the Service's goals and values."*

4. And there are six **Goals** and eight **KPIs** all remaining unchanged in the 1995-98 Corporate Plan. These are related, as shown in the table below. Although purpose, vision, values, goals and strategic priorities are unexceptionable as sentiments, the Inquiry has been unable to understand their relationship with each other or with the KPIs chosen. Staff in

establishments are equally confused and this may have some bearing on why so few hopes have been fulfilled.

The relationship between Service Goals and KPIs		
	Goals	KPIs
1.	Keeping prisoners in custody.	Escapes from establishments or escorts.
2.	Maintaining order, control, discipline and a safe environment.	Assaults on staff, inmates and others.
3.	Providing decent conditions for prisoners and meeting their needs, including health care.	Prisoners held in Units intended for fewer numbers. Prisoners with 24 hour access to sanitation.
4.	Providing positive regimes which help prisoners address their offending behaviour and allow them as full and responsible a life as possible.	Hours spent in purposeful activity. Proportion of prisoners held in establishments where they are unlocked on weekdays for at least 12 hours.
5.	Helping prisoners prepare for their return to the community.	Proportion of prisoners held in establishments where they can exceed the minimum visiting entitlement.
6.	Delivering prison services using the resources provided by parliament with maximum efficiency.	Average cost per prisoner per place.

KPI 1 - Escapes

5. The KPI on escapes is the only one with any direct implication for custody and that sends out a poor message as to the importance of security. The number of escapes is a necessary item of management information but it is a negative measure and indicates degree of failure rather than success. As the Service has discovered, most recently at Parkhurst, an escape-free record does not mean that an establishment is secure.

6. Prison Service data on escapes is produced in the following categories:

- Escapes from establishments - prisoners who have had to overcome a physical barrier to escape.
- Escapes from escorts - prisoners who have escaped while being escorted outside a secure perimeter.
- Absconds - prisoners who escape without having to overcome a physical barrier, including those who escape from external work parties but also from open Category C and D prisons.
- Temporary release failures (TRFs) - prisoners who have been given leave of absence and failed to return at the due time.

7. These figures can easily be misleading, especially when quoted in isolation. The Director General has shown the ambiguity of such statistics by announcing to a conference of the Howard League in September 1994 that:

> *"The Prison Service has been increasingly successful in achieving its key performance indicators, most notably in terms of escapes which have fallen by some 20% this year so far."*

8. By the time the 1993/94 Annual Report was published, that statistic had improved further and was quoted as an overall reduction of 25%. The statistics quoted are accurate but hide a situation that the public might consider less of a cause for congratulation. First, they relate only to escapes from establishments and escorts, amounting to 273 from a total of 4,796 illicit absences in 1993/94. The latter figure equates to nearly 10% of the total prison population.

9. Second, hidden within the escape figures, are a number of escapes by very dangerous individuals, who only count as 'one' each in the bald statistics. Whatever the semantics of the statistical argument, in a period of less than four months, from September 1994 to January 1995, nine of the most dangerous prisoners in the system escaped from two of the very highest security prisons, the worst escape record in the history of the Service. The 1994/95 KPI statistics in their present format are unlikely to convey the seriousness of the situation or stimulate action to prevent further escapes.

10. The Scottish Prison Service uses, as a performance measure, the number of Category A and B prisoners unlawfully at large, which usefully concentrates attention on the most dangerous prisoners. The Key Targets are:

> *"No 'A' Category prisoners should escape.*

The number of escapes by 'B' Category prisoners should be no higher than 2.5 per 1,000 prisoners."

11. It was encouraging to read in the latest Business Plan (1995/96), published 1st April 1995, that the Prison Service is moving towards similar performance measures.

12. Four more positive measures of security are suggested by the Inquiry:

- The number of months since the last escape of a high security prisoner.
- The percentage of establishments in which no escape has occurred in the preceeding 12 months.
- The number of prisoners kept in prisons where no escape has occurred in the preceeding 12 months.
- The percentage of establishments meeting recognised security standards (appropriate to their category).

KPI 2 - Assaults

13. Assaults are an important indicator but the way the Prison Service calculates them is a curious combination of all assaults, including those on staff, inmates and any other person, expressed as a percentage of the overall prison population. In recent years, this calculation has produced a steady and continuous increase, from 7.7% in 1989/90 to 12.3% in 1993/94. The Prison Service draws comfort from the outturn figure for 1994/95 of 11.6%.

14. If the individual components of the calculation are examined, a more mixed and less comforting picture emerges. Assaults on staff have continued to increase but this is hidden by the statistics, because of the reduction in assaults on inmates and the increase in prison population. Between 1989 and 1994, the number of assaults on staff almost doubled, from 1,750 to 3,204 (the projected figure for 1994/95 is a further increase to 3,318). Whilst the 1994 Annual Report suggests that this increase could result from a more strenuous approach to deterring and punishing perpetrators of violence, it should concern the Service that the numbers of assaults on staff shows no evidence of falling.

KPI 3 - Prisoners held in Units intended for fewer numbers

15. Genuine progress has been made, with no prisoners now held three to a cell in accommodation intended for single occupancy. The Annual Report revealed that the number held two to a single cell increased in 1993/94 and that a number of prisoners were still housed in police cells towards the end of the year; but the situation had improved overall.

KPI 4 - Access to 24 hour sanitation

16. Although statistics supporting this KPI indicate considerable success, the Inquiry found that the introduction of sanitation to individual cells had brought problems. Some prisoners were complaining that they were now eating food in a lavatory. Others have made strong representations over the lack of privacy, since male or female Officers can view the lavatory from the door portholes. In some establishments, the privacy argument has been used to justify the covering of portholes, with obvious security implications.

KPI 5 - Time in purposeful activity

17. Whilst the Service seeks to increase time spent in purposeful activity, other aspects of prison life militate against this objective. The time permitted in workshop activity is restricted, due to prison routines and increased visiting entitlements. In any case, the attraction of such work to inmates is severely limited by the unimaginative nature of the work and the lack of any realistic incentive to work or sanction against not working.

18. Staff commented that the official statistics on this KPI were exaggerated. They seemed unaware of the definitive description of what is 'purposeful activity' and each establishment has applied its own interpretation. Whilst time spent in classrooms was virtually always logged as purposeful activity, the reality was often that it amounted to no more than free association, since inmates did not take part in classes but simply sat together at the rear of the class and chatted. Even in prisons where great effort has been made to provide genuinely purposeful activities, the total of such activity is limited because of staff and instructor shortages. This makes targets difficult to achieve legitimately.

KPI 6 - Time out of cell

19. This KPI is potentially dangerous to good order and control within the establishments. In 1993/94, 29% of prisoners were in establishments where the time out of cells exceeded 12 hours per day. Ideally, much of the time should be devoted to purposeful activity but that was rarely found to be the case.

20. Because there is a target, staff have attempted to reach it, regardless of a widespread concern, often shared by the inmates themselves, that the additional time only leads to aimless or, worse, mischievous activity. The Prison Service Inspectorate have officially recognised that, in the absence of positive alternatives, extra time out of cell makes for increased boredom, which generates trouble.

21. This KPI is supposed to support the Goal of providing more positive regimes but it has been counterproductive in many cases.

KPI 7 - Exceeding visiting hours

22. Visiting hours are related to the Goal of assisting prisoners to prepare for their return to the community. Liberal allowances, and a lack of any true measure of the end result, make any such correlation tenuous.

23. Because the KPI dictates an absolute target, no attempt has been made to focus the privilege of additional visits on the most deserving prisoners, such as those in drug-free Wings, nor to use it as any other form of incentive. As with time out of cell, there was simply a compulsion on the staff to squeeze in as many visits as humanly possible, to meet and exceed targets.

KPI 8 - Average cost per prisoner place

24. This is an understandable and potentially useful measure, provided care is exercised to measure like with like. There are inherent dangers if the only motive is to drive down costs, because the Inquiry learnt that security measures are often the first to be cut. It is not clear whether the statistics produced by the Prison Service are a genuine measure of "maximum efficiency", in accordance with the Goal.

Areas omitted from KPIs

25. In addition to examining those indicators chosen by the Service, the Inquiry found a number of areas within the stated aims or objectives of the organisation which were not covered by KPIs. They were: Headquarters staff reductions, staff development and commitment, recidivism, physical security, discipline, drugs and suicides.

26. Previous business plans had contained targets covering devolution or the further reduction of Headquarters staffing. It is a matter of concern that these were removed, despite lack of progress.

27. An omission with both organisational and morale implications is the absence of any KPI linked to staff development and commitment. In the USA, the importance of prison staff is recognised and written into the 'core values' and published priorities of the Prison Service. The Federal Bureau of Prisons has eight core values, of which four relate directly to staff, and six strategic long-term goals, of which human resource management appears as second highest. The goal is supported by a commitment to effective recruitment, selection, training and development strategies.

28. It is interesting to contrast this with the published priorities of HM Prison Service. Although the Values within the Prison Service Corporate Plan, 1994-97 include a commitment to staff, as 'the most important asset of the Prison Service', none of the six Goals are staff-related. Only the last of seven Strategic Priorities relates to staff, namely:

"Developing a well trained, well motivated staff with a shared commitment to the Service's goals and values."

29. The Inquiry found scant evidence that this strategic priority has significantly influenced either policy or practice in any area, including training. Staff consistently highlighted the absence of a KPI linked to staff development. It was clear that this had a significantly detrimental effect on morale.

30. On the question of recidivism the measurement of performance is not straightforward and calls for co-operation with other Agencies, for example the Courts, the Police and the Probation Service. One problem is the time lapse, because offender behaviour in any one year could depend on regimes experienced years before. Nevertheless, it is difficult to see how the Service can retain the overall objective without measuring the results. Although one year's figures may not indicate whether efforts that same year have been successful, there are still important conclusions to be drawn, in particular from the trend.

31. There are no indicators on physical security, discipline, drugs or suicides. Identifying appropriate measures for these is not easy and more work is needed but if, for example, a goal is to make prisons, or at least parts of them, drug-free, there should be some measure of the results of drug-testing and searching for drugs.

32. There are indications in the Prison Service 1995/96 Business Plan that some of these areas are to be considered in the next two years. This timescale may be too slow.

APPENDIX K
THE ORGANISATION OF THE PRISON SERVICE
(as at start of the Inquiry)

THE ORGANISATION OF THE
PRISON SERVICE

(As at start of the Inquiry)

HM PRISON SERVICE

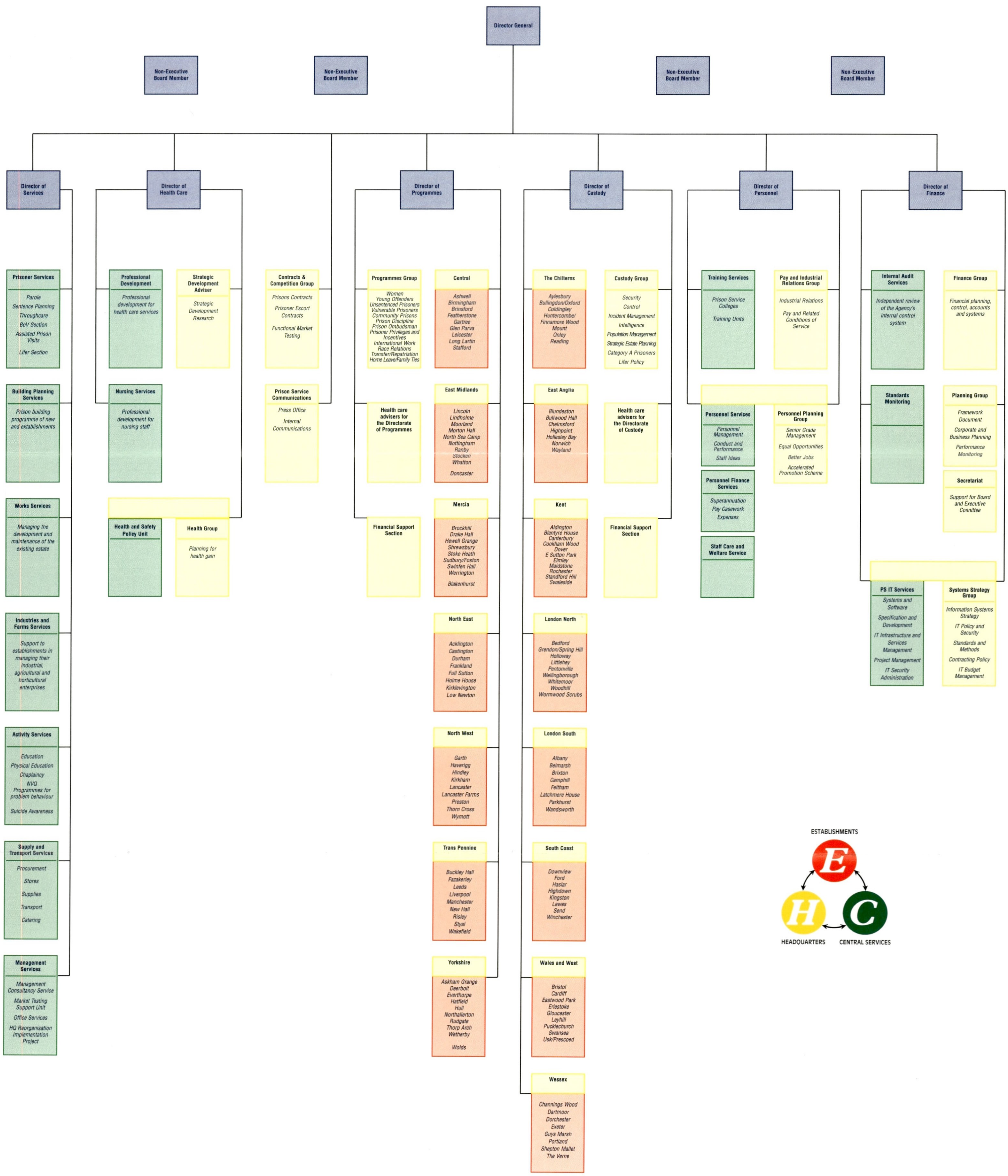

APPENDIX L
LIST OF PRISON SERVICE INITIATIVES

List of Prison Service Initiatives

Agency Status.

Business & Strategic Plans (new system introduced 1994/95).

Development of KPIs: Reduce escapes, reduce assaults, more regime hours, decent conditions, more out of cell time.

Devolved Budgets and greater local involvement.

Headquarters Reorganisation - impact on establishments.

Market Testing - education example, contracts with Probation.

Service Level Agreements, more work, no extra resources - effect on morale.

Implementation of Woolf recommendations and Government's White Paper.

Race Relations.

Equal Opportunities.

Suicide Awareness.

Sentence Planning/Compacts.

Through-care Policy.

New Staff Reporting System (late edition within current year).

Change in escort procedures (some prioritised).

Dealing with increase in prison population.

Loss of Crown Immunity - food regulations.

New parole system, discretionary lifer panels, open reporting.

More local involvement in dealing with MPs' cases, solicitors etc.

Changes on home leave, adjudication procedures, prisoners' shopping.

Pay & Grading Review.

Area Manager's Review.

Post Incident Care.

Building Programme across estate.

20% allowance not sufficient for leave, training, sickness but more and more training initiatives and budgets being cut.

Introduction of new breathing apparatus for cell rescue.

Greater involvement of Governors in Headquarters Committees, Workshops, Seminars - taking Governors out of establishments more and more.

Drive to develop offending behaviour programmes, anger management, pre- release, drug advice groups, HIV/AIDs awareness, lifer groups (excluding the operational management of lifers through the Allocation Unit), staff/inmates consultative committees, family visits.

Change of status of POA, PGA - High Court Injunctions.

New minimum standards.

Flattening of management structures.

Hard charging for services.

Personal responsibility project.

"Realising our Potential" project.

Devolution of some personnel work.

Impact of major IT programmes.

Policy reviews.

Review of training requirements.

APPENDIX M
PAPERWORK CALCULATION

Paperwork Calculation

*One sheet of A4 paper (80gm/m2, 210 x 297mm) weighs approximately 5gm.
1,000 sheets weighs approximately 5kg.*

Result of survey: A local prison received 4,391 letters, 650 faxes and 474 e-mails during 20 working days in February 1995.

These communications comprised approximately 17,344 sheets of paper.

Extrapolating this to the 83 working days covered by the 'submissions' exercise, the establishment would have received 71,978 sheets of A4 weighing in at 360kg.

Assuming all establishments received about the same, total weight in the period would have been 47,880kg or 47 tons.

This represents a pile of paper nearly a mile high (0.88 miles).

APPENDIX N
FACET RESEARCH:
A NEW APPROACH TO THE CATEGORISATION OF PRISONERS

Facet Research: A New Approach to the Categorisation of Prisoners

1. The definitions in paragraphs 2.146-147 of the Report initially appear to cover all eventualities but this is not the case, as can be demonstrated by presenting the elements within the classifications in a table format:

Danger to public	*Escape risk*	*External resources*
1. Not dangerous	1. Trusted	1. No resources
2. Dangerous	2. Opportunistic	2. Outside resources
3. Highly dangerous	3. Determined and skilled	3. Outside resources and valued member of a terrorist or organised crime group

2. Using this format, an inmate can be rated with reference to each column. For example, a prisoner who presents no danger to the public, can be trusted not to escape and has no external resources, would have the profile:

1 1 1

while a leading member of a terrorist group who is highly dangerous, determined to escape and has access to external resources would have the profile:

3 3 3

3. With this in mind, it is possible to allocate profiles to the current security classifications and to allocate a numerical value to each profile as a total of the ratings on each element:

Category A Exceptional Risk:	3 3 3 = 9
Category A High Risk:	3 3 2 = 8
Category A Standard Risk:	3 2 1 = 6
Category B:	2 2 1 = 5
Category C:	1 2 1 = 4
Category D:	1 1 1 = 3

4. It is possible to produce the following profile of two of the escapees (see Appendix G) whom the Inquiry found to be anomalies:

Danger to Public	Escape Risk	External Resources	
3	3	1	= 7

As can be seen, they both achieve a score that does not sit within either Category A Standard or High Escape Risk, which is exactly the dilemma brought to notice by the Inquiry. The mathematics show that there is a gap in the quantitative scores due to the failure to take proper account of individual ability. It could be properly argued that this gap is filled by the Escape List, which is an arbitrary facility open to Prison Governors; inmates suspected of planning or conspiring to escape can be placed on the list and subject to additional security. However, the three who escaped from Parkhurst were not on the list which indicates its unreliability.

5. From the table above, it can be seen that there are a total of 27 possible profiles (3 x 3 x 3), yet it is implicitly assumed in the present categorisation system that only six profiles exist, which fails to account for the other profiles and for qualitative differences between prisoners. The present system fails to allow for the true spread of profiles within the prison population, thereby forcing inmates into categories to which they do not properly belong. This is clearer to see when the 27 possible profiles are written as a simplified scalogram:

			Profiles				*Total score*
			111				3
		211	121	112			4
	311	221	212 131	122	113		5
321	312	231	222	132	213	123	6
	322	331	313 232	133	223		7
		332	323	233			8
			333				9

6. It is immediately obvious that, out of the 27 profiles, some will not arise in practice while others will predominate. For example it is extremely improbable that someone would have the profile 3 1 3, ie be highly dangerous, trusted not to escape and a valued member of a terrorist or organised crime group with access to outside resources. This is the point at which detailed research is required, initially to establish the empirical existence of profiles and secondly to explore the whole domain of prisoner categorisation, with the objective of developing a more reliable system.

7. The short-term approach is simply a matter of examining data held by the Prison Service, while the long-term solution requires a more radical overhaul of the system. The following paragraphs outline the research methodologies which have direct application to the short and long-term solutions.

8. The categorisation system, as it currently stands, assumes that prisoners can be categorised on a unidimensional scale. In other words, prisoner X needs more physical and procedural security than prisoner Y. It fails to take into account the fact that two prisoners may share a similar total score in terms of security requirements but they may be very different in terms of the type of security required. Theoretical representations of prisoners as mathematical profiles is of little value. What is required is processing of empirical data to present the findings in a relatively simple and interpretable structure.

9. This is achievable through Partial Order Scalogram Analysis (POSA), which provides the researcher with the ability to work with data which does not conform to a perfect, unidimensional scale and reduces the potential complexity of the mathematical profiles to a much simpler system of related co-ordinates (Canter, 1991). To quote Shye (1985), who has done most to develop this approach:

> *"When empirical observations result in many profiles that are mutually incomparable ... scales can often be found which ... reveal something about the structure of the concept measured. Two purposes can thereby be served. First, every ... individual can be assigned a new and shorter profile, which lists his scores on the derived scales. Second, an opportunity is created to abstract fewer and possibly more fundamental variables for the contents investigated."*
>
> *(Quoted in Canter, 1991)*

10. POSA is a computer programme which attempts to place profiles in a two dimensional space and, in doing so, to represent their common order. However, due to the multidimensionality of the system, this can only ever be achieved partially. In essence, POSA provides the means to test data currently held by the Prison Service and to establish the existence and frequency of profiles and their relationships to each other. The intention is the production of a categorisation scale that is representative of the true variations between prisoners, based on the components being measured.

11. The scientifically more appropriate long-term solution hinges on the need to establish a clear conceptual underpinning to the "fundamental distinctions inherent in the classification of offenders" (Canter, 1991).

12. An interesting broadening of the area of research would be to add another facet covering control aspects. It has in the past been presumed

undesirable to produce a control categorisation system (Control Review Committee (CRC) Report, 1984). Psychological research following the CRC Report led to the development of a computer-based prisoner behaviour profiling system (PROBE). The Inquiry examined this issue and recommends research to validate and improve on PROBE, which in essence produces up-to-date prisoner control ratings. Facet research has the capability to address this issue, either as a separate piece of research or, probably more sensibly, as a distinct component of research into prisoner categorisation.

CONCLUSIONS

13. It is not possible, nor practicable, to explain the facet approach in any detail. Suffice it to say that it provides a powerful means of scientifically researching prisoner categorisation. The contention here is that properly funded and co-ordinated research is essential to produce a categorisation procedure based on scientific study of empirical data. Such research, which should encompass the issues of security and control, would require time to achieve the desired aims. This paper offers a short-term solution which is to enhance the current system on the basis of simple research to identify and remove anomalies.

14. The potential rewards to the Prison Service, prisoners and the public through efficient categorisation of prisoners have been clear for all to see ever since 1968. The prison population has changed considerably since then and will continue to change. Applied research is the key to coping with this change.

REFERENCES

Canter D (ed) (1985)	Facet Theory: Approaches to Social Research, New York: Springer-Verlag.
Canter D (1991)	A Facet Approach to Offender Profiling, Final Report to the Home Office: Surrey University.
Control Review Committee (1984)	Managing the Long-term Prison System, London: HMSO.
Shye S (1985)	Multiple Scaling: The Theory and Application of Partial Order Scalogram Analysis, North-Holland.
Shye S (ed) (1978)	Theory Construction and Data Analysis in the Behavioural Sciences, San Francisco: Jossey-Bass.
Shye S, Elizur D, and Hoffman M (1994)	Content Design and Intrinsic Data Analysis in Behavioural Research, California: Sage.

APPENDIX O
RECOMMENDATIONS FROM THE REPORT OF THE WOODCOCK ENQUIRY INTO THE ESCAPE FROM WHITEMOOR PRISON

Recommendations from the Report of the Woodcock Enquiry into the Escape from Whitemoor Prison

A SURVEILLANCE AND OBSERVATION - SECTION 4 (PARAS. 4.13 - 4.28)

1. CCTV should be extended to give coverage of all internal and external areas of the Unit, including the staff office but excluding personal cells and showers.

2. All curtains, blinds and obstructions should be removed from internal observation windows throughout the Unit. The size and location of windows in the staff office should be reviewed as the present arrangement does not afford a view into one of the cell corridors. Consideration should be given to incorporating one-way glass to increase unobtrusive surveillance.

3. Officers should patrol all areas of the Unit throughout their shift, entering all communal areas unannounced and at frequent but irregular intervals. The tasks allocated should rotate at least hourly, to guard against boredom and retain alertness.

4. All materials, tools and equipment in communal/association rooms should be subject of daily formal audit. Consideration should be given to implementing good practice as at Full Sutton who have a tally system for knives and kitchen utensils. This could usefully be extended to include all tools and other potentially dangerous items. All items should be retained in, and allocated from, the staff office.

5. Night duty staff to make regular, thorough and documented searches of all communal areas on a nightly basis, for unauthorised or suspicious items, as part of a certified searching pattern.

B. PROPERTY AND SEARCHING - SECTION 5 (PARAS. 5.3 - 5.32)

6. A volumetric control of all prisoners' possessions should be introduced forthwith to reduce dramatically the amount of property in possession/storage and facilitate effective searching. The volume allowed should be standard to all inmates, whatever their category.

   Prisoners should only be allowed that which fits into the authorised cupboard, wardrobe and shelf space of a cell plus a maximum of two transit boxes, to be stored under the bed. Over time it may be possible to issue inmates with a large trunk which would represent the total volume of property permitted and act as part of the cell furniture once unpacked (eg as a table). Compliance with this recommendation would remove the need for prisoners' property to be stored elsewhere. Prisoners should not be allowed to add to their property if it would then exceed the allowance until arrangements are made for excess property to be collected by relatives/friends.

All remaining recommendations concerning property are reliant on the above volumetric controls being in place.

7. The present Dispersal Prisons privilege list has fallen into disrepute and should be dispensed with. Every Governor is responsible for the security of their establishment and the types of property allowed to inmates should be assessed with security in mind.

   When approving specific items, Governors should be mindful of difficulties which might occur on inmate transfer but Governors must not be committed by the actions or decisions made at another establishment.

8. Searching of cells and property should be carried out at frequent but irregular intervals in accordance with the searching strategy agreed by the Area Manager. The procedure should be :-

   - individual strip search of prisoner;
   - prisoner then excluded from cell during search, to avoid intimidation;
   - no other inmates to be permitted in the vicinity;
   - searches to declare any accidental damage;
   - search to meet the evidential requirements of adjudication.

9. The Lakes/Hadfield proposal for dedicated and specially equipped search teams in prisons holding Category A inmates should be mandatory. Such teams should have available to them on a regular basis dogs trained to identify firearms, explosives and drugs.

10. Each establishment should be required to identify the availability of specialist explosive detection equipment (MOD and/or Police).

    Contingency plans should include the standing arrangements for obtaining such equipment.

C. VISITS - SECTION 6 (PARAS. 6.4 - 6.58)

Gatehouse

11. A clear written policy on searching procedures should be available to all staff, inmates and visitors.

12. All staff expected to work in the gatehouse to be fully trained on the X-ray and metal detection equipment, searching procedures and relevant rules/legislation. These procedures should be regularly supervised.

13. Sufficient accommodation and equipment should be provided at the main gate of all prisons holding Category A inmates to enable searching of all staff and visitors to take place at all times. This should be subject to CCTV observation to enhance security and safety.

14. Visitors to prisons holding Category A inmates must be subject of a 'rub-down' search and X-ray check, in accordance with existing instructions. All hand baggage and loose items (eg coats) to be X-rayed. All baggage and property, except for coins for vending machines, where appropriate, to be left in secure containers at the gate house or in a Visitors Centre situated outside the prison perimeter.

15. No food whatsoever to be admitted with visitors.

16. Only property brought in for prisoners with prior approval will be accepted by gate staff. This property must be subjected to full X-ray and security check prior to being passed to the inmate within 24 hours. This property should be dealt with in accordance with property recording guidelines.

17. There should be random searches of visitors and staff leaving the prison.

High Risk Visits

18. The high risk visits area at Whitemoor should be up-graded to provide CCTV coverage and fixed furniture within the open plan design.

SSU

19. SSU inmates should not be eligible for more visits than other Category A prisoners.

20. All SSU visitors to have a second full search on entry to the Unit. SSU to be issued with X-ray machinery for this purpose. Exit searches should also be undertaken.

21. Accepting that only closed visits would provide completely secure conditions, if open visits are to continue, visits area should be totally open plan with fixed furniture providing a permanent barrier between prisoners and visitors to prevent circulation. Construction and design should allow for conversion to closed visit facilities where circumstances require this.

    CCTV to cover all parts of the visits area and to be recorded. Lenses to be covered for protection against tampering and to disguise movement.

22. Visits to be supervised by non-SSU staff to counteract conditioning, familiarity and intimidation. These staff will be responsible for completing a record of the visit and for fully searching the visits area before and after each visit.

23. The visits area should be further isolated from the remainder of the Unit to restrict direct access. No other inmates should be allowed to enter the area during visits.

24. Inmates must have no access to the visits area before or after visits for any purpose, including personalisation (ie placing photographs etc) or the provision of food.

25. Items such as disposable nappies should be made available in the visits area as required.

26. Cleaning of the visits rooms and staff areas to be carried out by regular cleaning staff, under Prison Officer supervision.

D. SEARCHING OF STAFF - SECTION 6 (PARAS. 6.59 - 6.64)

27. To minimise the risk of coercion, and guard against unauthorised items passing via staff, and to protect their integrity all staff should be searched on every occasion they enter the prison.

28. Facilities should be provided for all staff to leave civilian clothes and personal possessions outside the prison perimeter.

29. When commencing duty all SSU staff should additionally be searched on entry to the Unit by Specialist Search Officers; all subsequent searches at the Unit should then be by SSU staff.

30. The infrastructure (space and equipment) must be made available at the entrance to the SSU to accommodate the requirement for staff and visitor searching.

E. INMATES' PROPERTY TRANSFER - SECTION 6 (PARAS. 6.65 - 6.73)

31. Commensurate with the reduction of prisoners' property, a simplified and standardised system of property handling and recording should be established which is easily understood and items added to or removed from a prisoner's property must be properly recorded on the inventory and certified as having been searched.

32. Other than in exceptional circumstances, all property should accompany a prisoner on transfer and be checked against the inventory, searched and X-rayed by fully trained staff at each prison establishment.

33. Each prison establishment should have its own unique prisoners' property seals, which should be controlled and accounted for at the prison Reception.

34. Any items under construction by an inmate (eg in hobbies classes) should be subjected to physical examination during routine searches. If perceived as a security risk such items should also be subjected to an X-ray search examination.

F. NEW PRISON CONSTRUCTION - SECTION 6 (PARAS. 6.74 - 6.79)

35. There should be a co-ordinated security strategy in respect of all new building and refurbishment of prison premises. This should include

- strict procedures regarding access to plans and information, with a system for booking out and retrieval of all plans issued. Each plan should have its own unique security identification feature.

- Regular security checks to be carried out throughout the construction, to prevent any secretion of weapons, tools or other items.

36. A thorough pre-occupation search should be carried out at all new and refurbished establishments by specialist trained and equipped Officers or private consultants.

37. All security measures should be thoroughly tested prior to inmate occupation of the establishment, eg exercises should be staged to simulate escape attempts, hostage situations, to allow testing of access and manoeuvrability within the establishment.

G. PHYSICAL SECURITY MEASURES - SECTION 7 (PARAS. 7.3 - 7.24)

38. The review of security at Whitemoor, carried out by the Prison Service following the events of 9.9.94 should be implemented immediately. Any additional or amended measures at the SSU should form part of any recommendations for future SSU construction and be implemented as necessary, at other SSUs within the Prison Service.

39. There should be a review of contingency planning with particular reference to facilitating the rapid deployment of staff and emergency services inside and on the perimeter of the prison when serious incidents occur or are anticipated.

40. The location and type of CCTV cameras used should be reviewed, with a view to providing a more effective and comprehensive coverage, including light sensitivity, in particular eliminating "blind spots", and making their operation less obvious.

41. Inmates should not be permitted into the exercise yard without staff being present to provide supervision.

42. To remove the opportunity for intimidation of control staff the functions presently carried out in the SSU control room should be transferred permanently to the ECR with the necessary personnel allowing the continuous CCTV monitoring of inmates with any unusual patterns of activity reported to the Senior Officer and actioned.

43. Inmates should be totally excluded from the staff areas of the Unit, unless invited in for specific and exceptional reasons.

44. Immediate line managers with responsibility for the SSU, including the Duty Governor, should visit the Unit and walk through all areas at least on a daily basis, completing the Occurrence Book to record their visit, its duration and details of decisions made. The Head of Operations and Prison Governor should also visit frequently. A matrix of supervisory visits should be produced monthly to the Prison Governor. Additionally, the CCTV monitoring facilities in the ECR should be regularly utilised to monitor practices.

45. The Senior Officer on each shift should be required to keep a daily record of observations about each individual prisoner within the Unit, reporting attitudes, trends and activities. Security Information Reports (SIRs) should be submitted, as appropriate.

H. DOG SECTION DEPLOYMENT - SECTION 7 (PARAS. 7.25 - 7.33)

46. There should be a review of the training of dogs and handlers which should cover their terms of reference and reflect the need to co-ordinate deployment to respond collectively and effectively in emergencies. Training should reflect a variety of situations and weapons.

47. Patrols of the outside perimeter should be increased and carried out at irregular times throughout the day whilst inmates are unlocked.

48. A more flexible deployment of dogs in all areas of the prison, in support of staff, would ensure a more effective use of a valuable resource.

I. COMMISSIONING - SECTION 8 (PARAS. 8.2 - 8.8)

49. The Prison Service should review the procedure for opening a new prison, especially with regard to the :-

- provision of expert advice from people with relevant expertise to support management in the commissioning stage, which may include outside consultants,
- recruitment and selection of staff, and
- allocation and mix of prisoners.

J. INMATE PRIVILEGES - SECTION 8 (PARAS. 8.9 - 8.49)

50. Work presently being carried out by the working party examining incentives in prison regimes and its implementation should be time limited, to ensure that these long standing issues are finally resolved.

The underlying premise should be that all allowances are 'privileges', to be earned by good behaviour and work performance, with sanctions for bad behaviour. The unlimited availability of private cash to inmates is recognised by the Service as totally unsatisfactory and should be strictly limited.

51. All foodstuffs to be provided or purchased, or any other items allowed to inmates (eg batteries, electrical goods) should only be obtainable through the on-site shop (canteen) or catering department. There should be no external shopping whatsoever on behalf of inmates by any member of staff.

52. All use of official telephones should cease forthwith other than urgent legal and compassionate calls. On these occasions there should be a written application from the inmate. The authority of a Governor Grade should be mandatory and officially recorded.

All calls, other than those described above, should be paid for by the inmate.

53. A cardphone with appropriate recording/monitoring facilities should be installed in the SSU. It will be necessary, however, to take account of the implications of cards as a second 'currency', by having a system for the regulation of their purchase and use.

K. STAFF SELECTION AND TRAINING - SECTION 8 (PARAS. 8.50 - 8.59)

54. Deployment in an SSU should be considered a key post by selecting only experienced staff. Selection should be based on ability and skills, with due account taken of their background and personal circumstances. There should be a firm policy for the rotation of staff to reduce the threat of conditioning.

55. Specific training to nationally agreed standards should be given to all prospective SSU staff, in particular on conditioning and dealing with exceptional risk inmates. Supervisors should receive additional training for their specific role and should not be promoted directly into the Unit.

56. There should be a proactive use of Security Information Reports with a structured system for submission, analysis, action and feedback.

57. Sufficient numbers of staff should be trained at each establishment to ensure that all X-ray and metal detection equipment is operated by qualified staff.

L. CONDITIONING - SECTION 8 (PARAS. 8.60 - 8.69)

58. There should be regular local training for all Prison Officers to improve awareness and recognition of the importance of patterns of inmate activity, potential abuses of innocent articles and improve the gathering and utilisation of intelligence. Such training should be applicable to all levels, including Governor Grades.

M. MANAGEMENT AND SUPERVISION - SECTION 8 (PARAS. 8.70 - 8.97)

59. There should be nationally agreed written instructions and job descriptions setting out the expectations and requirements of all SSU personnel. These instructions should include the relevant daily routines and operating standards. Daily briefing and debriefing of staff should be carried out by supervisors and monitored by managers.

60. The Prison Service must provide a clear framework within which Governors are expected to operate. Levels of autonomy, responsibility and accountability should be clearly published making it plain which aspects of existing manuals and national instructions are mandatory, advisory or purely informative. Disparities of practice between SSUs, and indeed Dispersal Prisons, should be avoided with a continuous programme of independent audit introduced to identify good and bad practice, supplemented by self-inspection processes such as recently introduced at Belmarsh Prison.

61. The preparation of concise pocket handbooks on security to be provided to all Prison Officers should be expedited.

62. The Prison Service at all levels must continue to emphasise the central importance of security in all aspects of activity. Wherever changes are proposed in policy or practice should be tested against whether they add to or detract from security standards.

63. Consideration should be given to having a single Director specifically responsible for all aspects of security, policy formation and implementation.

    This Director should have executive authority with the independent auditing team working directly to her/him.

64. The co-ordination of SSU policy practice and line command should be by one nominated Director with executive authority. This person should chair and co-ordinate regular meetings of the Governors of prisons housing SSUs.

APPENDIX P
LEARMONT INQUIRY RECOMMENDATIONS

Learmont Inquiry Recommendations

1 Throughout the prison estate, establishments with workshops should set up daily audits of tools and materials. Workshops should be designed to ensure that prisoners can be observed at all times and, subject to health and safety regulations, safety screens should be made of transparent material.
(Paras. 2.21 and 2.29)

2 Such establishments should also ensure that Officers supervising workshops have basic knowledge and understanding of the work they are supervising, to ensure that they can identify security breaches and risks.
(Para. 2.23)

3 The Prison Service should review the type of work and training available to inmates in Dispersal Prisons, with emphasis on the central importance of security in all aspects of activity.
(Para. 2.29)

4 Sufficient accommodation and equipment should be provided, at the main gate of all prisons holding Category A inmates, to enable searching of all staff and visitors to take place at all times. This should be subject to CCTV observation. The main reception area should have direct communication with the visits reception area.
(Paras. 2.31) **[See Woodcock recommendation 13]**

5 Sufficient numbers of staff should be trained at each establishment to ensure that all X-ray and metal detection equipment, in particular at the gatehouse, is operated by qualified staff, who should be fully aware of searching procedures and relevant rules/legislation. Searching procedures should be regularly supervised.
(Paras. 2.31 and 2.41) **[See recommendation 86 and Woodcock recommendation 12]**

6 Visitors to prisons holding Category A inmates must be subject to a 'rub-down' search and X-ray check, in accordance with existing instructions. All hand baggage and loose items (eg coats) should be X-rayed. All baggage and property, except cash for canteens and vending machines, should be left in secure containers at the gatehouse or in a Visitors Centre situated outside the prison perimeter.
(Paras. 2.32 and 2.42) **[See recommendation 14 and Woodcock recommendation 14]**

7 There should be full 360° fixed CCTV cover in visits rooms in secure establishments, with video recording facilities.
(Para. 2.34) **[See Woodcock recommendation 18]**

8 Visits rooms in secure establishments should have fixed furniture with a formal and observable layout.
(Para. 2.35) **[See Woodcock recommendation 18]**

9 Inmates on visits should wear some form of distinguishable clothing.
(Para. 2.35)

10 A visitor recognition system should be introduced.
(Paras. 2.36-37)

11 The closed visits room at Parkhurst should be reconstructed to an appropriate design and brought back into use for all prisoners suspected of receiving illegal items from visitors and for inmates on the escape list.
(Para. 2.40)

12 A clear written policy on searching procedures should be available to all staff, inmates and visitors and should be monitored and supervised to ensure implementation.
(Para. 2.41) **[See recommendation 87 and Woodcock recommendation 11]**

13 Any prisoner or visitor needing to use the toilet facilities during a visit should be searched before and after visits to the toilet. In addition, all toilets should be searched before the end of a visits session and before inmates and visitors are allowed to leave.
(Para. 2.41)

14 Visitors should not make cash transactions in visits rooms except at canteens or vending machines.
(Para. 2.42) **[See recommendation 6]**

15 Family visits are not appropriate for Dispersal Prisons and should cease.
(Para. 2.47)

16 In high security prisons, visiting children should be restricted to toys provided in the children's area. In other prisons, imitation weapons should be banned and other toys brought in by children should be checked.
(Para. 2.50)

17 All staff at Dispersal Prisons should be searched each time they enter the prison and there should be random searches of staff leaving these prisons.
(Para. 2.52) **[See recommendation 95 and Woodcock recommendation 27]**

18 Facilities should be provided for all staff at Dispersal Prisons to leave civilian clothes and personal possessions outside the prison perimeter.
(Para. 2.52) **[See Woodcock recommendation 28]**

19 Other than in exceptional circumstances, a prisoner's property should accompany its owner on transfer and should be checked against the inventory, searched and X-rayed by fully trained staff at each prison establishment.
(Paras. 2.54 and 2.68) [See **Woodcock recommendation 32**]

20 'Rub-down' searches should be carried out consistently and to a standard specified in the annual security audit, agreed by the Area Manager.
(Para. 2.56)

21 Cell searches should be undertaken in accordance with the Manual on Security.
(Paras. 2.57-65) [See **recommendations 92 and 94 and Woodcock recommendation 8**]

22 The Hadfield/Lakes proposal, for dedicated and specially equipped search teams in prisons holding Category A inmates, should be mandatory in Dispersal Prisons. Such teams should have available to them, on a regular basis, dogs trained to identify firearms, explosives and drugs.
(Para. 2.59) [**See recommendations 93 and 94 and Woodcock recommendation 9**]

23 A volumetric control of all prisoners' possessions should be introduced forthwith, to reduce dramatically the amount of property in possession/storage and facilitate effective searching. The volume allowed should be standard to all inmates, whatever their category. Prisoners should be allowed only that amount of property which fits into a maximum of two transit boxes. Prisoners should not be allowed to add to their property, if it would then exceed the allowance, until arrangements are made for excess property to be collected by relatives/friends or stored centrally.
(Para. 2.68) [See **Woodcock recommendation 6**]

24 There must be a coherent strategy for searching of communal areas and appropriate records must be maintained.
(Para. 2.73) [See **recommendation 92 and Woodcock recommendation 5**]

25 Minimum physical security standards need to be set for all establishments and applied.
(Paras. 2.74-101) [See **recommendation 80**]

26 Locking schedules for secure establishments need to be reviewed with modern electronic or magnetic systems in mind. Current policy in respect of locks for non-residential buildings should be urgently reviewed.
(Paras. 2.75-76)

27 Home Office recommended standards for CCTV systems should be applied throughout the Prison Service.
(Para. 2.100) [**See Woodcock recommendation 40**]

28 Before Officers are deployed to an ECR, they must be fully trained to nationally agreed standards and familiar with the establishment.
(Paras. 2.108-109) [**See recommendation 82**]

29 The ECR at Parkhurst must be upgraded in accordance with the findings of the Director of Works.
(Para. 2.110) [**See recommendation 82**]

30 Supervisors must ensure that high standards of control on the movement of dangerous inmates are enforced and that movement books always accompany Exceptional and High Risk prisoners.
(Paras. 2.111-114)

31 Inmates should not be allowed access to the Wing Office.
(Para. 2.116)

32 In Dispersal Prisons, a prisoner movement system must be introduced in a form which provides a permanent record and is not accessible to inmates. Inmates must be required to give advance notification of discretionary movements off the Wing. Such movements should be co-ordinated, monitored and properly controlled.
(Para. 2.117)

33 Contingency plans must be regularly tested and practised, with all staff trained in realistic situations, in line with the instructions in the Manual on Security. Emergency packs must be subject to regular testing.
(Paras. 2.118-122)

34 Contingency plans must be reviewed annually, as part of the security audit.
(Para. 2.122)

35 Directions in the Manual on Security, in respect of Duty Governors, must be strictly followed.
(Paras. 2.123-126)

36 Clear instructions must be issued throughout the Service directing that staff must co-operate fully with any police investigation and, if requested, make a verbal and/or written statement without delay.
(Paras. 2.127-129)

37 A working party should be set up to review intelligence and management information needs throughout the Prison Service, building on best practice, available IT systems and experience of other Agencies.
(Paras. 2.131-145)

38 Security categorisation should be reviewed and researched to remove dangerous anomalies produced by the current system.
(Paras. 2.146-149) [**See recommendations 102 and 103**]

39 The decision to retain a hospital at Parkhurst, as a Service-wide resource, should be reviewed.
(Para. 2.178)

40 Parkhurst should be down-graded as soon as possible and consideration given to its replacement as a Dispersal Prison by a more appropriate establishment. The relevance of current building work should be examined so that unnecessary work can be stopped.
(Para. 2.179) [**See recommendation 106**]

41 The SSU at Parkhurst should not be re-opened in that capacity. The accommodation should be put to other use.
(Para. 2.179)

42 Visible leadership must be demonstrated by Wing Managers, who should work from an office located on their Wing.
(Paras. 2.194-196 and 2.228)

43 Telephone monitoring should be intelligence driven. Improved facilities need to be in place to monitor foreign language conversations.
(Paras. 2.201-205)

44 In the short term, the current £40 limit per week for phonecards at Parkhurst must be reviewed and set at a lower level. In the long term, the issue of phonecards needs to be re-assessed throughout the Service, to remove abuses of the system.
(Paras. 2.201-209) [**See Woodcock recommendation 53**]

45 Prisoners should be offered sufficient, regular and meaningful employment or education facilities. Those not taking up work places should be locked in their cells during the day.
(Paras. 2.210-213) [**See recommendation 117**]

46 Cooking facilities on Wings should be treated as a privilege and not a right. Access to stores of food must be supervised and regulated.
(Paras. 2.214-216) [**See Woodcock recommendation 51**]

47 All curtains, blinds and obstructions should be removed from the association areas.
(Para. 2.217) [**See Woodcock recommendation 2**]

48 Officers should patrol all areas of each Wing unannounced and at frequent but irregular intervals.
(Para. 2.217) [**See Woodcock recommendation 3**]

49 A coherent personnel policy needs to be established and reflected in the Establishment Plan.
(Para. 2.220)

50 Training should not be regarded as a dispensible task.
(Paras. 2.220-222)

51 Additional training should be given to Dispersal Prison staff to counter the extra problems inherent in dealing with the Dispersal population.
(Para. 2.227) [**See recommendation 99 and Woodcock recommendations 55 and 58**]

52 Procedures need to be put in place to select, for Dispersal Prisons, staff with the necessary skills and experience for the work, with additional incentives to enhance the status of those selected.
(Paras. 2.225-227) [**See Woodcock recommendation 54**]

53 Prison managers should set aside a minimum number of hours to walk around their establishments.
(Para. 2.228)

54 The applications system should be urgently reviewed so that minor matters are resolved at the appropriate level and only serious issues are referred to Governor Grades.
(Para. 2.229)

55 The procedures for handling disputes with the Prison Officers Association need to be reviewed.
(Para. 2.230)

56 Wings and Units should each have a single Manager, empowered through direct access to a Senior Management Team oriented towards operational needs. The management structure should be built from the bottom up and have only five levels.
(Paras. 2.231-238)

57 Officers should work in regular teams under a Senior Officer responsible to one Manager. Wing and Unit Managers should report directly to the Head of Operations and Security. The Head of Operations and Security and the governing Governor should both be supported by a Secretariat, including a Staff Officer for the Governor.
(Paras. 2.235-237)

58 The Director General and Board should have regular contact with those who have operational responsibilities so that security weaknesses do not go unnoticed.
(Para. 3.16)

59 Headquarters and other senior appointments should be filled largely by Prison Service professionals.
(Para. 3.18)

60 The Service must rapidly become a more caring and people-oriented organisation. Gallantry and good service should be recognised.
(Paras. 3.22-23 and 3.25)

61 Positive and visible leadership must be shown at all levels.
(Para. 3.27)

62 The Service Statement of Purpose should be clarified, to make custody the primary purpose.
(Paras. 3.35-40)

63 All staff, including Governors, should normally wear uniform, with name badges. Civilian members of staff should be clearly identifiable from inmates.
(Paras. 3.46 and 3.48)

64 The Board should build on the willingness of staff associations to co-operate in taking the Service forward.
(Para. 3.50)

65 The Board should review its approach to Key Performance Indicators, to reinforce the main objectives of the Service and to ensure meaningful and valid interpretation:

(a) "Escapes" is too negative an indicator on its own and should be supplemented by indicators that show progress towards preventing escapes.

(b) Figures for assaults should show percentage changes separately for assaults on staff, inmates and others.

(c) Greater care should be taken to monitor the way "purposeful activity" data is captured to prevent exaggeration and ensure credibility.

(d) The Service should develop new KPIs to indicate:

(i) the extent to which staff training fulfils a clear staff development policy (the Service having first introduced a clear development policy).

(ii) staff morale. Three obvious indicators are turnover, sickness and absence. Complaints by staff are also an indicator, if a sufficiently well-developed scheme is in place.

(iii) recidivism rates. Examples might be the percentage of new inmates who have a previous conviction, the percentage of inmates released during the past two, five and ten years who have been re-convicted and the average number of years before released inmates re-offend. There are difficulties in expressing these figures meaningfully but there are ways of handling them.

(iv) the degree of success in dealing with the drug problem in prisons.

(v) inmate behaviour, eg disciplinary cases and suicides.

(vi) standards of physical security.

(vii) reduction in Headquarters personnel.

(viii) reduction in the percentage of total Prison Service budget absorbed by Headquarters and support (ie non-operational) activities.
(Paras. 3.54-56 and Appendix J)

66 Deficiencies in training must be rectified without delay. The identification of core competencies, for training purposes, should be extended to all grades. Before line managers take up new posts, they should receive leadership and management training. Over the next five years, annual training for all staff should rise to 14 days.
(Paras. 3.66-69)

67 Personnel management systems should be introduced to ensure equal opportunities and common standards, to identify talent for fast-streaming and to develop top managers.
(Paras. 3.71-72)

68 The operational chain of command should be the core of the business. Functional activities should play a supporting role. The number of layers in the structure should be minimised.
(Para. 3.75)

69 An "owner" should be nominated for the Service, to fulfil the role of line manager for the Director General. A small, professional unit should be formed to support the "owner".
(Para. 3.82)

70 The problem of the Director General's pre-occupation with Parliamentary matters must be overcome. He must redress the balance between keeping Ministers informed and running the Service.
(Paras. 3.83-86)

71 The Home Office should undertake an in-depth study of the relationship between itself and the Prison Service.
(Para 3.87)

72 Service structure should deliver the right messages to the organisation and the Board should be re-structured to strengthen operations:

(a) Operational Directors should have previous experience as a governing Governor and should be increased from two to four as outlined in Section 5. They should be in the chain of command in emergency situations.

(b) Responsibility for policy at Board level should be vested in one Policy Director, with operational experience gained, ideally, from within the Prison Service.

(c) The Head of Health Care should report to the Policy Director and need attend Board meetings only when medical matters are discussed.

(d) The Finance Director should be a professional, with financial experience gained in an operational environment.

(e) The Director of Personnel appointment should be reviewed within the next three years, after devolution of personnel matters to operational directorates, areas and establishments, when responsibility for personnel policy at Board level could pass to the Policy Director, supported by a professional personnel manager.

(f) Services should be contractorised by competitive tendering, with contracts renewable only if standards are met. The Director post might then be reviewed.

(g) The number of non-Executive Directors should be reviewed.
(Paras. 3.92 and 3.100-114)

73 The momentum to downsize Headquarters and Central Services, by at least 500 posts by 1998, must be maintained. Activities not essential to operational management, such as the Lifer Group (excluding the operational management of lifers through the Allocation Unit), Parole Unit and Superannuation Section, should be moved out of Headquarters.
(Paras. 3.123-124)

74 The Service must look for better ways of dealing with the proliferation of paperwork and take urgent action to reduce it.
(Paras. 3.129-132 and Appendix M)

75 Area Managers should be an integral part of the corporate planning process, monitor service delivery and manage the area's resources. They should be located in their areas and hold their own budgets. They must

concentrate on operational management of establishments and make their voices heard at Board level through the Operational Directors.
(Paras. 3.133-136)

76 The Service should ensure that, when contracts are drawn up for private prisons, staffing levels are set on the basis of staff and prisoner safety and the protection of the public.
(Paras. 3.137-138)

77 A substantial public Prison Service should be retained but the advantages arising from competition and private sector involvement should be applied across the Service.
(Paras. 3.140-141)

78 Boards of Visitors should be properly resourced and the Liaison Section should be moved out of Headquarters.
(Paras. 3.142-143)

79 Designs for all prisons must be agreed nationally.
(Para. 4.3)

80 Appropriate facilities, including CCTV, must be provided at the entrances to Dispersal Prisons. The prison estate must conform to up-to-date security standards.
(Para. 4.4) [**See recommendation 25**]

81 The Prison Service Headquarters Security Survey, on electronic security defences, should be actioned without delay. The Service must provide national solutions to technical problems. Remedial work identified by security audits should be a high priority.
(Paras. 4.7-9)

82 Each Dispersal Prison must have a properly equipped ECR. All staff must be properly trained for their various tasks and every Governor of a Dispersal Prison must have a Command Suite for use in emergencies.
(Paras. 4.10-12) [**See recommendations 28 and 29**]

83 The Manual on Security should be mandatory and used as the basic document for training purposes. Copies should be widely distributed in all establishments and concise versions should be available to operational staff.
(Paras. 4.14-15)

84 The concepts of drugs-free Wings and of drugs testing should be implemented where appropriate.
(Para. 4.16)

85 To deal with drug abuse, all prisons must have programmes which inform, educate and help prisoners combat the drug habit. Success on such programmes should be rewarded through the incentive scheme.
(Para 4.18)

86 Procedures for searching visitors are laid down in the Manual on Security and must be obeyed, to minimise the risk of smuggling. Staff must have the latest equipment and be properly trained and proficient in the use of X-ray and metal detecting machinery.
(Paras. 4.19 and 4.25) [**See recommendation 5 and Woodcock recommendation 12**]

87 The Prison Service must develop visitor searching standards for each type of prison and maintain a system for auditing performance.
(Para. 4.21) [**See recommendation 12**]

88 The Prison Service must develop standard designs for visits rooms, commensurate with the levels of security and facilities required for differing establishments or circumstances. Existing rooms should be surveyed and, where practicable, brought to these standards.
(Para. 4.23)

89 CCTV cameras should be covered for protection against tampering and to disguise movement. Full video recording facilities must be available.
(Para. 4.25)

90 In most cases, some physical contact should be allowed between inmates and family. Mandatory closed visits are recommended only for Exceptional Risk Category A prisoners.
(Paras. 4.26-27)

91 For other than Exceptional Risk Category A prisoners, the option of imposing closed visits should be available in all secure establishments, to be used at the Governor's discretion. Governors should make more use of the option, when they have reasonable grounds for suspicion, and Headquarters should support them.
(Para. 4.28)

92 All prison establishments must implement a searching programme in accordance with the Manual on Security.
(Paras. 4.29 and 4.31) [**See recommendations 21, 24 and 94 and Woodcock recommendations 5 and 8**]

93 The Prison Service should establish dedicated search teams at all Dispersal Prisons and at the two new prisons recommended in Section 5.
(Para. 4.31) [**See recommendations 22 and 94 and Woodcock recommendation 9**]

94 Across the rest of the estate, better use must be made of search teams,

supported by appropriate equipment and the wider deployment of trained dogs to search for drugs, guns and explosives.
(Para. 4.31) [**See recommendations 21, 22, 92 and 93**]

95 All staff entering Dispersal Prisons, and the two new establishments, should be searched and there should be random searches of staff leaving these prisons. Elsewhere, programmes for searching staff should be agreed between Governors and Area Managers.
(Para. 4.32) [**See recommendation 17 and Woodcock recommendation 27**]

96 Prison establishments must properly supervise on-site contractors and their vehicles particularly when entering and leaving establishments.
(Para. 4.33)

97 In the short term, wherever possible, remand Category A prisoners should be held in Dispersal Prisons but it will be necessary for many of them to be held in other strategically placed prisons with accommodation to Category A standard.
(Para. 4.35)

98 The practicality of installing TV links between prisons holding remand prisoners and Magistrates' Courts should be explored.
(Paras 4.36-38)

99 The problems of intimidation, manipulation and boredom must be thoroughly addressed during recruitment and training, continuously monitored by line managers and carefully studied by the Service with a view to appropriate action. More important still is visible leadership which recognises the human dimension, shows enthusiasm for people's efforts and promotes feelings of self-respect and self-confidence.
(Paras. 4.39-48) [**See recommendation 51 and Woodcock recommendations 55 and 58**]

100 The Prison Service should ensure that the contribution of civilian staff is properly recognised.
(Paras. 4.49-50)

101 The Service must keep abreast of work on chemical incapacitants and consider the use of CS gas to quell riotous behaviour. There is a need also for the Service to re-examine the argument for an armed response capability.
(Paras. 4.53-55)

102 The Prison Service should introduce a new interim categorisation system as soon as possible.
(Paras. 5.4-5) [**See recommendations 38 and 103**]

103 The Prison Service should further refine the system, drawing on the work of Professor David Canter.
(Para. 5.7) **[See recommendations 38 and 102]**

104 Prisoners in new Categories 1 and 2 should be housed in a new purpose-built High Security Prison.
(Paras. 5.14-16)

105 Prisoners in the new Category 3 should be housed in the existing Dispersal system.
(Paras. 5.17-18)

106 Parkhurst should be downgraded as soon as possible to become an establishment for prisoners in the new Category 4 and should be replaced in the present Dispersal (Category 3) estate by a more suitable establishment, perhaps Belmarsh Prison.
(Para. 5.18) **[See recommendation 40]**

107 In the long term, subject to revised arrangements for remand hearings (see recommendation 98), remand prisoners in the new Categories 1 and 2 should be held in the proposed High Security Prison when awaiting trial. During trial, they should be held in the High Security Prison, if it is geographically convenient, in an SSU within the Dispersal system or in one of a small number of suitable establishments across the country.
(Para. 5.19)

108 The Prison Service should provide suitable accommodation for high risk women prisoners and young offenders.
(Para. 5.20)

109 Prisoners in the new Category 4 should be housed in closed, cellular prisons with secure perimeters.
(Para. 5.23)

110 Prisoners in the new Category 5 should be housed in the present Category C, non-cellular establishments with adequate perimeter security and CCTV coverage of vulnerable areas.
(Para. 5.25)

111 The Prison Service should evaluate the concept of Industrial Prisons as a matter of urgency. Prisoners from any part of the new Category 4 and 5 estate should be eligible to work in them. They would earn this right by virtue of good behaviour and the recommendation of staff and Governors.
(Paras. 5.27-31)

112 The Prison Service should undertake a review to assess the present open estate and to decide what is required for resettlement Units, what should be retained as open accommodation and what should be upgraded to new security standards.
(Paras. 5.32-37)

113 Women's prisons should be the responsibility of one Area Manager. All women prisoners should be housed in women's prisons. In the longer term, there should be a thorough review of the female prisoners' estate.
(Paras. 5.38-40)

114 A Control Prison should be established for particularly disruptive prisoners including disruptive prisoners who are mentally ill.
(Paras. 5.48-54)

115 Prisoner programmes should be adopted nationally. Every sentenced prisoner serving more than 12 months should have a sentence plan and should be allocated a Personal Officer.
(Para. 5.59)

116 Early release should be a privilege earned through good behaviour and the Prison Service initiative on this matter should be taken forward urgently.
(Paras. 5.67-70)

117 All prisons should offer meaningful work and wages. Prisons should be allowed to keep the profits from their commercial activities and commercial advice should be available to Governors.
(Paras. 5.71-74) [**See recommendation 45**]

118 Private cash should be phased out.
(Paras. 5.75-76)

119 There must be a mandatory minimum entitlement to visits which takes account of the need to retain family links. Additional visits can be used as incentives to good behaviour.
(Paras. 5.77-78)

120 Telephone privileges should feature in an incentive scheme.
(Para. 5.79)

121 Television in cells could provide a calming influence and a powerful incentive to good conduct. It could also be used for educational and communication purposes. The right to this privilege should be earned by good behaviour, once the prisoner has earned the right to electricity in the cell.
(Paras. 5.80-83)

122 The Prison Service should explore ways of increasing the availability of home leave and apply firm sanctions to those who abuse the privilege.
(Paras. 5.84-85)

123 The high security estate should be managed as a whole rather than piecemeal. An Operational Director should be appointed with the sole task of managing the High Security Prison, the Control Prison and the six Dispersal Prisons. This Director should be a full member of the Prisons

Board, have operational experience as the Governor of a Dispersal Prison and have no substantial work other than the management of these prisons. The High Security, Control and Dispersal Prisons should remain in the public sector.
(Paras. 5.86-87)

124 The remainder of the prison estate should be organised into 11 clusters, each cluster working to an Area Manager, supported by sufficient staff to run the Area. The 12th Area Manager would control the women's estate.
(Paras. 5.89-94)

125 An Operational Director at Board level should control no more than four Area Managers. The number of Operational Directors should be increased from the current two to four, reducing their span of control, putting substantial extra operational weight onto the Board and enhancing security across the Prison Service.
(Paras. 5.94-95)

126 The Prison Service must introduce, as a matter of urgency, an accreditation system which would require each establishment to hold a certificate, awarded following the objective measurement of performance against approved national standards. Where an establishment's performance failed to meet the required standard, the certificate would be withdrawn and sanctions would follow.
(Paras. 5.96-97)

127 The role of HM Chief Inspector of Prisons should be extended to include security issues and he should be provided with staff for this purpose.
(Para. 5.99)

APPENDIX Q
COSTINGS OF THE LEARMONT INQUIRY RECOMMENDATIONS

Costings of the Learmont Inquiry Recommendations

INTRODUCTION

1. This Appendix has been prepared over a three month period from 1st July 1995 in order to provide the Home Secretary with the Inquiry's assessment of the financial implications of implementing the recommendations shown in Appendix P.

2. Recommendations that reaffirm Woodcock Proposals and those that reinforce existing Prison Service policy or can be identified in the Business and Corporate plans have not been costed. Only recommendations which are in addition to these have been highlighted.

3. The specific figures relating to costs and savings, both real and potential, are contained in Schedule 1 of this Appendix. These have been divided into current and capital expenditure. The potential for future costs/savings have been identified but no figures have been estimated. The remaining recommendations carry a nil or negligible penalty and are not included.

METHODOLOGY

4. Schedule 1 has been drawn up from information received from the Prison Service, professional Prison Service advice from within the Inquiry Team, input from an independent architect (in relation to the new High Security and Control Prisons), a Home Office management accountant and the judgement of the Assessors.

5. Schedule 2 shows the general costing assumptions applied.

SUMMARY OF COSTS AND SAVINGS

6. The Inquiry has identified 21 recommendations which attract costs/potential costs, with a further 10 recommendations showing savings/potential savings. The remaining 96 recommendations have a nil or negligible additional cost and are not considered further.

7. Overall the total cost of the Learmont recommendations for Year 1 (£36 million) represents only about 2% of the 1995/96 financial provision for the Prison Service. The four year forecast up to 1999/2000 is shown on page Q11 of this Appendix. By far the largest proportion of these costs is related to recommendations covering the provision and running of two÷ new High Security Prisons and increased staff training.

8. Information provided by the Prison Service has been used to calculate the costs or savings where applicable. It will be appreciated that until the Report was submitted to the Home Secretary the recommendations contained in Appendix P could not be disclosed. For this reason the general costing assumptions used, together with the specific costs and savings shown in Schedule 1, have not been discussed with the Prison Service.

LEARMONT RECOMMENDATIONS : SUMMARY OF COSTS AND SAVINGS SCHEDULE 1

Learmont Recommendation

Structure

72 Service structure should deliver the right messages to the organisation and the Board should be re-structured to strengthen operations. (Paras. 3.92 and 3.100-114)

(a) Operational Directors should have previous experience as a governing Governor and should be increased from two to four as outlined in Section 5. They should be in the chain of command in emergency situations.

125 An Operational Director at Board level should control no more than four Area Managers. The number of Operational Directors should be increased from the current two to four, reducing their span of control, putting substantial extra operational weight onto the Board and enhancing security across the Prison Service. (Paras. 5.94-95)

72 Service structure should deliver the right messages to the organisation and the Board should be re-structured to strengthen operations. (Paras. 3.92 and 3.100-114)

(e) The Director of Personnel appointment should be reviewed within the next three years, after devolution of personnel matters to operational directorates, areas and establishments, when responsibility for personnel policy at Board level could pass to the Policy Director, supported by a professional personnel manager.

(f) Services should be contractorised by competitive tendering, with contracts renewable only if standards are met. The Director post might then be reviewed.

(g) The number of non-Executive Directors should be reviewed.

Service Management

62 The Service Statement of Purpose should be clarified, to make custody the primary purpose. (Paras. 3.35-40)

Prison Management

56 Wings and Units should each have a single Manager, empowered through direct access to a Senior Management Team oriented towards operational needs. The management structure should be built from the bottom up and have only five levels. (Paras. 2.231-238)

63 All staff, including Governors, should normally wear uniform, with name badges. Civilian members of staff should be clearly identifiable from inmates. (Paras. 3.46 and 3.48)

COSTS AND SAVINGS (£000's)							
CAPITAL				CURRENT			
96/97	97/98	98/99	99/00	96/97	97/98	98/99	99/00
				554	554	554	554
				Future Potential Savings			
				Future Potential Savings			
				Future Potential Savings			
				37			
				Future Potential Savings			
				592	345	345	345

LEARMONT RECOMMENDATIONS : SUMMARY OF COSTS AND SAVINGS SCHEDULE 1

Learmont Recommendation

Personnel Policy

52 Procedures need to be put in place to select, for Dispersal Prisons, staff with the necessary skills and experience for the work, with additional incentives to enhance the status of those selected. (Paras. 2.225-227)

Training

66 Deficiencies in training must be rectified without delay. The identification of core competencies, for training purposes, should be extended to all grades. Before line managers take up new posts, they should receive leadership and management training. Over the next five years, annual training for all staff should rise to 14 days. (Paras. 3.66-69)

Conduct of Visits

7 There should be full 360° fixed CCTV cover in visits rooms in secure establishments, with video recording facilities. (Para. 2.34)

88 The Prison Service must develop standard designs for visits rooms, commensurate with the levels of security and facilities required for differing establishments or circumstances. Existing rooms should be surveyed and, where practicable, brought to these standards. (Para. 4.23)

9 Inmates on visits should wear some form of distinguishable clothing. (Para. 2.35)

10 A visitor recognition system should be introduced. (Paras. 2.36-37)

Closed Visits

90 In most cases, some physical contact should be allowed between inmates and family. Mandatory closed visits are recommended only for Exceptional Risk Category A prisoners. (Paras. 4.26-27)

91 For other than Exceptional Risk Category A prisoners, the option of imposing closed visits should be available in all secure establishments, to be used at the Governor's discretion. Governors should make more use of the option, when they have reasonable grounds for suspicion, and Headquarters should support them. (Para. 4.28)

Family Visits

15 Family visits are not appropriate for Dispersal Prisons and should cease. (Para. 2.47)

COSTS AND SAVINGS (£000's)							
CAPITAL				CURRENT			
96/97	97/98	98/99	99/00	96/97	97/98	98/99	99/00
				1,350	1,350	1,350	1,350
				13,196	27,287	42,193	57,903
1,080					22	22	22
				42	21	21	21
				3			
191	190						
				Future Potential Savings			

LEARMONT RECOMMENDATIONS : SUMMARY OF COSTS AND SAVINGS SCHEDULE 1

Learmont Recommendation

Physical Security

26 Locking schedules for secure establishments need to be reviewed with modern electronic or magnetic systems in mind. Current policy in respect of locks for non-residential buildings should be urgently reviewed. (Paras. 2.75-76)

Electronic Security

27 Home Office recommended standards for CCTV systems should be applied throughout the Prison Service. (Para. 2.100)

Intelligence

37 A working party should be set up to review intelligence and management information needs throughout the Prison Service, building on best practice, available IT systems and experience of other agencies. (Paras. 2.131-145)

Parkhurst

39 The decision to retain a hospital at Parkhurst, as a Service-wide resource, should be reviewed. (Para. 2.178)

41 The SSU at Parkhurst should not be re-opened in that capacity. The accommodation should be put to other use. (Para. 2.179)

Purposeful Activities

111 The Prison Service should evaluate the concept of Industrial Prisons as a matter of urgency. Prisoners from any part of the new Category 4 and 5 estate should be eligible to work in them. They would earn this right by virtue of good behaviour and the recommendation of staff and Governors. (Paras. 5.27-31)

117 All prisons should offer meaningful work and wages. Prisons should be allowed to keep the profits from their commercial activities and commercial advice should be available to Governors. (Paras. 5.71-74)

45 Prisoners should be offered sufficient, regular and meaningful employment or education facilities. Those not taking up work places should be locked in their cells during the day. (Paras. 2.210-213)

Privileges and Incentives

116 Early release should be a privilege earned through good behaviour and the Prison Service initiative on this matter should be taken forward urgently. (Paras. 5.67-70)

COSTS AND SAVINGS (£000's)							
CAPITAL				CURRENT			
96/97	97/98	98/99	99/00	96/97	97/98	98/99	99/00
	Future Potential Costs						
1,650							
	Future Potential Costs						
	Future Potential Costs						
					Future Potential Savings		
					Future Potential Savings		
					Future Potential Savings		
					Future Potential Savings		
	Future Potential Savings				Future Potential Savings		

LEARMONT RECOMMENDATIONS : SUMMARY OF COSTS AND SAVINGS SCHEDULE 1

Learmont Recommendation

The High Security Estate

104 Prisoners in new Categories 1 and 2 should be housed in a new purpose-built High Security Prison. (Paras. 5.14-16)

114 A Control Prison should be established for particularly disruptive prisoners including disruptive prisoners who are mentally ill. (Paras. 5.48-54)

Other Establishments

108 The Prison Service should provide suitable accommodation for high risk women prisoners and young offenders. (Para. 5.20)

113 Women's prisons should be the responsibility of one Area Manager. All women prisoners should be housed in women's prisons. In the longer term, there should be a thorough review of the female prisoners' estate. (Paras. 5.38-40)

124 The remainder of the prison estate should be organised into 11 clusters, each cluster working to an Area Manager, supported by sufficient staff to run the Area. The 12th Area Manager would control the women's estate. (Paras. 5.89-94)

75 Area Managers should be an integral part of the corporate planning process, monitor service delivery and manage the area's resources. They should be located in their areas and hold their own budgets. They must concentrate on operational management of establishments and make their voices heard at Board level through the Operational Directors. (Paras. 3.133-136)

Remand Prisoners

97 In the short term, whenever possible, remand Category A prisoners should be held in Dispersal Prisons, but it will be necessary for many of them to be held in other strategically placed prisons with accommodation to Category A standard.(Para. 4.35)

98 The practicality of installing TV links between prisons holding remand prisoners and Magistrates' Courts should be explored. (Paras. 4.36-38)

Private Prisons

77 A substantial public Prison Service should be retained but the advantages arising from competition and private sector involvement should be applied across the Service. (Paras. 3.140-141)

TOTAL COSTS

TOTAL SAVINGS

COSTS AND SAVINGS (£000's)							
CAPITAL				CURRENT			
96/97	97/98	98/99	99/00	96/97	97/98	98/99	99/00
7,620	22,900	24,732					2,313
9,060	28,393	29,223					2,763
79		3,050					
			6,030				
				-123	-483	-483	-483
393							
					Future Potential Savings		
					Future Potential Savings		
20,073	51,483	57,005	6,030	15,774	29,579	44,485	65,271
				-123	-483	-483	-483

GENERAL COSTING ASSUMPTIONS

SCHEDULE 2

1. All costs are at 1995/96 prices.

2. Total costs and savings are the sum of estimates over the period 1996/97 to 1999/2000.

3. Current costs include:

   - Staff
   - Travelling and subsistence
   - Accommodation
   - Maintenance of buildings and equipment
   - Electricity and heating
   - Replacement items
   - Training costs

4. Salary costs have been calculated to include superannuation and Earnings Related National Insurance Contributions (ERNIC).

5. Accommodation costs/savings for Prison Service Headquarters are notional but have been treated as current costs/savings for the purposes of this costing exercise.

6. No account has been taken of the Private Finance Initiative in the construction of two new High Security Prisons.

7. Capital costs have been restricted to items costing more than £1,000 and relate to:

   - Equipment
   - Building

8. No account has been taken of inflation or depreciation of capital items.

9. All costs exclude VAT.

Printed in the United Kingdom for HMSO
Dd 5065713, C50, 10/95, 51-1347, 39462